THE INTERNATIONAL ECONOMY AND THE UNDEVELOPED WORLD 1865-1914

THE INTERNATIONAL ECONOMY AND THE UNDEVELOPED WORLD 1865-1914

A. J. H. LATHAM

CROOM HELM LONDON

ROWMAN AND LITTLEFIELD TOTOWA N.J.

Croom Helm Ltd, 2-10 St John's Road, London SW11

British Library Cataloguing in Publication Data

Latham, A J H
The international economy and the undeveloped world 1865-1914.
1. Underdeveloped areas – Economic conditions
I. Title
330.9'172'4 HC59.7

ISBN 0-85664-825-6

First published in the United States 1978 by
Rowman and Littlefield
81 Adams Drive
Totowa, New Jersey

ISBN 0-8476-6088-5

Printed in Great Britain by offset lithography by
Billing & Sons Ltd, Guildford, London and Worcester

CONTENTS

MAPS, GRAPHS AND DIAGRAMS

TABLES

APPENDICES

INTRODUCTION

The idea for writing this book came to me when attending the conference 'Britain in the World's Economy, 1860-1914' at Eliot House, Harvard University, in September 1973, organised by Paul David, Charles Feinstein, Roderick Floud, Donald McCloskey and Barry Supple. For while many sophisticated papers were heard, it was frankly staggering to witness the myopia of British and American economic historians, who, almost without exception, seemed to believe that the world economy at the end of the nineteenth century consisted mainly of Britain and the United States, with Asia and Africa hardly figuring at all in the discussions.[1] To one who had just completed eight years of research in African economic history, and who was currently teaching a course demonstrating the vital importance of India as a keystone in the international economy in the late nineteenth century, this distorted view seemed truly amazing. In the mid-1960s the first lesson which a prospective Africanist had to learn was to see Africa from African eyes, not British ones. Clearly British and American economic historians in the early seventies had not yet learned this lesson, and were still looking at the rest of the world from their own vantage point, having made little attempt to obtain a truly global view of what the world's economy really was. The aim of this book, then, is to press the claim that the working of the world economy at the turn of the century cannot be understood without comprehending what was happening in Asia and Africa. Another reason for writing the book is to counteract the tendency in recent years for Africanists and Asianists to produce excellent monographs on various regions, without trying to obtain a more international view of economic trends. Whilst this is undoubtedly a result of the worthy desire to study African and Asian economic history from an internal point of view, it has nevertheless brought with it its own distortion. So it is also hoped that this book will help place Asia and Africa in the international economy from a neutral, world-wide point of view.

In so doing the book argues the case that the undeveloped world of Asia and Africa was of considerable importance to the overall development of the international economy in the fifty years before the First World War. Developments there made it possible for the world economy to evolve as it did. Without the part which the undeveloped world played in the system it is doubtful if the so-called free-trade era could ever have continued, and its termination would have meant considerable readjustment both in Europe and America.

There will inevitably be criticism that I have not dealt with the topic of Imperialism. Indeed that emotive word is only used here in the entire text. The reason for this is that there have been innumerable works on this theme, and I have been more concerned with trying to show how the international economy actually worked than in dissipating my time in tired controversies about limiting ideologies. There will also be criticism from specialists of Asia and Africa that I have dealt only superficially with their specialist areas. Regrettably this is inevitable in one short book trying to take a global view of an enormous subject to meet a publisher's deadline. There may also be criticism that at times excessive detail has been provided, but my justification is that I am making available information which is not easily accessible, so that others might use it. On the railways, for example, there is no available study of the development of the world's railways; nor, to take another example, is there any convenient handbook of world freight rates. Another criticism which could well be levelled is that Latin America has not been referred to, as perhaps might be expected from the title. Again, limitations of space prohibited this, together with the realisation that the contribution of Latin America to the international economy in these years was really rather different from that of Asia and Africa. Others might equally complain of South Africa's inclusion in a study of the undeveloped world. However, the fact remains that the South African economy was dependent for its workers on Africans, and to a lesser extent Indians and Chinese, all of whom obviously originated in the undeveloped world. It could also be pointed out that the Philippines have been omitted, but as with Latin America, and one might add Madagascar, Mauritius, Réunion, Fernando Po and many others, there are limitations to what one can cope with in one small book. Lastly, complaint may be made that the book is written too simply. For this I make no apology; long experience of teaching, writing and, worst of all, university committees, has convinced me that information and arguments not presented as simply as possible are likely to be misconstrued. Even then that fate may still occur.

So my intention is just to show that Asia and Africa were of vital integral importance to the international economy in these years. If that lesson comes across I shall have achieved my purpose. Of course much more research needs to be done in this entire area, and what I have presented here is really only a preliminary investigation. But that research will not be done so long as the main body of economic historians are oblivious to the existence of Asia and Africa in the international economy at this time. If in getting this message across it is also shown that the spirit of economic enterprise was just as present in the undeveloped world as it was in Wichita or Wigan, it will help to serve as a useful antidote to those who see Asia and Africa as locked in backwardness by inhibiting social attitudes.

In writing this book I am grateful to W.A. Cole, Ian Drummond, Jack Fisher, A.G. Hopkins, Tom Kemp, Donald McCloskey, Larry Neal, David Richardson and John Saville for discussions we had on various points, although they are in no way responsible for any errors, or nonsense, which the reader may think the book contains. I am also grateful to Mrs Jean Davies, who was responsible for the typing and to my wife, who put up with the whole process.

A.J.H. Latham
Department of Economic History
University College
Swansea 1 December 1977

Note

1. *Explorations in Economic History,* 11 (1974), pp.317-444.

1 COMMUNICATIONS

The Railways

The construction of railways brought Asia and Africa into the expanding international economy of the late nineteenth century. Railways ran inland from the seaports, opening new hinterlands for the export of wheat, rice, tea, copra, groundnuts, cocoa, rubber, diamonds, gold, tin and copper, and creating new markets for the manufactured goods of the industrial world. Some of the railways were built with military and strategic purposes in mind, so that troops could be moved quickly to trouble spots, or territorial claims asserted. By linking centres of population, or staking out desirable areas, they still served to open new economic possibilities to the people who lived there.

The Indian railways were the major achievement of railway engineers working in the undeveloped world. The first line, of 21 miles, was opened in 1853 from Bombay to Thana, and it opened the railway era not only for India but for the whole of Asia. Its purpose was essentially economic, as it was to link the cotton fields of the Deccan to the port of Bombay. The next line opened in India was also built for economic reasons, to link Calcutta to the coalfields to the northwest. In this way the pattern of India's early railways reflected her need to provide transport for her exports. But after the troubles of 1857, military considerations became important, and the Government actively participated in the development of the system, by guaranteeing the companies the funds to pay a 5 per cent dividend, if sufficient revenue was not being made. So it was that by 1864 passengers could travel by rail the 1,020 miles from Calcutta to Delhi, and by 1870 the basic network linking Madras, Bombay, Calcutta, Delhi and Lahore was almost complete. During the 1870s the guarantee system was replaced by a vigorous programme of construction by government agency, but the bad famine years of 1874-9 brought financial problems for the Government and private enterprise was brought back from 1880 with modified guarantees. Feeder and subsidiary lines were now encouraged, and although substantial additions had already been made to the basic system by 1882, between then and 1913 India acquired an extremely substantial mesh of major and minor lines. It was the most extensive railway system in the two continents, as can be seen from Map 1 (p.18). There were nearly 35,000 miles of line, some 5 per cent of the world's total

Map 1: Railways in Asia and Africa, 1913

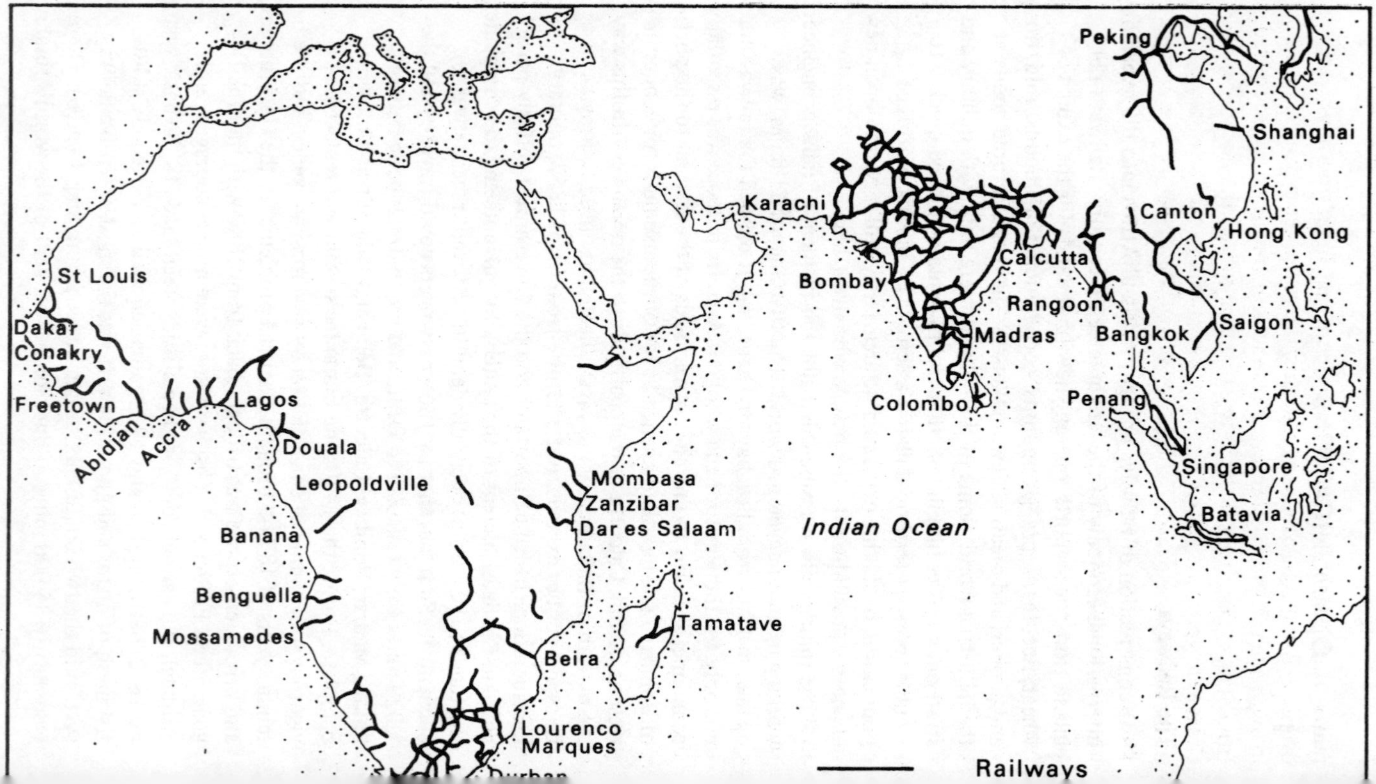

railways. Although there has been criticism that India's railways were overloaded and congested, and also that the guarantee system resulted in excessively high freight rates, the amount of freight carried increased from 4.75 million tons in 1873 to 81 million tons at the outbreak of the Great War. India was better served by her railways than any other part of the undeveloped world.[1] Burmese railways developed as part of the Indian system, but it is worth noting that the first line was built to provide famine relief in Bengal, and was opened in 1877. Later extensions ran to the Chinese border, and across lower Burma, which had previously been served only by footpaths and fords across the numerous creeks.[2] By contrast, in Ceylon the railways developed independently, the first line being opened from Colombo in 1865. By 1913 Ceylon had an adequate system of some 606 miles.[3]

To the east, on the Malayan peninsula, the first railway was not opened until 1885. But between then and 1899 all the major tin-mining towns on the west coast were connected to ports, enabling them to ship equipment in and ore out. After 1899 a railway was built running north-south, joining the mining centres, and by 1909 it was possible to travel by rail all the way down the peninsula, save only for the ferry from Penang to the mainland in the north, and the ferry from the mainland to Singapore in the south. Although servicing tin production had been the original purpose of the railways, rubber plantations were soon established along the tracks, using the facilities to get the latex to the ports. After 1910 railway building began up the east side of the peninsula, and by 1913 there were 862 miles in operation.[4] In the Dutch territory of Java further south the first lines opened in 1867, and by 1873 there were 162 miles, one line linking the port of Samarang to the main area of sugar plantations, the other linking Batavia to the hills where tea and coffee were grown. Further expansion took place in Java to serve the sugar planters, and in neighbouring Sumatra lines were built, some for political reasons, others to export tobacco and coal. Mileage doubled in Java and Sumatra from 1,073 miles in 1891 to 2,256 miles in 1900, including light railways or tramways which linked the plantations to the main system. By 1913 there were 1,783 miles of proper railway, plus approximately another 1,592 miles of tramway.[5]

Siam, which remained an independent state, did not embark upon railway building until 1891, and by 1893 the first 12 miles ran inland from Bangkok. Political considerations dominated, and by 1900 164 miles were open to the north and north east. There was further expansion north, and a start made on a line south towards the Malay states, so that by 1913 706 miles were in operation. As proved the case elsewhere, although the original motivation for the lines was political and strategic, the spread of lines to the north encouraged the development of rice cultivation there, and exports rose substantially.[6] Political and economic considerations went hand in hand in determining the railway structure in French Indo-China. Between 1881 and 1885 a line was built from Saigon through the most densely populated part of the country in the south. Then the conquest of Tonkin to the north made it necessary to build a railway for military purposes. Technical and financial difficulties were great, and in 1896 private capital was brought in, guaranteed by the French Government. Now the aim was to build across Indo-China to connect the two populous deltas of the north and south, and enable direct communication between the Chinese and Siamese frontiers. In this way essential defence considerations would be satisfied, and economic exchange stimulated between the different regions. Branches into the interior were planned, and an extension north into the Chinese province of Yunnan. Most of this work was complete by the outbreak of the First World War, when there were 2,310 miles of line open.[7]

The story of the construction of railways in China is a sorry and confused tale. Even in 1913 there were only 6,158 miles of line there, less than 1 per cent of the world's railways. The first line, built by British merchants in the face of much local opposition, opened from the port of Woosung to Shanghai in 1876, some nine miles. But soon after it was opened, a Chinese was run over by the locomotive and killed. Protests followed, the Chinese Government bought the railway, and in 1877 the line was torn up and dumped in the sea. So the real beginning of railways in China came in 1880 when the Kaiping Coal Mining Company opened a six-mile line to carry coal to the coast for bunkering steam ships. Although mules and horses pulled the trucks to begin with, in 1881 Mr Kinder, the engineer, built a home-made locomotive out of an old boiler, which he named the *Rocket of China.* This successful line was later incorporated into the Peking-Mukden line. In the meantime, it demonstrated to the Chinese officials that railways were of practical use. Yet internal politics determined that railway development should be slow, and in 1894 only two short lines were working, one to shift coal as described, and the other to move iron ore. China's disastrous defeat by the Japanese in 1894 changed all this. Because they believed China to be on the point of breakup, the various Western nations now clamoured for railway concessions there, to obtain a toehold and sphere of influence. By 1898 China had signed contracts with companies in Britain, Russia, Germany, Belgium, France and the United States, for a total of 6,250 miles of line. The lines were mostly constructed with foreign loans, which gave control of the project to the foreign creditors, whose antics provoked the chauvinistic backlash of 1900 known as the Boxer Movement. Certainly little attention was paid to the real needs of the Chinese economy, and there was widespread corruption. The resulting network, if it can be called that, showed a lack of planning and uniformity. Yet railway building did now begin in earnest, and by 1906 there were 2,448 miles of line open. The shock of the Russo-Japanese war of that year led to a new wave of locally sponsored railway schemes, but sufficient capital could not be raised, and work was either never started or halted after it had begun. This confused situation, together with the need to centralise military communications against foreign aggression and possible internal rebellion, led to the nationalisation of the railways in 1911. Fear that the railways would now be used as an instrument of oppression encouraged the revolution the same year which overthrew the Ching Dynasty, although the railways were to remain nationalised. In 1913 there was still only a pitiful amount of lines by comparison with India, and not even a north-south link from Peking to Canton.[8]

In Africa for the most part railway development came later than it did in Asia, and the mileage laid down by 1913 was much less, as Table 1 (p.22) shows. This reflects Africa's unimportance in the international economy until the 1880s, and her relative insignificance, except for Southern Africa, from then until the First World War. The original line in Africa was the two-mile line from Point to Durban in Natal, opened in 1860. This was extended a further 4 miles in 1874 to cope with the production of sugar, maize, coffee and arrowroot in the neighbourhood. Meanwhile a longer line had been opened in 1864 from Cape Town to Wellington. So by 1874 only 69 miles of line had been opened in the subcontinent of Africa, all in the south.[9] This situation changed with the discovery of diamonds at Kimberley, which created a sudden need for lines inland from the ports. During the late 1870s lines were built from the three principal ports of the Cape, Cape Town, Port Elizabeth and East London, which converged at De Aar Junction, from where the line extended north to Kimberley. At the same time, a line had been built from Durban to Pietermaritzburg. Then in 1886 came the gold discoveries on the Witwatersrand, creating a new need for railways, as the reef could be reached only by ox wagon from Kimberley or Pietermaritzburg. So the Cape railway was extended to Johannesburg and Pretoria, giving in 1892 a through line from the Cape ports to

Table 1: World Railways, 1913

World	Total	%	Private	State
Europe	216,396	31.36	100,285	116,111
America	356,317	51.63	328,094	28,223
Asia	67,591	9.79	23,298	44,293
Africa	27,693	4.01	11,129	16,564
Australasia	22,136	3.21	1,615	20,521
TOTAL	690,133	100.00	464,421	225,712
Asia*	Total	%	Private	State
British India	33,850	73.64	4,362	29,488
Ceylon	606	1.28	606	–
Malay States	862	1.82	862	–
Dutch Indies	1,783	3.77	238	1,545
Siam	706	1.49	105	601
French Indo-China	2,310	4.88	2,310	–
China	6,158	13.01	6,158	–
TOTAL	46,275	99.89	14,641	31,634
Africa**	Total	%	Private	State
South Africa	8,596	43.23	705	7,891
Rhodesia	2,420	12.17	2,420	–
French Colonies	2,011	10.11	2,011	–
British Colonies	2,368	11.91	1,047	1,321
German Colonies	2,608	13.11	–	2,608
Belgian Congo	868	4.36	868	–
Portuguese Colonies	1,015	5.10	1,015	–
TOTAL	19,886	99.99	8,066	11,820

* These figures exclude Russian Central Asia and Siberia, Japan, Asia Minor, Persia, etc.

** These figures exclude Algieria and Tunisia, Egypt, etc.

Source: *Railway Year Book* (1916), pp.48-9.

the Rand. In 1894, a line was completed from Pretoria to Komati Port on the Mozambique border, and from there to Lourenço Marques in Delagoa Bay, giving the Rand another outlet to the sea. So all the lines in South Africa converged from the ports to the diamond city of Kimberley, and the gold city of Johannesburg. From the 1890s to the outbreak of the Boer War attention turned to branch and feeder lines to develop other industries, especially copper and coal. Then in the remaining years before the war substantial railway building took place aimed at developing the agricultural resources of the country. At the outbreak of war there were 8,596 miles of line.[10] In Rhodesia, railway development took place under the influence of Cecil Rhodes. The Cape line was extended from Kimberley, reaching Bulawayo in 1897, 1,362 miles from Cape Town. Although Rhodesia was well suited to maize, tobacco, cotton, wheat, barley and other commercial crops, the main incentives for the railway builders were the gold and diamond deposits, together with the silver near Umtali, and other deposits of copper, tin and antimony. Salisbury was connected to Beira in Mozambique in 1899, giving her direct access to a port, and when the line was completed to Bulawayo in 1902, there was also a connection to the ports of the Cape. A line was built to the Wankie collieries in 1903, which provided coal for the whole system, and with the discovery of the mineral wealth of Broken Hill the line was extended in that direction. Then the line was carried towards the Congo border, and the newly discovered mineral wealth of Katanga. By 1913 there were 2,420 miles of line in Rhodesia.[11]

Outside of Southern Africa the French were the most active initially, starting construction on a line in Senegal in 1879, linking St Louis to Dakar, some 163 miles, so that the products which came down-river could be transferred to a good port. This was achieved in 1885. Subsequently the line was carried through the interior to the Senegal river at Keyes, although this was not finished in 1914. Keyes was also connected to the Niger, for political and strategic considerations. These motives, to secure the hinterland from British encroachment, and break British economic domination there, were the force behind the line from Konakry in French Guinea to the Niger, of which there were 365 miles by 1913.[12] Further west, on the Ivory Coast, a line was built from Abidjan to Bouaké, 194 miles up country, both to secure the hinterland and to open it up. For similar reasons lines were being established in Dahomey at the same time, comprising a track from Cotonou to Save, and a line from Porto Novo to Pobe, of which 178 miles were open in 1913. To the south, in French Equatorial Africa, the Compagnie Minière du Congo Français opened a private line of 102 miles from Mindouli to Brazzaville in 1912.[13]

In the British colonies in Africa, military and economic aims ran together, the Pax Britannica leading to greater economic activity. Most of these lines were built comparatively late. It was not until 1896 that the first line was laid down in Sierra Leone, the 32 miles from Freetown to Songo Town being completed in 1898. Further extensions were added, and by 1913 there were 317 miles open. In the Gold Coast, 40 miles were open in 1901, and 168 by 1903, linking the port of Sekondi to Kumasi. The other important line ran inland from Accra, but little of this had been finished by 1913, when there were 217 miles not including a short mining railway 11 miles long, which opened in 1905. In Nigeria too, military and economic intentions were served by the railways. The first 20 miles were opened in 1897 from Lagos, and construction continued by way of Ibadan to Minna, which was reached in 1911, a distance of 479 miles. The line was pushed forward towards Kano, so that on the eve of the war there were 927 miles of track, including the Bauchi light railway, opened in 1912 to the tin mines.[14] In East Africa political and strategic purposes determined the railway programme. Railway construction began from Mombasa, and by 1899 the engineers had reached Nairobi. The intention was to provide a direct link to Uganda, in order to secure a sound defensive position at the source of the Nile. So the line was pushed on to Lake Victoria, and by 1904 there were 584 miles of line open. While this line was essentially political, there can be no doubt that it was the initial stimulus to economic development not only in Uganda but in Kenya as well. With the addition of branch lines, there were 618 miles in 1913.[15] Also in East Africa, 113 miles of line had been laid in Nyasaland by 1913, although they were not to be a really effective force for development until they were linked to Beira after the war.[16] Thus, including minor lines, there were 2,368 miles of railway in the British African colonies in 1913, excluding Rhodesia and South Africa.

Germany was fairly active in providing her African colonies with railways. In Togo 27 miles were open in 1905, running inland from Lomé. Further additions were made and by 1913 there were 204 miles open. In the Cameroons 31 miles were open in 1901, and by the war there were 193 miles, comprising three separate routes towards the interior, from Victoria, Douala and Bonaberi. But it was South West Africa which had the most lines. There the first lines were opened in 1897 from Swakopmund. In 1906 another line was opened from Luderitz in the south, and by 1912 these two lines were joined to form a loop passing inland from Swakopmund through Windhoek and Keetmanshoop to Luderitz, a network of 1,315 miles.[17] The remaining German colony was of course in East Africa, namely Tanganyika. By 1896 the first 25 miles of line were opened from Dar Es Salaam, the intention being to build two branches of penetration, one to Lake Victoria, the other to Lake Tanganyika. At the outbreak of war 896 miles of line were open, to the benefit of sisal and rubber cultivation.[18]

Although the Belgians had only one colony in Africa, it was extremely important. The first three miles of railway in the Congo were working in 1891, being part of a scheme to connect Matadi on the Congo estuary to Leopoldville and Kinshasa, bypassing the waterfalls which made the lower reaches of the river unnavigable. The whole project came into operation in 1898. Subsequently the major incentive for railway building was the exploitation of the copper resources of Katanga. After 1900 the amount of track was increased from 279 miles to 868, in 1913.[19]

The only other colonial power of importance was Portugal, which had two major territories, Angola and Mozambique. In Angola 37 miles of line were laid between 1886 and 1889, from Loanda towards Ambaca, which was not finally reached until 1899. Later this line was pushed on towards the border of the Belgian Congo. Another line was built inland from Benguela, or rather the nearby harbour of Lobito Bay. The first section of this line was opened in 1906, with further links being opened year by year to 1913. In the south another line was built from Mossamedes, the first section also being opened in 1906. In Mozambique in East Africa, a line of some 50 miles came into operation from Lourenço Marques in 1887. This was to serve as an access route to the sea for the Transvaal, and subsequently South Africa in general. Much the same applies to the line from Beira, which opened in 1896, and provided Rhodesia with a port after through traffic was established in 1900. So although there were only 302 miles of line in Mozambique in 1913, these lines were of a significance and importance quite out of proportion to their length. In 1913 there were 1,015 miles of railway in the Portuguese colonies.[20]

Having outlined the course of railway construction in Asia and Africa before the Great War, it remains to make a few general observations. The first point to note is the overwhelming importance of Indian railways in the two continents, a point brought home forcibly by Graph 1 (p.26). Secondly, for the most part the railways began at convenient ports and ran inland. While strategic and economic ends were both important in determining railway building, it is obvious that railways which could carry troops inland could also carry exports to the coast. Lastly, it may be said that whatever criticisms may be made of these railway systems, introduced largely by colonial powers, they were nevertheless vital in the process of linking the undeveloped world more fully with the international economy. China remained something of an anomaly, a vast subcontinent meanly provided with lines in a state of chronic disarray, the outcome of her own weakness.

Graph 1: Railways in Asia and Africa, 1850-1913

The Steam Ship and the Suez Canal

If the railways linked the ports to their hinterlands, it was the steam ship which linked the railway networks of the world into an international transport system. Steam engines had been used to power ships during the 1820s, when the railway first became a practical proposition. But because of the low efficiency of the early marine engines, the steam engine was used only on short voyages initially. Long voyages were not technically impossible, but so much coal had to be carried that there was not enough room for cargo. This did not matter in the passenger trade, and here steam successfully took over from sail, gradually extending its range. The Irish Sea and North Sea were served in the 1820s and the Mediterranean in the early 1830s. By 1840 there were regular scheduled passenger services to the United States, and during the 1850s regular steamship services began to West Africa and South Africa.[21] So steamships gradually ousted sailing ships on more and more distant routes, as the marine engine improved in efficiency and reliability. If the steamship triumphed first on passenger routes, by the late 1860s steam was establishing itself on cargo routes up to about 3,000 miles.[22]

In West Africa, the arrival of a new steam-ship service in 1869 virtually marked the end of sail.[23] But although Alfred Holt's Blue Funnel line began a steamship service in 1866 calling at Mauritius, Penang, Singapore, Hong Kong, and Shanghai, this long voyage round the Cape still remained largely the preserve of the sailing ship.[24] Presumably it would have continued to do so until the closing years of the century, had it not been for the opening of the Suez Canal in 1869. At a stroke Asia was brought some 4,000 miles nearer to Europe, with the voyage from Britain to Bombay cut from 10,667 miles to 6,224 miles, and the voyage to Calcutta from 11,900 miles to 8,083. This of itself would not have necessitated the Asian trade switching to steamships, for it was still cheaper to ship by sail on voyages over about 6,000 miles, the new distance to Bombay. However, the canal was not suitable for sailing ships, which had to be towed through the cutting, only to meet unsatisfactory wind conditions in the Red Sea. Indeed, the first sailing vessel to pass through was wrecked on the very evening it emerged. So in practical terms, the canal shortened the steamship route, but not the sailing-ship route. There were other specific advantages for the steamship. Coal was easier to obtain on the voyage through the Mediterranean than it would have been round the coast of Africa, so less coal and more cargo could be carried. And because the route went through more populous and economically developed regions than the long, deserted coasts of Southern Africa, there were more opportunities for picking up and discharging cargo on the voyage.[25] But even so, the Suez Canal alone would not have driven the sailing ship from the coasts of India and China. Coal prices rose very steeply east of Suez, and the sailing ship would have held its own for some years, had it not been for improvements in the marine engine. The single-cylinder marine engine's consumption of coal per horsepower per hour had been lowered from 8-10½ lbs in the 1830s to about 4 lbs by the 1860s. But John Elder's compound engines, introduced in 1854-6, reduced coal consumption to 2-2½ lbs per hour. Where coal was cheap this did not matter, and the compound engine did not oust the single cylinder. But the incentive of the Suez Canal, plus the high price of coal east of the

Canal, gave the compound engine an advantage that the single cylinder could not match.[26] Yet sail still continued in the Indian and Far Eastern trades until after the turn of the century. Far from being driven from the seas by the Suez Canal and the compound engine, after an initial setback, there was a revival of sailing ships in the late 1870s. These new sailing ships were built of iron, were steel masted and were double the size of the ships of the 1850s. It took the new high-pressure triple-expansion engine of the 1880s to beat these new sailing ships, and it is only from that time that the final demise of sail can be dated. Paradoxically, one of the bulk trades which prolonged the life of the sailing ship was the carrying of coal to the steamship bunkering stations of Asia. The sailing ships which continued to carry rice from India usually returned from Europe with coal for the great bunkering stations of Singapore and Hong Kong. Apart from this, the sailing ship had a special advantage in the bulk trades, as it was the cheapest form of warehousing there was. So the sailing ship continued in existence as a floating warehouse, carrying low-value bulk items such as rice, jute and millet, on their long journey round the Cape to Europe. But from the 1880s their use even in this role declined.[27] Although Parson's steam turbine, and the Diesel engine were to supersede the triple-expansion engine, they had little impact on the Asian and African trades until after the war, and Alfred Holt's was still laying down ships with triple-expansion engines in 1914.[28]

The opening of the Suez Canal led directly to a boom in steam-ship building, the new steamers going on the much shortened Bombay route, where they had the greatest advantage over sailing ships. Although hardly any steam ships came to Britain from Bombay before the opening of the canal, the year after its inauguration 28 per cent were steam, and by the early 1890s all the cargo from Bombay was carried by steam. On the rather more distant route to Calcutta, about a quarter of the tonnage was still sail in the 1890s, mainly rice and jute. Surprisingly, the biggest shift from sail to steam took place in the China trade, although the distance from Britain to Shanghai was reduced only from 14,000 miles to 11,000 miles by the canal. In 1869 14 per cent of the tonnage to Britain from China was steam, but by 1873 70 per cent was borne by steam ship, and by 1880 over 90 per cent. This was because the China trade was in high-value goods, particularly tea, whose shippers were prepared to pay for fast passage. The steam ship using the canal halved the time for the voyage from China, but charged approximately the same freight rate as the tea clippers. So it made obvious sense to ship by steam, especially as lower insurance premiums were paid for tea carried in steamships.[29] One other area affected by the opening of the Suez Canal, and the steamship was East Africa, as the canal created a new sea route to this direction. Now it was possible to link South Africa to Europe via East Africa.[30]

As regards the development of Asia and Africa, the crucial effect of the introduction of the steam ship and the opening of the Suez Canal was that freight rates fell, as shown on Graph 2 (p.30). This drastic fall caused consternation among the shipping companies, and led to the creation of conferences to maintain rates.[31] The conference system worked by all the main shipping lines on a particular route agreeing to charge the same freight rate, and to share the trade amongst themselves according to an agreed division. Outsiders were excluded by allowing customers a percentage rebate payable a fixed number of months after shipment, but only if they continued to ship with conference lines. This ingenious scheme was introduced in the Calcutta trade in 1875, and then in the China trade in 1879.[32] Although the conferences now stabilised rates, it was at the new low levels, and the overall decline in rates was to continue.[33] This fall in rates was to be a vital factor in the decline in the price of Eastern commodities between 1873 and 1896. Cotton, jute, indigo, rice, tea from India; gutta-percha, sago and tin from the Straits Settlements; coconut oil and cinnamon from Ceylon; silk and tea from China; all gained from this fall in transport costs to the European market.[34]

The pattern and organisation of trade was profoundly altered by the opening of the Suez Canal. So much so that the London *Economist* attributed the commercial crisis of 1873 to the disruption resulting from the redirection of trade.[35] French shipping lines in particular had hoped to exploit the advantage of their geographical position in the Mediterranean to capture much of Britain's share of the Eastern trade, but 80 per cent of gross tonnage passing through the canal in 1880 was still British, and 76 per cent in 1890. The reason for the failure of the French was that unless their lines went to Britain first, to pick up a cargo of coal, salt or railway iron, they could not get an outward cargo, and had to go out in ballast. So they could not offer a competitive freight rate. The shipping of other Mediterranean countries faced the same problem, even though they were subsidised by their governments. It was not until Germany challenged Britain's position in the last years of the century that Britain's share of the traffic decreased substantially. In 1910 Britain accounted for 62 per cent of the canal's trade, and Germany 16 per cent. Yet although Britain retained her hold of the shipping trade, often her ships now sailed direct to European

Graph 2: Freight Rates, 1870-1913

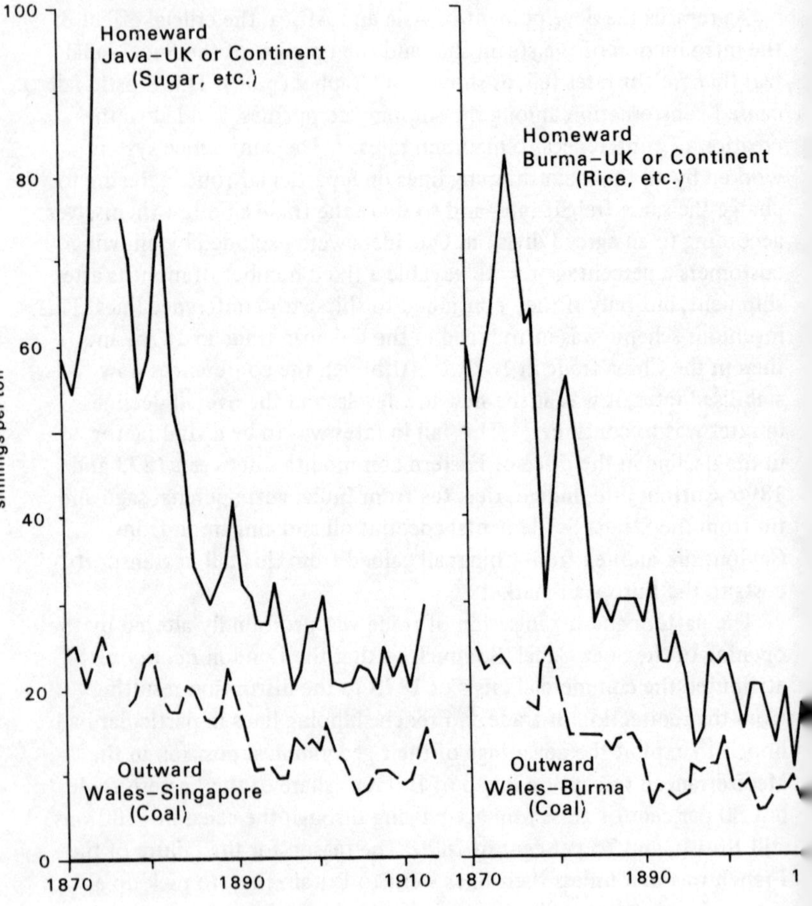

Source: Fairplay, Jan.-June 1920; see Appendix 1.

ports, without docking in Britain first. In the past Britain had stockpiled the products of the East for Europe and the United States, because of the uncertainties of trade by sail round Africa. But with the opening of the Suez Canal, European buyers increasingly had these goods consigned direct to them, avoiding the rake-off of the London or Liverpool middlemen. Indian cotton, indigo and hides now went straight to Europe, as did Chinese silk, even though British ships carried them there. Rice and raw jute only switched to direct shipment to Europe as the sailing ship disappeared. Only in the tea trade did shipments come straight to Britain, but then Britain was the major consumer. As regards the United States, the products of the East still came to Britain first, for transpacific routes were as yet unimportant. Between 1873 and 1913, re-exports to the United States of foreign and colonial produce, particularly rubber and tin, increased tenfold from £3.1 million to £30.2 million.[36] The increase in direct trade to Europe cannot be attributed entirely to the Suez Canal, as it applied even to the West African trade, which was unaffected by the canal. This was probably a result of the terms of the British-dominated conference agreements, which sought to keep European ships from British ports, but allowed British ships into those of Europe.[37] The development of transcontinental and submarine cables also played a vital role in this process by putting purchaser and producer in contact without an intermediary. The fact that Europe was now consuming enormous quantities of Asian and African foodstuffs and raw materials was a force in the same direction, as direct shipment kept handling costs to a minimum.[38]

India was particularly affected by the canal. Suddenly she was 4,000 miles nearer Europe, and served by regular steamships. Freight rates dropped, lowering the prices of her goods in Europe. By 1883-4 85 per cent of total trade between Britain and India went via the canal, and British ships carried the bulk of India's trade, even when the destination was Europe. They carried manufactured goods, and textiles, from Britain out to India, filling any extra cargo space with coal or iron, and then returned to Europe with Indian foodstuffs and raw materials. In 1912 British ships sailing through the canal for India were using 76 per cent of potential capacity, and they returned using 98 per cent. On the Atlantic trade, by contrast, they used only 20 per cent on the outward journey and 63 per cent sailing back. Indeed British tonnage on the Indian trade roughly equalled her tonnage on the route to the United States.[39]

Thus the opening of the Suez Canal opened the vast trading area of the East to the efficient steam ship, in due course forcing the sailing ship out of existence, completing a process already begun in West Africa. The consequent fall in freight rates revolutionised trading conditions from Dakar to Shanghai. African and Asian produce flooded on to the European and American markets, giving Africans and Asians the means to buy the manufactured goods of the industrial countries. This new pattern of world shipping routes is shown in Map 2 (p.33).

The Telegraph

The railways broke open the hinterlands of the ports in the undeveloped world, increasing the export of primary goods and the reciprocal import of manufactured goods. The steamship, aided by the Suez Canal, linked the ports into the international transport system. Now it only remained for the telegraph to connect sellers to buyers to bring Asia and Africa fully into the international market.

The electric telegraph dates back before 1830, but the spread of railways made it a practical necessity, and it was to accompany the railways as they spread abroad from Britain.[40] Although there had been experiments with telegraphs in India as early as 1839, which proved they were practicable, it was not until 1850 that the Indian Government became interested and sanctioned tests. The tests proved successful, and the first telegraph in Asia opened in 1854. When the Calcutta-Bombay cable was inaugurated in 1855, the period for communication to London was cut from 35 days to 26.[41] The railway was not to reach Calcutta from Bombay until 1870.[42] Within a few years of its introduction, most of the important Indian towns and cities were linked by telegraph.[43] But elsewhere in Asia and Africa the telegraph did not exist. Nor was there a means of direct communication from India to Europe, except by sea, or dromedary across the Syrian desert. The submarine cable was to change this situation.

In 1857 the Red Sea and India Telegraph Company was promoted to establish communication between Britain and India. The British Government, aware of the need for rapid communication made evident by the troubles of that year, gave a guarantee of 4½ per cent on its capital for 50 years. But it soon became clear that the problems of laying long submarine cables had not been conquered. The first transatlantic cable opened in 1858, but within a month had failed. And the 3,043 nautical miles of cable laid in 1859 and 1860 from Suez to Karachi via Aden proved equally unsuccessful, and was abandoned. A government committee was set up to inquire into the whole question of the construction, laying and maintenance of submarine cables, and their findings encouraged the Government of India to try to establish

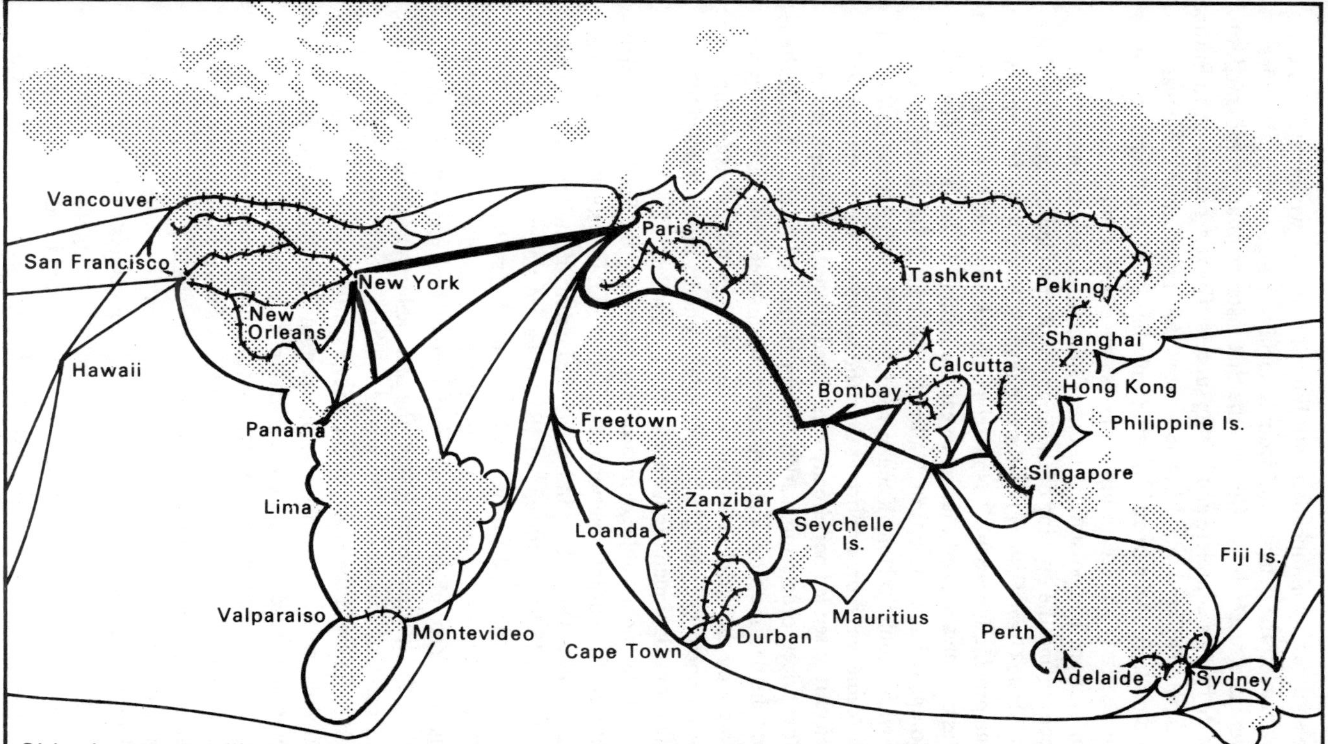

Shipping routes (line thickness indicates comparative importance of routes)

* Importance of route is measured by volume and value of trade, in F. Allen, *An Atlas of Commercial Geography* (Cambridge: Cambridge University Press, 1913), p.1

Source: After G. Philip & Sons, London Geographical Institute.

telegraphic communication with Europe on their own initiative. A cable was laid in the Persian Gulf from Karachi to Fao, and all 1,450 miles were laid successfully. This was the first instance of any great length of cable being a complete and lasting success. The rest of the link to Europe was made by land line. In 1866 a successful transatlantic cable was laid using Brunel's *Great Eastern,* symbolically linking the pioneer of both railway and steamship with this new element of communications innovation. The possibility of direct submarine cable to India now rearose, and the opening of the Suez Canal provided the incentive. In 1870 the *Great Eastern* laid the line from Suez via Aden to Bombay, the line proving successful.[44] Now telegraph communication to the Far East was conceivable, and that very year the Eastern Extension Telegraph Company laid a cable from Madras to Penang and Singapore, following it with a cable to Hong Kong in 1871.[45] As far as India was concerned, the cable was more important than the railway or the steamship, as in effect it extended her already completed domestic telegraph system. Now prices, orders and market information could be easily transmitted, and she became more a part of the world market than she could ever be simply by the introduction of railways and steamships. As for the Government of India, it was now able to end its monthly subsidy to the dromedary mail service across the Syrian desert.[46]

The laying of cables eastward linked not only the Straits Settlements into the flow of information which was the international marketplace, but also the Dutch East Indies, via the landing of the cable at Batavia in Java in 1870. By the end of 1871 it was possible to cable London from Shanghai, and Saigon was linked into the system by the French Government that same year, bringing French Indo-China into world markets. Yet unlike India, where the internal telegraph system pre-dated the submarine cable link, the new cables in the East remained to some extent peripheral. This was certainly true of China, where the cables followed the coast, and it was not until 1898 that China was provided with an internal telegraph system. This merely reflects the internal political weakness and isolationism which had delayed the introduction of railways. In Malaya, too, internal telegraphs were only introduced in the 1890s, along with the railways. Nevertheless the cable did bring the East more fully into the world market, and trade tended to centralise in the ports that were cable centres: Hong Kong, Shanghai and Singapore. New steamship companies entered the Shanghai trade, increasing competition and forcing the silk trade to use the newly opened Suez Canal. Silk was now sold in advance of its arrival, on information telegraphed to Europe. Indeed, the China cable became more profitable than the Indian cable, because it had no competitors such as the line through Persia and the Persian Gulf, and because the lucrative silk trade made such use of forward selling. London, as the centre of the world-wide cable system, became more than ever the centre of the world market, even if the produce in question was never landed in Britain but went direct to its destination.[47]

But connection by telegraph to the Far East via India did not bring Africa into the international communications system, and the comparatively late arrival there of the submarine cable reflects once more the relative unimportance of that continent in terms of international economic life. Only in South Africa were there early telegraphs, the first line being opened from Cape Town to Simonstown in 1860, with an extension to Kimberley opening in 1876, in response to the diamond rush. Later telegraphs, like the railways, were to be built in response to the gold rush in the mid-1880s. But it was only in 1879 that submarine cables were laid to South Africa, in response to the fact that the news of the annihilation of a British force at Isandlwana by the Zulus took 20 days to reach London. The cable ran down the east coast of Africa, from Aden via Zanzibar, Mozambique and Delagoa Bay to Durban. Thus from 1880 there was direct telegraphic communication from South Africa to London. Now Aden was a main cable junction like Singapore, with a southern and eastern cable.[48] West Africa was still neglected and it was not until 1886 that a cable was laid on the West Coast of Africa via Bathurst, Sierra Leone, Accra, Lagos, Brass and Bonny to Cape Town. Internal telegraphs did not come until the 1890s, and up to that time messages still had to be carried by messenger and canoe.[49]

With the African cables, the skeleton of a telegraph service had been created in the undeveloped world, and between then and the First World War, flesh was put on these bones by subsidiary cables, duplicate cables and the spread of domestic networks. But the Pacific was not crossed until 1902, with a line from Canada to Australia and New Zealand. It was followed in 1903 with a line to the Philippines from the West Coast of America, which established direct communication from the United States to China.[50] For as Map 3 of telegraph cables in 1897 shows (on page 36) the world telegraph system centralised in London, as did the international market. The Pacific was not a trading ocean.

The telegraph brought with it the telegraphic transfer, which came to be used instead of the bill of exchange, and it encouraged the rise of the tramp steamer, moving from port to port carrying goods according

Map 3: The Telegraph System in Asia and Africa, 1897

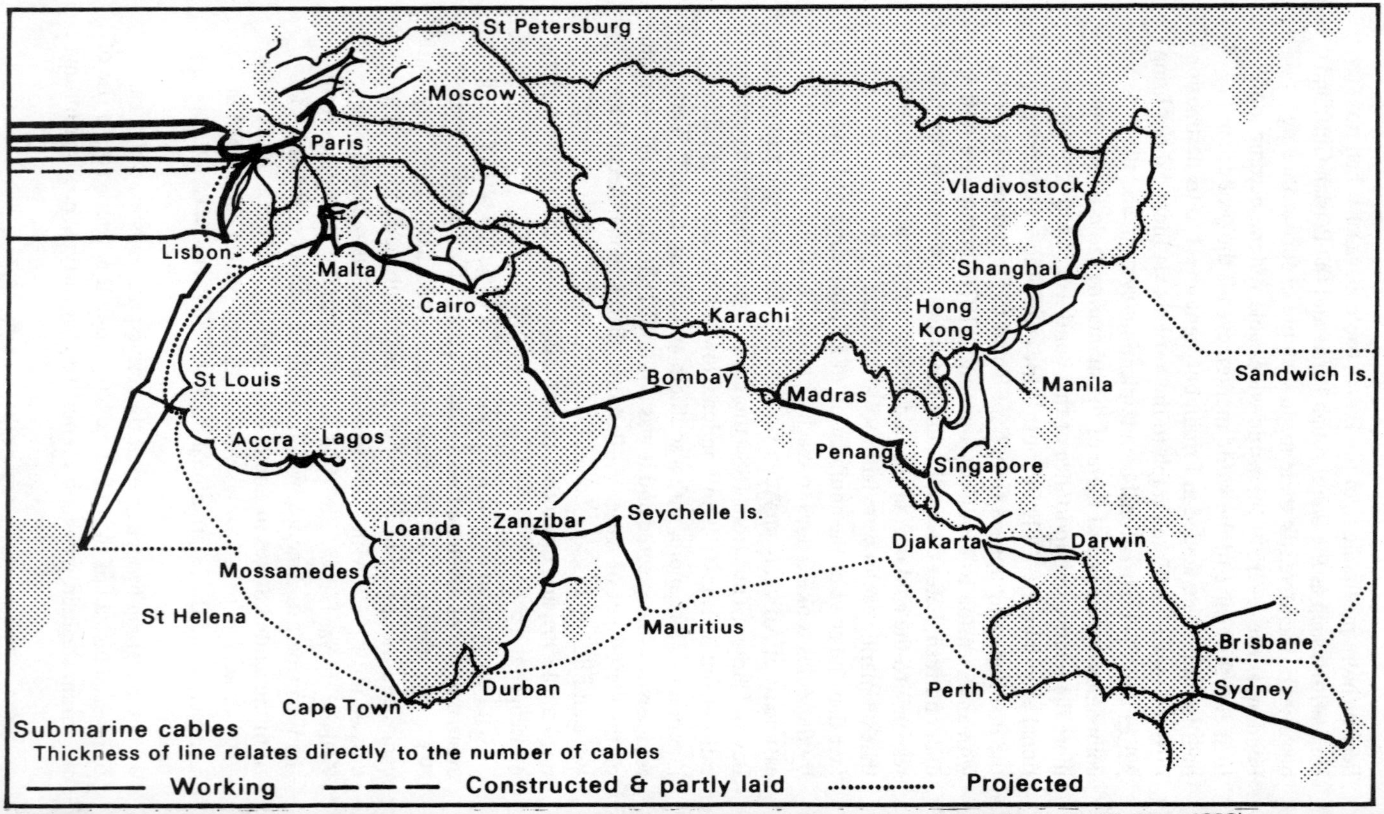

to instructions received from Europe.[51] But its real importance lay in the fact that it completed and crowned the communications revolution created by the railways, the steam ship and the Suez Canal. The transport innovations enabled primary produce to be brought to the ports from the hinterlands, and shipped to the industrial countries of the world. But it was the telegraph which carried the information about prices, quality and delivery dates, which enabled the goods to be bought and sold long before they arrived in Europe or America. Now deliveries could be made direct to buyers, without having to be stockpiled in London first. Yet the fact that the world's telegraph system was centred on London meant that the world market remained there. It was there that buyer met seller, that prices were set, and deals made. Even the commodities from India or China for the United States were bought by way of London. London was the centre of the international system, but Calcutta, Shanghai and Lagos were now as much a part of the international market as New York.

Notes

1. M.N. Das, *Studies in the Economic and Social Development of Modern India, 1848-56* (Calcutta: Mukhopadhyay, 1959); D.H. Buchanan, *The Development of Capitalistic Enterprise in India,* 2nd ed. (London: Cass, 1966); K.V. Iyer, *Indian Railways* (Calcutta: Oxford University Press, 1924); J.N. Sahni, *Indian Railways: One Hundred Years, 1853-1953* (New Delhi: Ministry of Railways, 1953); N. Sanyal, *Development of Indian Railways* (Calcutta: University of Calcutta, 1930); P.H. Middleton, *Railways of Thirty Nations: Government Versus Private Ownership* (New York: Prentice-Hall, 1937); D. Thorner, 'Great Britain and the Development of India's Railways', *Journal of Economic History,* xi (1951), pp.389-402; J.N. Westwood, *Railways of India* (Newton Abbot: David & Charles, 1974); M.D. Morris and C.B. Dudley, 'Selected Railway Statistics for the Indian Subcontinent, 1853-1946/7', *Artha Vijnana,* 17 (1975).

2. J.S. Furnivall, *Colonial Policy and Practice: A Comparative Study of Burma and Netherlands India* (Cambridge: Cambridge University Press, 1948), p.78.

3. *Railway Year Book* (1903), p.174; G.F. Perera, *The Ceylon Railway,* (Colombo: *Ceylon Observer,* 1925).

4. Federated Malay States Railways, *Fifty Years of Railways in Malaya, 1885-1935* (Kuala Lumpur: Federated Malay States Railways, 1935), pp.1-45; Lim Chong-Yah, *Economic Development of Modern Malaya* (Kuala Lumpur: Oxford University Press, 1967), pp.272-3.

5. J.S. Furnivall, *Netherlands India* (Cambridge: Cambridge University Press, 1944), pp.204, 329-30.

6. James C. Ingram, *Economic Change in Thailand* (Stanford: Stanford University Press, 1971), pp.85-6.

7. C. Robequain, *The Economic Development of French Indo-China* (London: Oxford University Press, 1944), pp.90-2.

8. Cheng Lin, *The Chinese Railways: A Historical Survey* (Shanghai: China United Press, 1935); P.H. Kent, *Railway Enterprise in China: An Account of its Origin and Development* (London: Edward Arnold, 1907); E-tu Zen Sun,

Chinese Railways and British Interests, 1898-1911 (New York: Kings Crown Press, 1954), Edouard de Laboulaye, *Les chemins de fer de China* (Paris, 1911); Middleton, *Thirty Nations,* pp.228-37; Mongton Chih Hsu, *Railway Problems in China,* 2nd ed. (New York: Ams Press, 1968).

9. *Railway Year Book* (1904), p.285.

10. M.H. De Kock, *Selected Subjects in the Economic History of South Africa* (Cape Town and Johannesburg: Juta, 1924), pp.345-52; J. Van Der Poel, *Railway and Customs Policies in South Africa, 1885-1910* (London, Longmans Green, 1933); Lionel Wiener, *Les chemins de fer coloniaux de l'Afrique* (Brussels: Goemaere, 1931), pp.337-407; *Railway Year Book* (1904), p.285.

11. De Kock, *Economic History of South Africa,* p.350; Wiener, *Chemins de fer de l'Afrique,* pp.433-7.

12. Wiener, *Chemins de fer de l'Afrique,* pp.82-92; Jaques Mangolte, 'Le chemin de fer de Konakry au Niger, 1890-1914', *Revue Française d'Histoire d'Outre-Mer,* 55 (1968), pp.37-105.

13. Wiener, *Chemins de fer de l'Afrique,* pp.94-124.

14. Wiener, *Chemins de fer de l'Afrique,* pp.296-320; *Railway Year Book* (1915), p.296.

15. Wiener, *Chemins de fer de l'Afrique,* pp.491-95; M.F. Hill, *Permanent Way: Vol.I, The Story of the Kenya and Uganda Railway,* 2nd ed. (Nairobi: East African Railways and Harbours, 1961), pp.191, 243-4; *Railway Year Book* (1915), p.298; A.M. O'Connor, *Railways and Development in Uganda. A Study in Economic Geography* (Nairobi: Oxford University Press, 1965), pp.35-7.

16. Wiener, *Chemins de fer de l'Afrique,* pp.179-81, 466-70. *Railway Year Book,* (1915), p.296.

17. Wiener, *Chemins de fer de l'Afrique,* pp.97-8, 109-11, 409-21; *Railway Year Book* (1916), p.49.

18. Wiener, *Chemins de fer de l'Afrique,* pp.474-82; *Railway Year Book* (1916), p.49; M.F. Hill, *Permanent Way:* Vol.II, *The Story of the Tanganyika Railways* (Nairobi: East African Railways and Harbours, 1962), pp.57-96.

19. Wiener, *Chemins de fer de l'Afrique,* p.191; *Railway Year Book* (1916), p.49; Andre Huybrechts, *Transports et structures de développement au Congo: Etude du progrès économique de 1900 à 1970* (Paris: Mouton, 1970), pp.14-19, 395.

20. Wiener, *Chemins de fer de l'Afrique,* pp.147-79; *Railway Year Book* (1915), p.296; *Railway Year Book* (1916), p.49.

21. G.S. Graham, 'The Ascendency of the Sailing Ship 1850-85', *Economic History Review, 9* (1956), p.74; A.J.H. Latham, 'A Trading Alliance: Sir John Tobin and Duke Ephraim', *History Today,* Dec. (1974), p.867; P.N. Davies, 'The African Steam Ship Company', in *Liverpool and Merseyside: Essays in the Economic and Social History of the Port and its Hinterland,* ed. J.R. Harris (London: Cass, 1969), pp.214-16; P.N. Davies, *The Trade Makers: Elder Dempster in West Africa, 1852-1972* (London: George Allen & Unwin, 1973), pp.42-3; M. Murray, *Union Castle Chronicle 1853-1953* (London: Longmans Green, 1953), p.14; De Kock, *Economic History of South Africa,* p.339.

22. C.K. Harley, 'The Shift from Sailing Ships to Steamships, 1850-1890: A Study in Technological Change and its Diffusion', in *Essays on a Mature Economy: Britain after 1840,* ed. D.N. McCloskey (London: Methuen, 1971), pp.221-3.

23. Davies, in *Liverpool and Merseyside,* pp.218-19; Davies, *Trade Makers,* pp.56-62; A.J.H. Latham, *Old Calabar 1600-1891: The Impact of the International Economy upon a Traditional Society* (Oxford: Clarendon Press, 1973), p.63; C. Leubuscher, *The West African Shipping Trade, 1909-1959* (Leyden: Sythoff, 1962), pp.14-15.

24. F.E. Hyde, *Blue Funnel: A History of Alfred Holt & Co., Liverpool, 1865-1914* (Liverpool: Liverpool University Press, 1957), p.24.

25. M.E. Fletcher, 'The Suez Canal and World Shipping, 1869-1914', *Journal of Economic History,* 18 (1958), pp.558-9; Harley, 'Sailing Ships to Steamships', pp.223-4.

26. Fletcher, 'Suez Canal', pp.556-7; A.W. Kirkaldy and A.D. Evans, *The History and Economics of Transport,* 3rd ed. (London: Pitmans, 1924), p.289.

27. Graham, 'Ascendancy of the Sailing Ship', pp.82-8; Fletcher, 'Suez Canal', pp.562-3.

28. Kirkaldy and Evans, *History of Transport,* pp.290-1; Hyde, *Blue Funnel,* pp.182-4.

29. Harley, 'Sailing Ships to Steamships', pp.224-5, Hyde, *Blue Funnel,* pp.37-9.

30. D.A. Farnie, *East and West of Suez: The Suez Canal in History* (Oxford: Clarendon Press, 1969), pp.207-11; Murray, *Union Castle,* pp.68-72.

31. Farnie, *East and West of Suez,* p.196.

32. Hyde, *Blue Funnel,* pp.56-61; F.E. Hyde, *Far Eastern Trade 1860-1914* (London: Black, 1973), pp.26-30; F.E. Hyde, *Shipping Enterprise and Management 1830-1939, Harrisons of Liverpool, 1830-1939* (Liverpool: Liverpool University Press, 1967), pp.63-81; B.M. Deakin and T. Seward, *Shipping Conferences – A Study of their Origins, Development and Economic Practices* (Cambridge: Cambridge University Press, 1973), pp.13-34.

33. A.W. Kirkaldy, *British Shipping: Its History, Organisation and Importance* (London: Kegan Paul, Trench, Trubner, 1914), Appendix xvi.

34. Farnie, *East and West of Suez,* p.196.

35. J.A. Fairlie, 'The Economic Effects of Ship Canals', *American Academy of Political and Social Science Annals.,* Jan. (1898), p.63.

36. Fletcher, 'Suez Canal', pp.565-7.

37. Fletcher, 'Suez Canal', p.567; Davies, *Trade Makers,* p.109; E. Hieke, *G.L. Gaiser: Hamburg-West Africa, 100 Jahre Handel mit Nigeria* (Hamburg: Hoffman und Campe Verlag, 1949), pp.34-45, 63-78.

38. Fletcher, 'Suez Canal', p.567.

39. Fletcher, 'Suez Canal', p.567-70.

40. J.L. Kieve, *The Electrical Telegraph: A Social and Economic History* (Newton Abbot: David & Charles, 1973), p.13.

41. Das, *Modern India,* pp.109-47.

42. Farnie, *East and West of Suez,* p.156.

43. Das, *Modern India,* p.160.

44. Kieve, *Electrical Telegraph,* pp.109-16.

45. G.L. Lawford and L.R. Nicholson, *The Telecon Story* (London: The Telegraph Construction and Maintenance Co. Ltd, 1950), pp.174-5; G.R.M. Garratt, *One Hundred Years of Submarine Cables* (London: HMSO 1950), p.29.

46. Farnie, *East and West of Suez,* pp.156-61.

47. Farnie, *East and West of Suez,* pp.186-7; Chong-Yah, *Modern Malaya,* p.48.

48. Farnie, *East and West of Suez,* p.272; De Kock, *Economic History of South Africa,* p.354.

49. Lawford and Nicholson, *Telecon Story,* pp.174-5; R.O. Ekundare, *An Economic History of Nigeria, 1860-1960* (London: Methuen, 1973), p.78; R.J. Hammond, 'Uneconomic Imperialism: Portugal in Africa before 1910', in *Colonialism in Africa, 1870-1914, Vol.1, The History and Politics of Colonialism 1870-1914,* eds L.H. Gann and Peter Dingnan (Cambridge: Cambridge University Press, 1969), p.359.

50. Lawford and Nicholson, *Telecon Story,* pp.174-5.

51. Farnie, *East and West of Suez,* p.161.

2 MONEY AND CAPITAL

The Gold Standard and the Silver Problem

The late nineteenth century is often portrayed as a period of stability in monetary affairs, thanks to the operation of the gold standard. But in fact this was no golden age, and the adoption of the gold standard by the major Western powers left much of the undeveloped world on a silver standard which depreciated rapidly. A marked contrast emerged between the monetary stability of the gold-standard industrial countries of Europe and North America and the silver-standard countries of Asia.

Britain had operated a gold standard since 1821, but from 1819 the French maintained a bimetallic system which gave them the opportunity for very profitable arbitrage operations. Portugal, however, went on to the gold standard in 1854, taking advantage of the sudden increase in international gold stocks resulting from the Californian and Australian gold rushes. In 1865 the Latin Union was formed by France, Belgium, Italy and Switzerland. This marked an extension of bimetallism, as the members of the union agreed to buy and sell silver and gold so as to maintain the traditional price ratio of 15½ to 1 between them. But elsewhere in Europe, and in the United States, there was widespread discussion of gold monometallism. So when Germany defeated France in 1871, and adopted the gold standard in 1873, bimetallism was dealt a severe blow. Denmark, Sweden and Norway followed the German example. During 1873 silver flowed into France and Belgium in such quantities from the new gold-standard areas that they could no longer automatically coin the inflow as before, and in 1874 the Latin Union as a whole declared it could no longer coin silver on demand, effectively moving to the gold standard. Holland adopted gold in 1875, Spain in 1878, and Austria-Hungary in 1879. Meanwhile the United States had moved in a similar direction, the Coinage Act of 1873 suspending the free coinage of silver and making gold legal tender for all sums over $5. This was confirmed by the Bland-Allison Act of 1878, which became effective in 1879. Thus by 1880 the gold standard was established as the international monetary mechanism between the leading economies of the world.[1]

From 1873 there was a steep and continuous decline in the value of silver, and hence in the exchange value of the remaining silver-standard countries of the world, which included India, Ceylon, the Straits

Settlements, Siam, French Indo-China and China. The Dutch East Indies seem to have been almost alone in adopting a form of gold exchange stability as early as 1877, following the Dutch decision.[2] The decline in the value of silver, and the consequent fall in the Indian rupee and the Chinese haikwan tael are shown on Graph 3 (page 43). As can be seen, the price of silver per ounce in London fell from 60d (£0.25p) in 1872 to 35d in 1893 and 28d in 1894. In 1890 there was a temporary jump in prices as the United States decided to purchase 54 million ounces annually, by the Sherman Act. This led to furious speculation on the world market and a consequent rise in prices. But prices soon resumed their previous path, and although they began to stabilise following the repeal of the act in 1893, they fluctuated downwards to 1913.[3]

The reasons for the decline in the value of silver have been the subject of much controversy. The British Royal Commission set up in 1888 to inquire into the matter came to the conclusion that the abandoning of the link between silver and gold by the Latin Union had been crucial. From then onwards the value of silver had moved according to demand and the supply for it.[4] So up to 1888 the relative value of gold increased as demand for it rose as countries moved on to the gold standard, at a time when the number of international transactions was increasing. But its supply was constrained by the lack of new gold discoveries. Simultaneously, the demand for silver was decreasing as countries abandoned the silver standard, while its supply was increasing owing to new discoveries such as the Big Bonanza, and the continued exploitation of the Comstock Lode. After 1888 the supply of gold greatly increased with the mining of the great gold reef of the Witwatersrand in South Africa. But the gold price of silver continued to fall, particularly when India abandoned silver in 1893, and other Asian countries followed suit at the turn of the century.[5] It is quite clear that supply changes alone were insufficient to explain the ever falling gold price of silver, as an examination of the ratio of gold stocks to silver stocks shows (*see* Table 2).[6]

Table 2: Ratio of Gold Stocks to Silver Stocks, 1872-1913 (end-of-year stocks)

	Gold (millions oz)	Silver (millions oz)	Gold/silver ratio
1872	288.58	5,624	19.49
1888	370.68	6,966	18.79
1913	734.88	11,322	15.41

Graph 3: The Fall of Silver and Silver Currencies, 1872-1913

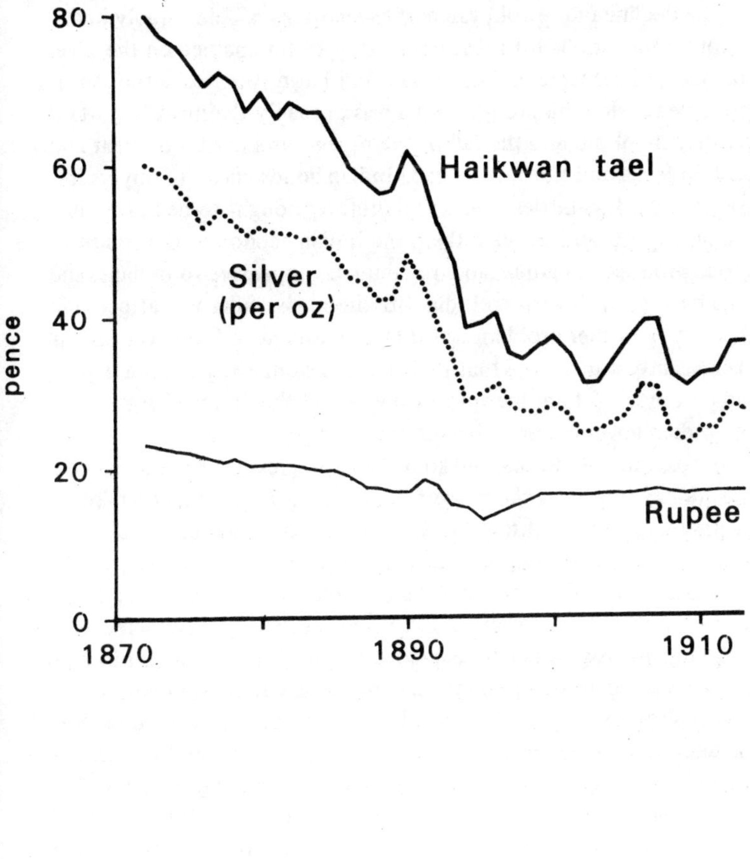

Sources: G.F. Shirras, *Indian Finance and Banking* (London: Macmillan 1919) pp.449-50, Table 6; 458, Table 12; C.F. Remer, *The Foreign Trade of China* (Shanghai: Commercial Press, 1926) p.250, Table 6; see Appendix 2.

In other words, the ratio of silver to gold actually decreased during the periods that silver was declining in gold value, both before the discovery of the Witwatersrand and after. So the fall in the gold price of silver must have been a result of the demand changes for each metal, not the supply changes. Indeed the ratio of stocks, at 15.41 in 1913, was closer to the traditional pre-1873 exchange rate of 15½ to 1 than it had been any time since the Latin Union was forced to abandon the link.

The decline in the gold value of silver after 1873 inevitably had serious implications for those countries which remained on the silver standard. These were mainly in Asia and Latin America, although the latter lie outside this study.[7] India was probably the most important country involved, and the fall of the rupee was a matter of great concern both in India and Europe. It made Indian goods cheap to buyers in gold-standard countries, and was therefore thought to be a stimulus to Indian exports and through them the Indian economy. But it also made goods produced in gold-standard countries expensive to Indians, and held back their exports to India. Britain in particular was affected in this way. Another problem was that investment to India was discouraged, as investors feared that their returns would be paid in a depreciated currency. Yet another problem was that the 'home charges' owed by the Indian government to Britain for a variety of goods and services were fixed in gold terms, and so became progressively burdensome to the administration as the rupee fell. However, no action was taken to tackle the problem, until 1890 when silver prices soared under the speculative pressure which was the international response to the silver-purchase clause of the Sherman Act. Trade between Britain and India became nothing but a gamble on the exchanges, and commerce was seriously disrupted. The Indian Government pressed London to allow it to adopt the gold standard, and a committee was set up under Lord Herschell to examine the matter. It reported in May 1893 in favour of closing the Indian mints to the free coinage of silver, and this was done, a fixed rate of exchange between gold and silver being announced. So India at last was on the gold standard, and after some fluctuations this settled down to a stable rate of about 16d from 1898. Further legislation in 1899 backed up the new situation, and made the sovereign and half-sovereign legal tender in India, at 15 rupees and 7½ rupees respectively. But the attempt to introduce the sovereign and half-sovereign as circulating coins was a failure, and they quickly returned to the government treasuries, leading to a shortage of rupees. So it was accepted that the rupee, augmented with paper notes, would be the best currency medium for India, its value being maintained at the declared rate through the purchase and sale of silver by the currency reserve. That was the system from 1900, and the Chamberlain commission of 1914 found that it had been very successful. Certainly the Indian economy prospered enormously between 1900 and 1914.[8]

The monetary history of Ceylon closely echoed that of India. The coin of Southern India had always tended to become the coin of Ceylon, and thus in 1873 the rupee became the legal currency. Accordingly, Ceylon suffered the same problems, and received the same advantages that India did, as silver prices fell. And when India adopted the gold standard in 1893, Ceylon went with her, although not without indignation and several protests. For it was felt that the depreciating silver standard had been a major factor in developing the tea industry when the coffee trade failed. Ceylon's major rivals in the tea trade were the Chinese, who remained on the silver standard, and would gain an advantage over the Ceylon planters as silver continued to depreciate. But Ceylon did reluctantly accept the situation, and remained part of the rupee area, sharing its fortunes.[9]

In the Straits Settlements the same problem existed. In 1867 the Straits were transferred from the control of the Indian Government to the British Colonial Office, and Indian coins were replaced by dollars from the Royal Mint at Hong Kong, together with Spanish, Mexican, Peruvian and Bolivian silver dollars. All previous laws of legal tender were repealed in 1890, and the Mexican dollar was declared the standard of value, with the Japanese yen, the Hong Kong dollar and half dollar, and the American trade dollar accorded the status of legal tender. The yen and the American dollar lost this status by Orders in Council of 1895 and 1898, although the British dollar recently coined by the unemployed Indian mints was to be accepted. So the Straits Settlements, the Federated Malay States, and Johore, which shared this common silver-based system, also experienced the problems of silver depreciation. Trade with Java and Sumatra was particularly affected as the Dutch East Indies had been on gold since 1877. The situation deteriorated after the closure of the Indian mints in 1893, but as exporting interests gained a competitive benefit from the depreciation, the committee set up to make recommendations could not agree. So it was not until 1903 that currency reform was decided upon, as a result of the uncertainty in exchange dealings caused by the recent sudden drop in the price of silver from 27d to 24d per oz. A Straits dollar was to be introduced, equal to the British dollar in weight and fineness, and it was to displace the British and Mexican dollar in circulation as soon as possible. Once in circulation its supply was to be restricted to force up its value to a suitable rate of exchange with the sovereign, when its rate would be fixed and declared. This operation took place in 1905, and in 1906 the rate was fixed at 28d, a reserve being established to maintain it. This new gold rate was a substantial increase on the old rate of under 19d, and the export and transit trades were badly affected until about 1910.[10]

As has already been mentioned, the first Asiatic country to make the change from silver to gold was Java, or the Dutch East Indies. When silver began to depreciate, Netherlands India was on the silver standard, with the guilder or florin the basic unit as in Holland. But when the Netherlands went on to the gold standard in 1875, Netherlands India remained on silver for two years, in which time she felt the consequences of the fall of silver. So in 1877 the colony was placed on the same basis as the mother country. In fact little gold actually circulated, and the silver token coins were accepted at their face value. Management of the exchange was in the hands of the Java Bank. As the trade balance was usually favourable, it was not difficult to maintain the gold standard.[11]

Siam was also a silver-standard country and was similarly affected by the depreciation of silver. From the 1850s the basic unit was the baht or tical, a bullet-shaped lump of silver, although as in Africa, and in China in the past, cowrie shells and salt often served as currency. As silver fell, so did the exchange value of the baht against sterling or gold, but not against the silver dollars of her neighbours. Although most of her exports went to the silver-standard countries nearby, many of her imports came from Britain, and the increasing cost of these imports, particularly railway equipment forced the Government to accept the recommendation of their British economic adviser and break the tie with silver. The baht had declined from 30d from the early 1870s to 11d in 1902, the year the mints were closed. The system adopted was a form of sterling exchange, but it served the purpose of stabilising the exchange in gold terms, the new rate being 14.11d. This proved to be too high, and the rate was finally fixed at 12d later that year. As the price of silver began to appreciate in 1904 further alterations had to be made to the rate to prevent an outflow of baht as bullion, and the rate finally reached 18.46d in 1907. The volume of rice exports was not much affected by this appreciation, being more dependent on rain than exchange rates.[12]

French-Indo China was not exempt from the silver problem. Before the French came, the currency situation was chaotic, coins of different weights, metals and standards all being used at the same time. But the principal trading currency was the Mexican dollar, together with Dutch, British and Spanish silver coins. Attempts were made by the French to introduce the franc, but this failed, and it was decided to coin a trade dollar or piastre, like the dollars which other countries were circulating. This was first coined in 1885, but although it exchanged at par with the Mexican dollar and Japanese yen, it contained a little more silver than either. Gresham's law operated, and the good piastre was driven out of circulation by the bad dollar, until a new piastre of equivalent silver content was introduced. As silver depreciated, and nearby countries turned to gold, French exporters and Indo-Chinese importers complained about their unfavourable position. The administration was also worried about the increasing cost of its contribution towards the French military occupation, and the fact that French capital investment was being inhibited to the detriment of development. So in 1902, as in Siam, the link between the piastre and silver was broken, and the Government began to control the issue of coinage. But unlike Siam, there was no attempt to fix the rate against gold. Imports of Mexican dollars were prohibited, and as they could still be exported, they slowly disappeared from circulation. In 1904 the export of piastres was also prohibited, because of the demands for specie resulting from the Russo-Chinese war. Under this 'closed vase' regime the rate of exchange could vary enormously. When the balance of trade was favourable and foreigners were unable to obtain piastres with silver, the exchange rate rose high above its intrinsic value. On the rare occasions that the trade balance was unfavourable, the exchange rate fell below the intrinsic value as specie could not be exported to settle the account. Despite severe criticism, the commissions that inquired into the situation could not agree and this unsatisfactory system, neither gold nor silver standard, continued until the First World War.[13]

In China, the currency situation was even more confused than it was in Indo-China. Cowrie shells had been used in China as money since 2400 BC but by the middle of the nineteenth century the system was based on silver and copper. There were copper 'cash' coins for small denominations, and the basic unit of account was the tael whose value was equivalent to one liang or Chinese ounce of silver. However there was no silver coinage, and no coin which represented the tael. Taels could be paid only by an equivalent amount of silver. This led to a very complicated situation as the silver in circulation varied in quality, most of it being the dollars and pieces of dollars of other countries. To make matters worse, there were several different interpretations of the value of the tael in operation at the various international ports. The haikwan tael was simply the tael used for customs purposes. This inadequate system lasted until the 1930s. China's persistence in remaining on a silver standard brought her the now familiar problems which other silver-standard countries experienced. Her exports were stimulated, as they appeared cheap to buyers in gold-standard countries. So the closing of the Indian mints in 1893 gave the Shanghai cotton industry an edge over Indian competitors, and the same was true of tea. The 'muck and truck' mixed-merchandise trade of China was stimulated, and this was reflected in increased general industrial activity in Shanghai. At the same time imports from gold-standard countries became more expensive, which was particularly serious for railway development. Foreign investment in China was also discouraged, for fear of repayment in a depreciated standard.[14]

The neighbouring British colony of Hong Kong also clung to silver, in her case until 1925. In 1863 the Mexican and equivalent dollars were made legal tender, and 1866-8 dollars were minted in Hong Kong. Later banknotes were introduced backed by Mexican dollars and the British dollars coined in Bombay from 1895. She retained the British dollar and its subsidiary silver coinage until the end.[15] Japan had gone on to the gold standard in 1897, and the Philippines in 1903, so at the outbreak of war only China, Hong Kong, French Indo-China (after a fashion) and a few Asian and Latin American countries of minor significance remained on the silver standard.[16]

The monetary situation in Africa was really rather different. For the most part Africans still used for their ordinary transactions their traditional monetary mediums such as cowrie shells, the brass bangles known as manillas, copper rods and wires, palm cloth mats, blocks of salt, cattle and grain. None of these were managed currencies, and their value depended upon supply and demand for them. Inflows of cowries and copper rods led to the depreciation of both these moneys during the second half of the century.[17] As might be expected, it was in Cape Colony, which dominated the monetary practices of the colonies which were to make up South Africa, that the first attempts were made to introduce a modern monetary system. Sterling was introduced in 1825, with subsidiary coinage. Gold coins from the Sydney mint were made legal tender in 1867, and in 1881 the subsidiary coinage was declared legal tender only up to 40 shillings, as in Britain. Natal shared this history after she became British in 1843, but in the Orange Free State and the Transvaal there were problems arising from the use of Boer rix dollars, and the overissue of paper money. These problems were solved by internal measures controlling the bank issue of paper, and the currency system was finally unified after the establishment of the Union of South Africa in 1909.[18]

Elsewhere in Africa, as has been pointed out already, traditional monetary systems operated, although as colonial authorities established themselves they tended to encourage the use of their own currencies. Thus in the British West African territories the shilling came into use as the medium of circulation from the 1890s. By 1912 British gold, silver and copper coins were legal tender, but in certain areas French, Spanish and American gold coins and the five-franc pieces of the Latin Union were also legal tender. In the Gold Coast there was a recently introduced nickel-bronze currency of pennies, half-pennies and tenth-pennies. Cowries, manillas, brass, copper and iron rods and gold dust were also legal tender in certain areas. Manillas continued to be used for many years in the Niger Delta, and when they were finally called in, in 1948-9, 30 million were collected. However a problem existed as shillings came into wider circulation, as they were only legal tender in Britain up to a limit of 40. Should a crisis arise and a mass conversion of shillings from West Africa be attempted, holders might be refused exchange, and lose their assets. Another problem was that there was no coinage denomination small enough to pay for the petty transactions of the local markets. So the committee set up to inquire into the situation recommended that a West African Currency Board be set up in London to manage a new silver-shilling coinage, the coinage profits going to establish a fund to guarantee convertibility if a crisis occurred. The value of the West African shilling would be maintained in sterling terms, and a new small denomination was to be issued as in the Gold Coast. These measures were effective from 1913.[19]

In British East Africa it was the rupee which was introduced as legal tender to displace traditional money, for when British traders and missionaries first entered the region, they did so from areas where the rupee was the standard unit. Reorganisation of the currency arrangements did not come until after the war in 1919, when an East African Currency Board was established on similar lines to that for West Africa.[20] So the currency systems of the British African territories in so far as they replaced traditional units were either an extension of sterling as in the South and West, or an extension of the rupee as in the East.

The French also took over territories with existing traditional systems, and gradually introduced their own currency medium, in this case the franc. They granted the Banque de l'Afrique Occidentale the privilege of becoming the sole bank of issue for French West Africa in

1901. The bank had to ensure that the currency circulating in French West Africa was freely convertible with the franc, and maintain a specified ratio between reserves and currency. It also had to make a financial contribution to the metropolis and the colonies. These arrangements lasted until 1945.[21]

In the German colonies a similar situation existed, with traditional monies slowly giving way to the metropolitan currency, in this case the mark. Silver coins were imported from Germany and made legal tender. In 1888 licences to import spirits costing 2,000 marks were being required of African traders in the Cameroons, and similar licences were introduced in Togo soon afterwards. In Tanganyika the situation was rather different, and the Germans had to bow to the predominance of the rupee. There they introduced a German rupee, divided into 100 heller, rather than annas and pies.[22]

In the Belgian Congo indigenous currencies had flourished before the establishment of the Congo State in 1885, and they continued to do so until the twentieth century, although an attempt was made to circulate some Congo State money. When the state became a Belgian Colony entirely in 1908 the currency situation was tackled and the Congo State money demonetised, Belgian francs being substituted in 1909. The Bank of the Belgian Congo, a private bank, was given authority to issue notes, but it had to share the profits with the metropolis. The charter giving Belgian currency validity in the colony assigned the profits of any coinage struck for the Congo to the colonial revenue.[23]

As with the other European colonial powers, Portugal introduced her domestic currency to her colonies, in this case the escudo. Portugal had been on the gold standard since 1854, but after a financial crisis in 1891 she was forced off the gold standard, leading to a loss in international confidence which made it difficult for her to raise capital for the development of the colonies.[24]

So Africa was largely unaffected by the collapse of silver, except in respect of the rupee in East Africa, but it can have been of little importance as the rupee was stabilised in 1893 when European penetration was not far advanced. Thus Africa's monetary experience in this period again reveals that she was only then being drawn into the international economy.

International Capital Movements

The development of the gold-standard system after 1873 encouraged and helped the flow of capital between the various countries which maintained the gold standard. But at the same time, the decline of silver discouraged the flow of capital to those parts of the world which remained on a silver standard, as investors feared, with justification, their returns being made in a depreciated currency. One of the major incentives to countries in the East to move on to the gold standard was the desire to increase investment from abroad. Africa was less affected by this problem, as few African currencies were based on silver, the currencies in operation being either traditional moneys or those of the colonial powers, most of whom operated the gold standard.

Beyond dispute, the major investor in the undeveloped world in these years was Britain. On Graph 4, page 52, is shown both the amount of new British portfolio investment in Asia and Africa in this period and the proportion of total British new-portfolio foreign investment which went to these areas. What is immediately striking is that, notwithstanding the problems of silver, the share of investment going to Asia and Africa was substantial. Indeed, in the 50 years up to 1914, no less than 25 per cent of aggregate new British portfolio foreign investment went to Asia and Africa. Asia alone received 14 per cent, which was 1 per cent more than Europe, and Africa received 11 per cent, as much as Australia. If the Americas dominated, with 17 per cent to South America, 21 per cent to the United States, and 13 per cent in the rest of North America, it is nonetheless significant that Asia and Africa absorbed a larger aggregate inflow of British capital than the United States, the single most important recipient. Of course, it must be noted that the figures for Africa include areas which really lie outside this study, in particular Egypt, and some might question the inclusion of the large flows to South Africa to develop the diamond and gold fields. But the fact remains that substantial British capital flows did take place to these areas, the most important single area being India. The tropical section of the British Empire, which included Egypt, India, Ceylon and Malayan settlements, took just over 14 per cent of total British overseas investment. Besides this, Britain also had substantial investments in the Dutch East Indies, and China.[25]

Details of the distribution of British overseas investment at the outbreak of the First World War may be obtained from Table 3 (page 53), which also includes the details of the investments of the major creditor nations. It is immediately apparent that Britain provided £1,016 million out of the world total investment of £1,561 million in these areas of Asia and Africa, some 65%. India and Ceylon received most British capital going to these regions, taking £380 million out of Britain's total Asian commitment of £575 million. China came next

Graph 4: New British Portfolio Foreign Investment, 1865-1914

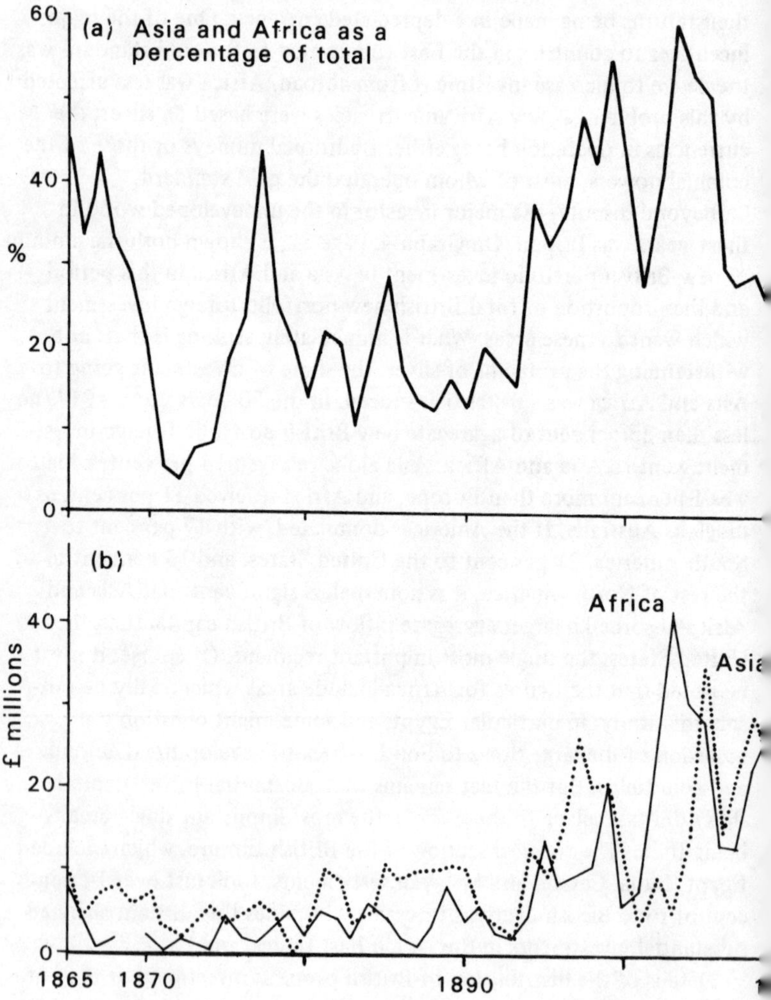

Source: Mathew Simon, 'The Pattern of New British Portfolio Foreign Investment, 1865-1914', in *The Export of Capital from Britain 1870-1914*, ed. A.R. Hall (London: Methuen & Co. 1968), pp.39-40, Appendix Table; see Appendix 3.

Table 3: Investment in Asia and Africa, 1914 (£ million)

	Britain	%	France	Germany	USA	Rest	Total	%
Asia								
India & Ceylon	380	37.40	–	–	–	–	380	24.34
Indo-China	–	–	41	–	–	–	41	2.62
Straits Sttmts	31	3.05	–	–	–	–	31	1.98
Dutch E. Indies	41	4.03	–	–	–	113	154	9.86
China	123	12.10	31	51	10	113	328	21.01
Asian total	575	56.59	72	51	10	226	934	59.83
Africa								
Brit. W. Africa	41	4.03	–	–	–	–	41	2.62
South Africa	318	31.29	21	–	–	–	339	21.71
Rhodesia	51	5.01	–	–	–	–	51	3.26
Brit. E. Africa	31	3.05	–	–	–	–	31	1.98
French Colonies	–	–	21	–	–	–	21	1.34
German Colonies	–	–	–	82	–	–	82	5.25
Belgian Congo	–	–	–	21	–	41	62	3.97
African total	441	43.40	42	103	–	41	627	40.16
Total	1,016	99.99	114	154	10	267	1,561	99.99
World total	4,107							

Source: William Woodruff, *Impact of Western Man, A Study of Europe's Role in the World Economy, 1750-1960* (New York: St Martin's Press, 1966), pp.154-5, Table IV/3.

with £123 million, followed by the Dutch East Indies with £41 million and the Straits Settlements with £31 million. In Africa, South Africa predominated, and together with Rhodesia it had taken £359 million from a total of £441 million. British West Africa came next with £41 million, then British East Africa with £31 million. So it can be said that British capital concentrated on British possessions to a greater extent in Africa than in Asia. After Britain, Germany was the most important investor in Asia and Africa, contributing £154 million or 10 per cent of the world total, with most of it, some £82 million, being in her African colonies. But she had also invested £51 million in China, and another £21 million in the Belgian Congo. To get an idea of the relative importance of German investment, it is worth noting that her total investments were less than Britain's investment in China and the Dutch East Indies. France came next with £114 million, just over 7 per cent of the world total. Although £41 million was in her colonies in Indo-China, she had also put nearly as much (£31 million) into China itself. Similarly, while £21 million was in her African colonies, another £21 million went to South Africa. However, her total investment was less than Britain's investment in China alone. Apart from the £10 million contributed by the United States, all of which was invested in China, the rest of the world, including the Netherlands, Belgium and Japan, put in £267 million, just £1 million less than the sums invested by Germany and France together. It also fell short of British investment in South Africa by £51 million. China received £113 million, and the Dutch East Indies another £113 million, the remaining £41 million being placed in the Belgian Congo.

The variations in the flow of capital to Asia and Africa from countries other than Britain from 1865 to 1914 is not known, but as British capital formed such a large proportion of the total, it is probably fair to assume that the aggregate flow must have resembled that from Britain. As can be seen on Graph 4 (page 52), over 46 per cent of British investment went to Asia and Africa in 1865; but this had fallen back to 5 per cent in 1872, the year preceding the financial crisis of 1873. From then on investment to both Asia and Africa grew slowly, and the share they received of total British investment also increased, to fluctuate at around 20 per cent. Despite the importance of India, the flows to Asia did not greatly exceed those to Africa, because of the influence of South African diamonds in the 1870s and gold from the late 1880s. Between 1891 and 1893 investment to both Asia and Africa plunged, and in the latter year India moved on to the gold standard with the closure of the mints. The following year there was a dramatic increase to both continents, which between them claimed over 37 per cent of British investment that year. This recovery was essentially maintained until 1903, when over 59 per cent of Britain's total went to these areas, Africa absorbing the most she was to do in any year before the Great War. The peak year for Asia was 1905, and thereafter investment to the undeveloped world began to fall away up to 1914.

For what purposes, then, was this investment used? It is quite clear that as far as total British international investment is concerned, railways were the major recipients of capital, absorbing no less than 41 per cent. Port facilities and roads took most of a further 5 per cent, which went to the creation of transport facilities. Another 23 per cent provided other kinds of public utilities and public works, so that in all 69 per cent went to the provision of social overhead capital. A further 12 per cent of British world investment went to mining and extractive industries, but less than 4 per cent was channelled into manufacturing. The remaining 15 per cent went into miscellaneous outlets, of which plantations must have been important.[26] It is now necessary to examine the pattern of foreign investment in the countries in question to see how true the overall pattern is of individual cases. This is also essential because there is no easily available evidence on the breakdown of the investments of other international creditor nations.

The railways had always dominated in India and Ceylon as an outlet for investment, and it has been estimated that between 1845 and 1875 nearly £103 million had been channelled into Indian guaranteed railway loans. From 1854 to 1869 about £154 million was invested in railways, shipping, tea plantations, jute mills, banking and other mercantile houses, establishing a pattern of investment which was to continue up to 1914. It must be noted, however, that the Indians themselves financed and controlled the early cotton mills, and in 1913 founded what was to become the vast Tata iron and steel corporation. Nevertheless, by the beginning of the First World War some 70 per cent to 75 per cent of recorded investment in India had come from abroad. Table 4 on page 56 shows the pattern of British investment as it stood in 1910. It confirms the importance of the railways, which had taken 37 per cent of investment up to that time, and of the 49 per cent invested in government a very large proportion had been used for railway construction. The next largest single outlet was the 5 per cent placed in tea and coffee plantations. Rubber plantations, and tramways, both with just over 1 per cent, and mines, which together with municipal investments took just under 1 per cent, follow. Then comes a long list of banks, commerce, oil, electricity, finance, telegraphs and telephones, coal and iron, gas and water, all with fractions of 1 per cent.[27]

At first sight, the pattern of investment in the Straits Settlements and Malay States appears to differ markedly from that in India and Ceylon. For there rubber attracted the biggest proportion of British capital in 1910, nearly 49 per cent. But the sum involved, £10.6 million, was not much more than double the £4.6 million invested in rubber in India and Ceylon. Apart from this, 36 per cent was in government, most of which was spent on the substantial dock works of Penang and Singapore, and also on railways, although the favourable current revenues of the Government made capital imports less necessary for railway building here than elsewhere. Another 9 per cent approximately

Table 4: Categories of British Investment in Asia, 1910 (£000)

	India & Ceylon	%	Straits Sttmts & Malay States	%	China	%
Government	178,995	48.98	7,943	36.04	22,477	83.84
Municipal	3,522	0.96	–	–	–	–
Railways	136,519	37.36	–	–	–	–
Banks	3,400	0.93	–	–	–	–
Commerce & industry	2,647	0.72	–	–	1,401	5.22
Electric light & power	1,763	0.48	–	–	9	.03
Finance, land & investment	1,853	0.50	1,485	6.73	1,879	7.00
Gas & water	659	0.18	–	–	373	1.39
Iron, coal, steel	803	0.21	–	–	–	–
Mines	3,531	0.96	1,912	8.67	350	1.30
Motor traction & manufacturing	90	0.02	–	–	–	–
Oil	3,184	0.87	–	–	–	–
Rubber	4,610	1.26	10,697	48.54	–	–
Tea & coffee	19,644	5.37	–	–	–	–
Telegraphs & telephones	43	0.01	–	–	–	–
Tramways	4,136	1.13	–	–	320	1.19
Total	365,399	99.94	22,037	99.98	26,809	99.97

Source: George Paish, 'Great Britain's Capital Investments in Individual Colonial and Foreign Countries', *Journal of the Royal Statistical Society,* 74 (1911), p.180.

was invested in tin mining, but it should be pointed out that much of the success of tin mining before the First World War was a result of the capital and enterprise of Malayan Chinese. The amount involved, £1.9 million, was actually less than the £3.5 million invested in Indian mining. A further 7 per cent went into finance, land and investment. In examining the record of foreign investment in Malaya, it is worth recording that there were some French, Belgian, Malayan Chinese and Shanghai interests in the rubber sector, although this does not show up in the statistics available.[28]

There is no such handy breakdown as Paish's for reference in discussing foreign investment in the Dutch East Indies. But from the information available, the pattern is much as one would expect. Of the £154 million invested there in 1914, £41 million was British, mainly financing rubber, tea and tobacco plantations. The remaining capital was mostly from the Netherlands, and was in plantations of all kinds, especially sugar, coffee, tea, tobacco and rubber. Railways, and the light railways known as tramways, which served the plantations, were important, as was petroleum. The Government also borrowed from abroad for railways and tramways, and other public works, and was directly involved in commercial undertakings in tin mining, coal mining and plantations of rubber, chinchona, coco-nuts, gutta-percha, oil palms, kapok and teak.[29]

In Siam there was foreign investment in teak from the 1880s, and by 1895 the British had invested nearly £1 million in this industry. By 1899 this figure had risen to £2 million out of a total foreign commitment of £2.5 million, much of the rest being Danish. There was investment in rice mills from Europe, the United States, and by Chinese at this time; and Chinese and Australians had interests in tin mining. Apart from this, the Siam Electric Company of 1887 was financed by European capital, and brought electricity and tramcars to Bangkok. In the first decade of the new century the Government obtained British loans to build the first railways, and by 1909 it had borrowed £4.63 million.[30]

French Indo-China was dependent mainly on France for its imported capital, and by 1914 there was £41 million invested there. The early railways had been built with government loans raised in France; and between 1901 and 1911 the Yunnan railway company borrowed over £10 million. Loans from France also paid for irrigation and flood-protection schemes, city sewers and electric power. Besides this, French capital had gone into the coal industry since 1888 when the Tonkin coal reserves were first exploited. After 1901-2 capital went into tin mining, and in 1906 into zinc as well. A cement factory was built with imported capital in 1899, and foreign capital was placed in rice alcohol production from 1900, and also cotton spinning. By 1908 there was also French capital in breweries, tobacco and match companies. Agriculture was relatively neglected until forestry attracted capital in 1905-8, and from 1910 there was investment in hevea plantations.[31]

China was the third most important recipient of foreign capital in Asia and Africa, after India and South Africa. There was £328 million invested there in 1914, of which Britain had supplied £123 million, Germany £51 million, France £31 million, the United States £10 million and the rest of the world, including Russia and Japan, £113 million. A slightly different set of estimates is given in Table 5 (p.58) which also shows how the shares of foreign investors changed between

Table 5: Foreign Investment in China, 1902, 1914

	1902 £ million	%	1914 £ million	%
Britain	53.44	33.0	124.74	37.7
Japan	0.20	0.1	45.09	13.6
Russia	50.61	31.3	55.29	16.7
United States	4.04	2.5	10.12	3.1
France	18.70	11.6	35.19	10.7
Germany	33.73	20.9	54.12	16.4
Belgium	0.90	0.6	4.70	1.4
Others	0.12	0.0	1.37	0.4
Total	161.74	100.0	330.62	100.0

Source: C.F. Remer, *Foreign Investments in China* (New York: Macmillan, 1933), p.76, Table 7.

1902 and 1914. It can be seen that the British share actually increased during the period from 33 per cent to nearly 38 per cent while the Russian share declined from 31 per cent to about 17 per cent, and the German share from 21 per cent to just over 16 per cent. The United States' share increased from 2.5 per cent to 10 per cent, but the most dramatic increase was Japan's rise from 0.1 per cent to nearly 14 per cent. At the same time, total foreign investment more than doubled from £162 million to £330 million. As might be expected, transport consumed the largest part of this investment, as Table 6 reveals. The general purposes of the Chinese Government were the next most important item, and included war and indemnity loans. Imports and exports also attracted capital, as did manufacturing, this being particularly interesting in view of the low contribution of British investment to manufacturing in both China and other parts of the world. Mining and real estate also attracted substantial sums. Another point worth noting about foreign investment in China at this time is that in 1914 Shanghai had received 18.1 per cent of the total and Manchuria 22.4 per cent, these being the two most important areas. British investment accords fairly well with the overall pattern of foreign investment, as can be seen in Table 4, page 56. Of British investment 84 per cent was in government in 1910 and although it is not clear how much of this was used for railways, it is a safe assumption that much of it was. Finance, land and investment came next with 7 per cent, followed by commerce and industry with 5 per cent. Then came gas and water,

Table 6: Categories of Foreign Investment in China, 1914

	£ million	%
Government	67.82	20.5
Transport	109.05	33.0
Communications & public utilities	5.46	1.7
Mining	12.13	3.7
Manufacturing	22.71	6.9
Banking and finance	1.29	0.4
Real estate	21.66	6.5
Imports and exports	29.28	8.8
Miscellaneous	61.23	18.5
Total	330.63	100.0

Source: Remer, *Foreign Investments in China*, p.70, Table 5.

mines and tramways, all with just over 1 per cent, and lastly electric lighting and power, with much less than 1 per cent.[32]

In Africa, South Africa attracted the overwhelming majority of foreign funds, £339 million out of a total of £637 million. Of British investment in Africa at the outbreak of the First World War, South Africa had received £318 million out of £441 million, some 72 per cent. Rhodesia had taken another 11.5 per cent of British African investment, making a total of 83.6 per cent for Rhodesia and South Africa together. Before examining the distribution of British funds in South Africa and Rhodesia, it is worth noting that France had invested £21 million in South Africa by 1914. Table 7 (p.60), shows the allocation of British funds in 1910. Diamonds and gold and other metals were the reason for the substantial investment in this area, as is borne out by the fact that mines attracted over 35 per cent of total investment, and the 21 per cent going to finance, land and investment can be regarded as supplementary to this. Government took the next highest amount, 28 per cent, most of which provided railway and transport facilities to service the mines; and besides this another 3 per cent went direct to railways. After these major outlets came the usual lists of municipal loans, commerce, iron, coal, steel, banks, electricity, breweries, etc.

There was £41 million invested in West Africa in 1914 which, perhaps, surprisingly, was £10 million more than in the Straits Settlements. In 1910 the pattern of investment there was very similar to that in South Africa, with mining being by far the most important sector, reflecting recent gold discoveries there. Some £12 million had

Table 7: Categories of British Investment in Africa, 1910 (£000)

	South Africa & Rhodesia	%	West Africa	%
Government	97.379	27.71	8,541	28.95
Municipal	17,701	5.03	—	—
Railways	9,354	2.66	—	—
Banks	4,558	1.29	257	0.87
Breweries	3,065	0.87	—	—
Commerce & industry	7,024	1.99	1,547	5.24
Electric light & power	3,667	1.04	—	—
Finance, land & investment	73,363	20.87	5,242	17.77
Gas & water	1,339	0.38	—	—
Iron, coal, steel	6,392	1.81	—	—
Mines	125,065	35.59	12,437	42.16
Nitrate	165	0.04	—	—
Oil	495	0.14	428	1.45
Rubber	—	—	1,046	3.54
Tramways	1,801	0.51	—	—
Total	351,368	99.93	29,498	99.98

Source: Paish, 'Great Britain's Capital Investments', p.180.

gone into this industry, 42 per cent of the total. Again Government came next, with 29 per cent, most of which had been spent on railways and ports. Also, as in South Africa, 18 per cent was in finance, land, and investment, supportive of mining. Commerce took 5 per cent and rubber 3.5 per cent, reflecting as in the Straits the rubber boom in response to the needs of the motor car. East Africa had taken £31 million in 1914, but unfortunately there is no breakdown of this investment available.[33]

There remains the question of capital investment in other parts of Africa; the French, German, Belgian and Portuguese colonies. Here information is scant. However, the French colonies had attracted £21 million by 1914, most of which was used for the railway programmes. Initially this finance took the form of loans to Government. Despite the acquisition of colonies, most of French foreign investment continued to go to Europe, and of her colonies, it was those in North Africa and Indo-China which took precedence. Yet there was some private investment in copper mines in the French Congo. The German colonies had received some £82 million, nearly all from Germany. South West Africa absorbed most of this, which went into the extensive railway system there. Railway construction was important too in Togo, Cameroon and Tanganyika. There was also investment in commerce, cotton, coffee and banana plantations, farms and mining enterprises. In the Belgian Congo in 1914, about half of the total investment of £62 million, only a third of which had come from Belgium, had gone into railways. A further 34 per cent was in mining, financial and exploration companies. Another 16 per cent had been put into commerce, agriculture, real estate and sundry industries, reflecting the pattern of the other colonial areas of Africa. As for Portuguese Africa, there was little capital there, owing both to the poverty of Portugal and the consequences of the financial crisis she faced in the 1890s. What capital there was went primarily to the provision of port and railway facilities, with Beira and Lourenço Marques being particularly important.[34]

In conclusion, then, it may be said that the capital flows to the undeveloped world in this period went primarily into railway and transport provisions, with smaller amounts going into mining and plantations which the transport facilities served.

Notes

1. Francis A. Walker, *International Bimetallism* (London: Macmillan, 1896), pp.131-7, 170-7, 184; H.P. Willis, *A History of the Latin Monetary Union,* 2nd ed. (New York: Greenwood Press, 1968), pp.59-60, 108-9, 112-22, 143-9; G.F. Shirras, *Indian Finance and Banking* (London: Macmillan, 1919), p.115; Ed. R. Robey, *The Monetary Problem, Gold and Silver: Final Report of the Royal Commission Appointed to Inquire Into the Recent Changes in the Relative Values of the Precious Metals, Presented to Both Houses of Parliament, 1888* (New York: Colombia University Press, 1936), pp.xiii, 26-8, 30, 64; Milton Friedman and Anna Jacobson Schwartz, *A Monetary History of the United States 1867-1960* (Princeton, Princeton University Press, 1963), pp.64, 89-90; Robert Triffin, *The Evolution of the International Monetary System: Historical Reappraisal and Future Perspectives* (Princeton: Princeton University, 1964), p.9; Count Matsukata Masayoshi, *Report on the Adoption of the Gold Standard in Japan* (Tokyo: Government Press, 1889), pp.vi-vii; B.R. Ambedkar, *The Problem of the Rupee, Its Origin and its Solution* (London: P.S. King & Son, 1923), pp.73-5; D.H. Leavens, *Silver Money* (Bloomington: Principia Press, 1939), pp.30-3.
2. Leavens, *Silver Money,* p.108.
3. Shirras, *Indian Finance,* p.133; Friedman and Schwartz, *Monetary History of the United States,* p.108.
4. Robey, *Monetary Problem,* pp.17-142.
5. Triffin, *Evolution of the Monetary System,* p.17; Benjamin White, *Silver, Its History and Romance* (London: Hodder and Stoughton, 1917), pp.46-60;

Benjamin White, *Gold, Its Place in the Economy of Mankind* (London: Sir Isaac Pitman, 1920), pp.48-50; R.A. Lehfeldt, *Gold Prices and the Witwatersrand* (London: P.S. King & Co., 1919), pp.3, 116.

6. Triffin, *Evolution of the Monetary System,* pp.79 (Table 17), 81 (Table 18).

7. David Williams, 'The Evolution of the Sterling System', in *Essays in Money and Banking in Honour of R.S. Sayers,* ed. C.R. Whittlesey and J.S.G. Wilson (Oxford: Clarendon Press, 1968), pp.272-3.

8. Shirras, *Indian Finance,* pp.113-223; Leavens, *Silver Money,* p.72; Marcello de Cecco, *Money and Empire: The International Gold Standard, 1890-1914* (Oxford: Basil Blackwell, 1974), pp.62-75; H.L. Singh, 'The Indian Currency Problem 1885-1900', in *Bengal, Past and Present,* 80 (1961), pp.16-37.

9. H.A. de S. Gunasekera, *From Dependent Currency to Central Banking in Ceylon. An Analysis of Monetary Experience, 1825-1957* (London: G. Bell & Sons, 1962), pp.1-6, 45-6, 59-60, 94-8, 128-40.

10. August Huttenbach, *The Silver Standard and the Straits Currency Question* (Singapore, Fraser and Neave, 1903); E.W. Kemmerer, *Modern Currency Reforms. A History and Discussion of Recent Currency Reforms in India, Porto Rico, Philippine Islands, Straits Settlements and Mexico* (New York: Macmillan, 1916), pp.391-409, 424-39, 445-63; Frank H.H. King, *Money in British East Asia* (London: HMSO, 1957), pp.1-14; Lim Chong-Yah, *Economic Development of Modern Malaya,* (Kuala Lumpur: Oxford University Press, 1967), pp.221-4.

11. Leavens, *Silver Money,* p.108.

12. James C. Ingram, *Economic Change in Thailand* (Stanford: Stanford University Press, 1971), pp.149-55.

13. C. Robequain, *The Economic Development of French Indo-China* (London: Oxford University Press, 1944), pp.137-43.

14. Lien-sheng Yang, *Money and Credit in China, A Short History* (Cambridge: Harvard University Press, 1952), pp.12-13; Frank H.H. King, *Money and Monetary Policy in China, 1845-1895* (Cambridge: Harvard University Press, 1965), pp.27-8, 189-210, 230; C.F. Remer, 'International Trade between Gold and Silver Countries: China, 1885-1913', *Quarterly Journal of Economics,* 40 (1926), pp.606-7; Leavens, *Silver Money,* pp.91-5.

15. G.L.M. Clauson, 'The British Colonial Currency System', *Economic Journal,* 54 (1944), p.19; King, *Money in East Asia,* pp.101-9; Leavens, *Silver Money,* p.99.

16. Leavens, *Silver Money,* p.128; Robequain, *Economic Development of French Indo-China,* p.141.

17. Marion Johnson, 'The Cowrie Currencies of West Africa', *Journal of African History,* 11 (1970), pp.17-49, 331-53; A.G. Hopkins, 'The Currency Revolution in South West Nigeria in the Late Nineteenth Century', *Journal of the Historical Society of Nigeria,* 3 (1966), pp.479-80; A.J.H. Latham, 'Currency, Credit and Capitalism on the Cross River in the Pre-Colonial Era', *Journal of African History,* 7 (1971), pp.599-605; Richard Grey and David Birmingham, *Pre-Colonial African Trade, Essays on Trade in Central and Eastern Africa before 1900* (London: Oxford University Press, 1970), Paul Einzig, *Primitive Money* (London: Eyre & Spottiswoode, 1951), pp.126-71.

18. M.H. de Kock, *The Economic Development of South Africa* (London: P.S. King & Son, 1936), pp.51-3; D. Hobart Houghton, 'Economic Development', in *The Oxford History of South Africa:* Vol.2, *South Africa 1870-1966,* ed. Monica Wilson and Leonard Thompson (Oxford: Clarendon Press, 1971), p.8; Williams, 'Evolution of the Sterling System', p.272; E.H.D. Arndt, *Banking and Currency Development in South Africa, 1652-1927* (Cape Town and Johannesburg: Juta & Co., 1928), pp.44-124; Robert Chalmers, *A History of*

Currency in the British Colonies (London: HMSO, 1893), pp.228-40.

19. Ida Greaves, *Colonial Monetary Conditions* (London: HMSO, 1953), pp.11-12; J.B. Loynes, *The West African Currency Board, 1912-1962* (London: West African Currency Board, 1962), pp.5-20; A.G. Hopkins, *An Economic History of West Africa* (London: Longmans, 1973), p.206; A.G. Hopkins, 'The Creation of a Colonial Monetary System, The Origins of the West African Currency Board', *African Historical Studies,* 3 (1970), pp.101-31; Chalmers, *Currency in the British Colonies,* pp.208-20; W.T. Newlyn and D.C. Rowan, *Money and Banking in British Colonial Africa* (Oxford: Clarendon Press, 1954), pp.25-45.

20. Clauson, 'British Colonial Currency System', p.11, Newlyn and Rowan, *Money and Banking,* pp.57-8.

21. Michel Luduc, *Les Institutions Monétaires Africaines des Pays Francophones* (Paris: A. Pedore, 1965), pp.11-25; Hopkins, 'West Africa', pp.207-8; Foreign Office, *Peace Handbooks; Vol.XVII, French African Possessions* (London: HMSO, 1920), 102, pp.40, 48; 104, p.36; 105, p.37; 107, p.48; 108, pp.59-60.

22. W.O. Henderson, *Studies in German Colonial History* (London: Frank Cass, 1962), p.53; Arthur J. Knoll, 'Taxation in the Gold Coast and Togo: A Study in Early Administration', in *Britain and Germany in Africa: Imperial Rivalry and Colonial Rule,* eds. Prosser Gifford and W.M. Roger Louis, (New Haven: Yale University Press, 1967), pp.443-8; Foreign Office, *Peace Handbooks: Vol. XVIII, German African Possessions (Late)* (London: HMSO, 1920), 110, p. 49; 111, p.69; 112, p.101; 113, p.103, John Iliffe, *Tanganyika under German Rule, 1905-12* (Cambridge: Cambridge University Press, 1969), pp.160-5; Harry R. Rudin, *Germans in the Cameroons, 1884-1914, A Case Study in Modern Imperialism* (London: Jonathan Cape, 1938), pp.335, 345; H. Brode, *British and German East Africa, Their Economic and Commercial Relations* (London: Edwin Arnold, 1911), pp.11-13; Clauson, 'British Colonial Currency System', p.11; A.J.H. Latham, *Old Calabar 1600-1891: The Impact of the International Economy upon a Traditional Society* (Oxford: Clarendon Press, 1973), p.89.

23. A.B. Keith, *The Belgian Congo and the Berlin Act* (Oxford: Clarendon Press, 1919), pp.199-200.

24. Elemer Bohm, *La mise en valeur des Colonies Portugaises* (Paris: Les Presses Universitaires de France, 1938), pp.145-6; James Duffy, *Portuguese Africa* (Cambridge, Mass: Harvard University Press, 1961), pp.261-4; R.J. Hammond, *Portugal and Africa, 1815-1910, A Study in Uneconomic Imperialism* (Stanford: Stanford University Press, 1966), pp.157, 205-7, 297-8; David M. Abshire, 'From the Scramble for Africa to the "New State"', in David M. Abshire and Michael A. Samuels, *Portuguese Africa, A Handbook* (London: Pall Mall Press, 1969), p.74; Leavens, *Silver Money,* p.30; Foreign Office, *Peace Handbooks: Vol.XIX, Portuguese Possessions* (London: HMSO, 1920), No.120, Angola, p.84, No.121, Mozambique, p.91.

25. Mathew Simon, 'The Pattern of New British Portfolio Foreign Investment, 1865-1914', in *The Export of Capital from Britain, 1870-1914,* ed. A.R. Hall (London: Methuen, 1968), pp.23-7.

26. Simon, 'New British Portfolio Foreign Investment', pp.23-6.

27. William Woodruff, *Impact of Western Man, A Study of Europe's Role in the World Economy, 1750-1960* (New York: St Martin's Press, 1966), pp.125-6; L.H. Jenks, *The Migration of British Capital to 1875,* 2nd ed. (London: Thos. Nelson & Sons, 1963), pp.214-30; Herbert Feis, *Europe, the World's Banker, 1870-1914,* 2nd ed. (New York: Augustus M. Kelley, 1961), pp.3-32; George Paish, 'Great Britain's Capital Investments in Individual Colonial and Foreign Countries', *Journal of The Royal Statistical Society,* 74 (1911), pp.178-80.

28. Woodruff, *Western Man,* p.129; G.C. Allen and Audrey G. Donnithorne,

Western Enterprise in Indonesia and Malaya, A Study in Economic Development (London: George Allen & Unwin, 1957), pp.40-44, 144, 150-2, 290, Appendix III; H.G. Callis, *Foreign Capital in South East Asia* (New York: Institute of Pacific Relations, 1942), p.48; Richard T. Stillson, 'The Financing of Malayan Rubber, 1905-23', *Economic History Review,* 2nd series, 24 (1971), pp.589-90; Paish, 'Britain's Capital Investments', pp.179-80.

29. Woodruff, *Western Man,* pp.129-30; Allen and Donnithorne, *Indonesia and Malaya,* pp.22-34; *The Economist,* 15 February 1913, p.334, and 15 March 1913, p.637; J.S. Furnivall, *Netherlands India* (Cambridge: Cambridge University Press, 1944), pp.227, 309-11, 406.

30. Ingram, *Economic Change in Thailand,* pp.70-1, 85-6, 98-101, 105-7, 133, 173, 181-2; Callis, *Capital in South East Asia,* p.59.

31. Robequain, *French Indo-China,* pp.90-1, 158-60; Callis, *Capital in South East Asia,* pp.71-2.

32. C.F. Remer, *Foreign Investments in China* (New York: Macmillan, 1933), pp.69-79; Paish, 'Britain's Capital Investments', pp.181-3; Chi-ming Hou, *Foreign Investment and Economic Development in China, 1840-1937* (Cambridge, Mass: Harvard University Press, 1965), pp.1-22.

33. S.H. Frankel, *Capital Investment in Africa, Its Course and Effects* (London: Oxford University Press, 1938), pp.149-50; Paish, 'Britain's Capital Investments', pp.179-80.

34. Feis, *Europe, The Worlds Banker,* pp.51-9, 71-8; Frankel, *Capital Investment in Africa,* pp.156, 164, 167, 169.

3 INTERNATIONAL TRADE

It has been shown that Asia and Africa benefited from improved communications in the fifty years before the First World War. To a large extent these consisted of railways, financed by foreign capital, most of which was British. The outcome was a substantial increase in external trade, which may also have been helped by the decline in the value of silver, the basis of most Asian currencies until the end of the nineteenth century.

Some impression of the increase in exports from the undeveloped world may be obtained from Table 8 (p.66), which shows the dollar values of the exports of the countries in question 1883, 1899 and 1913, as calculated by Lewis, with some additions. These figures, of course, can be used only as a very rough guide, as calculating in dollar terms tends to disguise the advance of those countries which experienced a depreciation of their exchange rate against the dollar and other gold-standard currencies. This includes the two most important countries, India and China, who together accounted for half of the total. Nor do the figures reveal volume changes, as the international price of the exports of many of these countries fell during the period. Nevertheless, the figures suggest an overall annual rate of export growth of 3.9 per cent in 1883-1913, with a rate of 2.0 per cent for the subperiod 1883-99, and of 6.0 per cent for the subperiod 1899-1913. Nearly every country experienced an increase in exports, only Zanzibar suffering a reversal.

But how important was the contribution of Asia and Africa to international trade in these years? Lamartine Yates has provided estimates of the shares of world trade by geographical region, shown in Tables 9 and 10 (page 67). While his use of the terms Asia and Africa cover wider areas than the more limited use here, his figures serve as a rough guide.

Although at first it might appear that the contribution of Asia and Africa was relatively small, it should be noted that in 1913 they provided slightly more of the world's exports than the United States and Canada, 15.5 per cent as against 14.8 per cent. The United Kingdom's contribution was only 13.1 per cent. Even taking account of their rapid development of Africa after the discovery of gold in South Africa at the end of the 1880s, Africa's share was still very small at

Table 8: Exports from the Undeveloped World, 1883-1913

	1883		1899		1913	
	$M	%	$M	%	$M	%
Asia						
Ceylon	13.9	2.0	32.8	3.4	72.7	3.3
India	336.6	48.5	353.9	36.8	792.4	36.0
Malaya[1]	72.7	10.4	102.8	10.7	192.5	8.7
Siam	8.0	1.1	15.2	1.5	43.1	1.9
Dutch East Indies	80.2	11.5	100.9	10.5	249.4	11.3
French Indo-China	15.7	2.2	26.6	2.7	66.9	3.0
China	95.1	13.7	142.9	14.8	294.4	13.3
Asia total	622.2	89.7	775.1	80.7	1,711.4	77.8
Africa						
Nigeria	7.9	1.1	8.5	0.8	33.0	1.5
Gold Coast	1.8	0.2	5.4	0.5	26.4	1.2
Sierra Leone	2.2	0.3	1.6	0.1	6.7	0.3
Gambia	1.0	0.1	1.2	0.1	3.2	0.1
South Africa	40.9	5.8	124.4	12.9	324.6	14.7
Northern Rhodesia	—	—	—	—	1.0	0.0
Southern Rhodesia	0.1	0.0	1.3	0.1	2.0	0.0
Kenya-Uganda	0.3	0.0	0.6	0.0	7.2	0.3
Nyasaland	—	—	0.2	0.0	1.1	0.0
Zanzibar	6.8	0.9	7.4	0.7	3.0	0.1
French West Africa	4.0	0.5	12.4	1.2	24.4	1.1
French Equatorial Africa	—	—	1.6	0.1	7.1	0.3
Togo	0.1*	0.0	0.5	0.0	0.6	0.0
Cameroons	0.6*	0.0	1.2	0.1	2.9	0.1
South West Africa	—	—	0.2[2]	0.0	17.1	0.7
Tanganyika	0.3*	0.0	1.0	0.1	3.9	0.1
Congo	2.2	0.3	7.0	0.7	11.7	0.5
Angola	2.0	0.2	8.6	0.8	5.6	0.2
Mozambique	1.1[3]	0.1	1.5	0.1	5.3	0.2
Africa total	71.3	10.2	184.6	19.2	486.8	22.1
Combined total	693.5		959.7		2,198.2	
£ million	142.4		197.0		451.3	

* Interpolation or guesstimate.

1. 1883 and 1899 (1900) Straits Settlements.
2. 1900.
3. 1884.

Sources: Charles C. Stover, 'Tropical Exports', in *Tropical Development, 1880-1913, Studies in Economic Progress,* ed. W.A. Lewis (London: George Allen & Unwin, 1970) pp.46-49; Ping-Yin Ho, *The Foreign Trade of China* (Shanghai: Commercial Press, 1935), pp.15-16; S.H. Frankel, *Capital Investment in Africa. Its Course and Effects* (London: Oxford University Press, 1938), p.219, *Statistical Abstract for British Colonies.*

Table 9: World Exports by Geographical Region, 1876-1913 (%)

	1876-80	1896-1900	1913
United States & Canada	11.7	14.5	14.8
United Kingdom & Ireland	16.3	14.2	13.1
North-West Europe	31.9	34.4	33.4
Other Europe	16.0	15.2	12.4
Oceania	–)	–)	2.5)
Latin America	–) 24.1	–) 21.7	8.3) 26.3
Africa	–)	–)	3.7)
Asia	–)	–)	11.8)

P. Lamartine Yates, *Forty Years of Foreign Trade: A Statistical Handbook with Special Reference to Primary Products and Under-developed Countries* (London: George Allen & Unwin, 1959), Table 6, p.32.

Table 10: World Imports by Geographical Region, 1876-1913 (%)

	1876-80	1896-1900	1913
United States & Canada	7.4	8.9	11.5
United Kingdom & Ireland	22.5	20.5	15.2
North West Europe	31.9	36.5	36.5
Other Europe	11.9	11.0	13.4
Oceania	–)	–)	2.4)
Latin America	–) 26.3	–) 23.0	7.0) 23.4
Africa	–)	–)	3.6)
Asia	–)	–)	10.4)

Source: Yates, *Forty Years of Foreign Trade,* Table 7, p.33.

3.7 per cent, Asia's being more than three times as great at 11.8 per cent. As for imports, in 1913 Asia accounted for very nearly as big a share as the United States and Canada, taking 10.4 per cent to the latter's 11.5 per cent. Africa and Asia together took 14 per cent of the world's imports, and substantially more than the United States and Canada, who received 11.5 per cent, and only 1.2 per cent less than the United Kingdom, which took 15.2 per cent.

However, to judge the relative importance of a region to the international economy, it is not the share of world exports and imports which is crucial, but as Saul has shown, the international balances which resulted from exports and imports, and other transactions of international business. Saul demonstrated that in the fifty years before 1914, a complicated web of international trade grew up. Countries no longer tried to strike a balance between their imports and exports with every country with which they traded, but allowed themselves to develop substantial deficits with some of their trading partners, which they met by earning considerable surpluses with the others. What happened in practical terms is that the rapidly industrialising countries of Western Europe and North America bought more and more raw materials and foodstuffs from the primary producers of the undeveloped world, and so ran up big deficits with these countries. Britain, because of her free-trade policy, was a major importer of manufactured goods from the new industrial countries, with whom she ran up substantial deficits. But she was also the chief exporter of manufactured goods to the undeveloped world, with whom she enjoyed a big surplus. Thus her surplus with the undeveloped world helped her to pay off her deficit with the newly industrialising countries. She also had a large income from interest payments on capital invested abroad, and other invisible earnings from shipping, insurance and banking which went to meet her deficits. As for the undeveloped world, the countries there were able to pay their deficit with Britain with their surplus earned by selling raw materials and foodstuffs to Europe and North America. Thus the circle of international payments was closed, as shown in the Diagram 1 on page 69.

Of course the account given above is a gross oversimplification of the World Pattern of Settlements, and Saul presents a more detailed diagram, reproduced in Diagram 2 on page 69. In this more detailed diagram, the chief point to be noted is the considerable surplus of £60 million which Britain had on her dealings with India, the main country of the undeveloped world so far as international trade is concerned. She also had a surplus of £13 million with Japan, and although it is not shown in Diagram 2, another surplus of £13 million on her trade with China. It was these Asian surpluses, together with those with Australia and Turkey, which enabled Britain to settle her deficits of £50 million with the United States and £45 million with industrial Europe, besides another £25 million resulting from wheat and timber imports from Canada. Saul's rough calculation of Britain's balance of payments in 1910 is shown in Table 11 (page 69).

The full list brings out the importance of China, with whom Britain had a surplus of £13 million, although as regards Asia as a whole, this is off-set to some extent by the debit with the Straits Settlements of £11 million. As regards Africa, the useful credit of £3 million with West Africa is more than offset by the £8 million debit with South Africa. So the significance of

Diagram 1: World Payments System about 1910

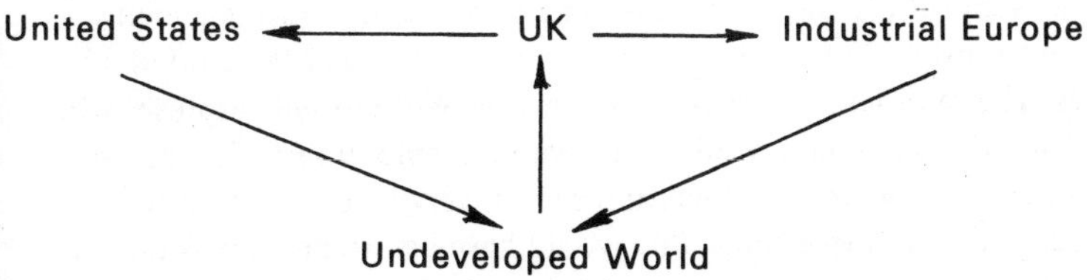

Diagram 2: World Pattern of Settlements, 1910

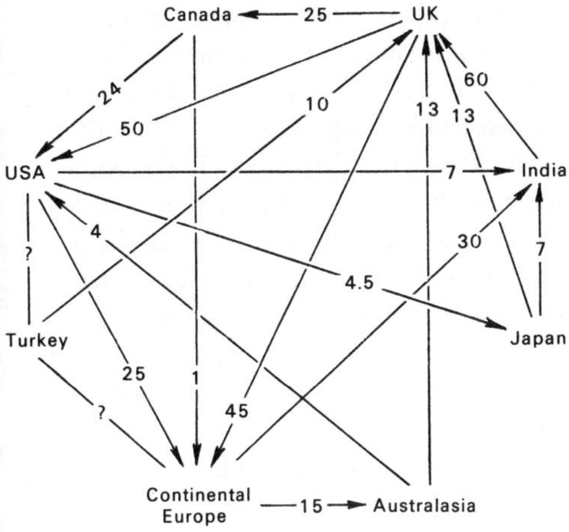

Arrows indicate flow of settlement

Table 11: Balance of Payments of the UK, 1910 (£ million)

Debit		Credit	
USA	50	India	60
Continental Europe	45	Australia	13
Canada	25	Japan	13
Straits Settlements	11	China (including Hong Kong)	13
South Africa	8	Turkey	10
New Zealand	4	Uruguay	6
Argentina	2	British West Africa	3
Total	145	Total	118

Source: S.B. Saul, *Studies in British Overseas Trade 1870-1914*, (Liverpool: Liverpool University Press, 1960), p.58.

India is confirmed. Of her dealings with the undeveloped world, it was her dealings with India, and to a lesser extent China, which enabled Britain to sustain her debits with industrial Europe and the United States. The ramifications of this are obvious. Without her surpluses with India and China, Britain would not have been able to settle her debits with the new industrial nations, and presumably would have been forced to abandon free trade. She would have had to put tariffs on her imports from these countries in order to make her imports from them balance her exports to them. This would have compelled the United States and industrial Europe either to have negotiated mutual tariff reductions, or to accept a lower rate of export growth, which would have retarded to some degree their overall development. The United States and industrial Europe, in particular Germany, were able to continue their policy of tariff protection only because of Britain's surplus with Asia. Without that Asian surplus, Britain would no longer have been able to subsidise their growth. So what emerges is that Asia in general, but India and China in particular, far from being peripheral to the evolution of the international economy at this time, was in fact crucial. Without the surpluses which Britain was able to earn there, the whole pattern of international economic development would have been severely constrained. Africa was less important to the international system, because Britain's surplus with West Africa was more than offset by her debit with South Africa, rendering the balance with Africa as a whole negative.[1]

Having indicated the vital role which India in particular played in the development of the world economy in these years, it is now necessary to examine in detail her international trade. For how was India able to sustain the massive debt she had on her transactions with the United Kingdom, the essential link in the network of international settlements? It is clear that the surpluses which she earned with the United States and industrial Europe, which amounted to £37 million in 1910, were not by themselves sufficient to meet her debit of £60 million with Britain.

Graph 5 (p.71) shows the progress of Indian trade in merchandise and treasure, by sea, for the period 1864-1914. There was a considerable increase in merchandise trade in this period, in terms of the rupee, with exports growing at a rate of 3.4 per cent per annum from 1868-70 to 1911-13, and imports growing at the slightly higher rate of 3.6 per cent. As has been mentioned earlier, if the rate of growth was measured in terms of the pound or dollar it would have been lower, as the rupee depreciated owing to the fall in silver. But as far as the Indian economy

Graph 5: Indian Overseas Trade, 1864-1914

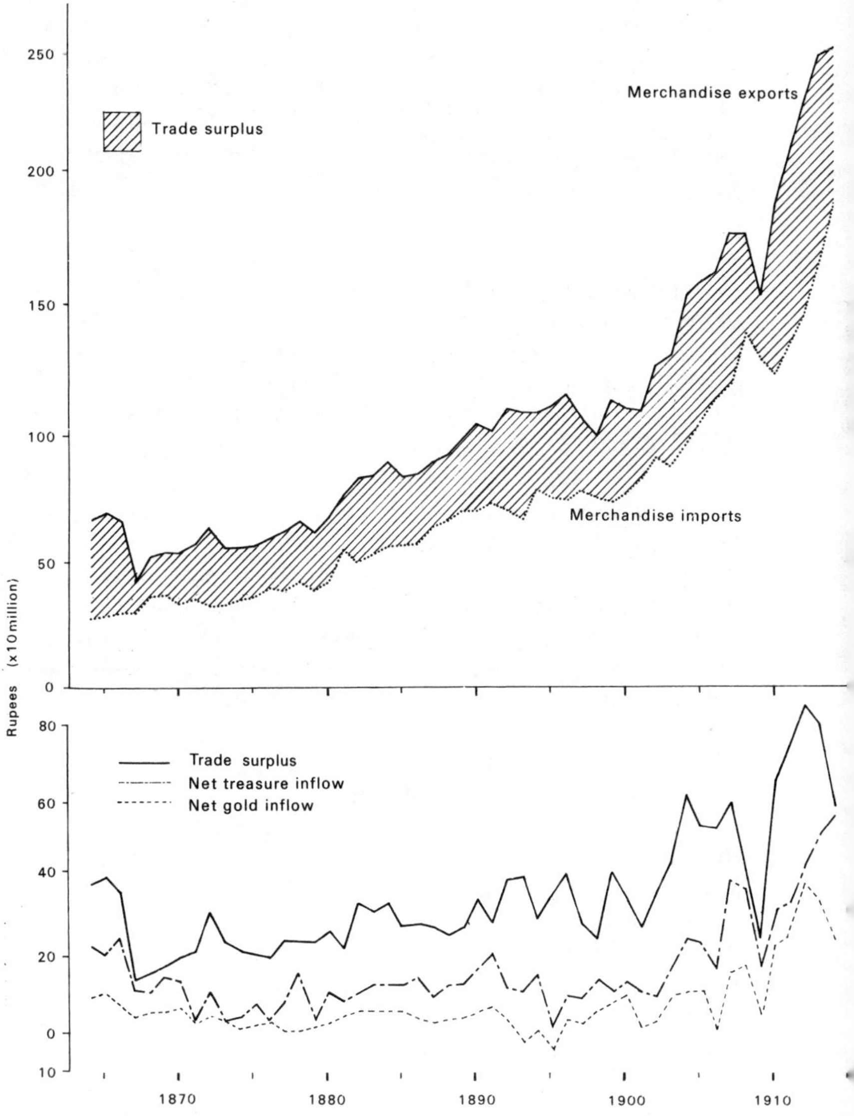

Source: Statistical Abstracts for British India; see Appendix 4.

was concerned, it was the rupee values which were important. There were two major phases in the development of India's trade in this period, the first being 1871-3 to 1896-8, from the beginning of the fall of the rupee until its stabilisation. Exports grew annually at 2.4 per cent in this period and imports at 3.3 per cent, exactly the opposite of what one might expect of a country with a depreciating exchange rate. However, this was not the only factor affecting Indian trade in this period. For the Suez Canal was completed, and freight rates fell. Several important links were added to the Indian railway network, lowering the cost of internal transport to and from the ports. Between 1867 and 1880 export tariffs were cut, and in 1882 all import duties were abolished and India was duty free until 1894, when a general rate of 5 per cent was reimposed. But Lancashire cotton yarns were allowed in free of duty from 1896, and other cotton goods given a reduced duty. Internationally, prices fell because of the great Victorian depression from 1873 to 1896, and internally business was affected by the famines of 1877-9 and 1896-7, the last coupled with bubonic plague in Bombay, Karachi and Sind, an earthquake in eastern India, and tribal rebellion on the north-west frontier. Besides all this, the Sino-Japanese war depressed trade in the important Chinese market in 1894-5. So the various commissions set up to inquire into the depreciation of the rupee did not find any support for the view that the depreciation had been a stimulus for Indian exports. This does not necessarily prove that there had been no stimulus, as Indians, who did most of the exporting, were not called upon to give evidence for the most part, and the opinions of European importers dominated the proceedings. In Ceylon, where exporters provided most of the evidence, the depreciation of the rupee was said to have had considerable effect.

The second major phase in the evolution of India's trade was from the stabilisation of the rupee in 1896-8 to the First World War, 1911-13. Exports grew annually at a rate of 5.2 per cent and imports at 4.7 per cent. However, the period began badly with the return of drought and disease in 1899-1900, and the Boxer disturbances in China. But from then on India participated in the general upturn in the international business activity, although there was a check 1908-9 following monsoon failure in the south west, international recession, and difficulties in the China trade owing to violently fluctuating exchanges. From 1909 there was continued expansion. India's very successful export performance in these years, by comparison with the period up to 1893, has led some observers to the view that this success proves that the depreciation of the rupee up to 1893 was not a stimulus to Indian exports. But it must be noted that up to 1896 Indian exports were selling in an international market where prices were in any case declining, which tended to nullify the stimulus of the falling exchange, and after 1896 exports were going to a world market where prices were rising, which tended to disguise any untoward affect of the stabilised exchange. Probably all that can be said is that the Indian experience of a falling exchange rate does not support the view that a falling rate of exchange should stimulate exports and inhibit imports. For it is impossible to separate the influence of the fall of the rupee from other influences which were making themselves felt at the same time. However, it is interesting to observe that in China, which also experienced a falling exchange rate, imports rose faster than exports, again contrary to theoretical expectations.[2]

From 1864 to the First World War India earned a considerable merchandise trade surplus, which is shown on Graph 5 (page 71). While merchandise trade is only one element in the Indian balance of payments, this trade surplus was obviously the main source of the surplus by which India was able to pay for her debit with Britain, for as Saul points out, India had only small earnings from transactions other than trade.[3] That she earned an overall balance of payments surplus in these years is indicated by the import surplus she had on her treasure transactions in gold and silver, which are again shown on Graph 5. This continuous inflow of precious metals is a classic indicator of an overall surplus. The gap between the line showing the trade surplus and the line showing the inflow of treasure is, of course, accounted for by the payments India had to make to other countries, particularly Britain, for her deficit on non-merchandise items in her balance of payments. Also shown on the graph are net gold imports; the gap between the treasure inflow and the gold inflow is filled by the inflow of silver. This sustained influx of gold and silver into India raises some very interesting questions, not least those prompted by Messrs McCloskey and Zecher in a recent paper. They suggest that under the gold standard, an inflow of gold will be the response to a rising demand for money by the people of a country, whose incomes are rising but whose demand for money is not met by the monetary authorities. If their surmise is correct, then the implication is that the inflow of gold, particularly after the stabilisation of the rupee against gold, indicates that demand for money was rising in India, because of increasing incomes there. Before this, when India was on the silver standard, the inflow of silver would point to the same conclusion. Rising incomes are precisely what one would expect in a country which enjoyed such a large and persistent export surplus.

Table 12: Indian Exports, 1870-1910: Five-year averages

	1870		1880		1890		1900		1910	
	%	Rank	%	Rank	%	Rank	%	Rank	%	Rank
Coffee	1.79	10	2.17	11	1.74	13	1.24	13	0.67	—
Cotton: raw	36.39	1	16.19	2	14.31	1	10.67	3	14.46	1
Cotton: twist, yarn	0.16	14	1.60	12	5.92	7	6.27	9	4.53	10
Cotton: manufactures	2.17	8	2.41	10	2.83	11	1.25	12	1.08	12
Indigo	5.38	4	4.99	7	3.54	10	1.91	11	0.17	—
Grain: rice	7.12	3	11.92	3	11.00	2	13.23	1	11.85	2
Grain: wheat	0.20	13	4.76	8	7.99	5	3.78	10	5.78	8
Hides and skins	3.08	7	5.11	6	4.80	9	8.12	5	6.92	6
Jute: raw	4.32	6	5.90	5	7.55	6	8.61	4	9.97	4
Jute: manufactures	0.44	12	1.51	14	2.63	12	6.65	8	8.84	5
Opium	21.41	2	18.79	1	9.45	4	7.29	7	5.55	9
Seeds	4.62	5	8.37	4	10.36	3	11.05	2	10.80	3
Tea	1.96	9	4.59	9	5.69	8	7.45	6	6.05	7
Wool	1.20	11	1.56	13	1.61	14	0.96	—	1.29	11
Others	9.76		10.13		10.31		11.52		12.04	

Source: *Statistical Abstracts for British India.*

What is more, India had been a 'sink' of gold and silver from the rest of the world from time immemorial![4]

How then did India earn her vast trade surplus? Table 12 (p.74) shows India's principal exports, and it is immediately clear that raw cotton was the leading item, and if twist and yarn and other cotton manufactures are added to it, then cotton goods headed the list throughout the period. But rice was the next important item, and if wheat exports are put with rice, these grain exports were the leading category of exports after 1880, and second only to cotton goods as a whole. Opium declined in importance, taking first place in 1880 but ninth in 1910. Oil seeds, however, increased in importance, as did hides and skins and jute and jute manufactures. Tea became more important, at the expense of coffee; wool remained fairly constant; and indigo declined. So by and large Indian exports were of agricultural and, with the exception of tea, of peasant origin. But manufactures, especially jute, and cotton, particularly twist and yarn, did increase their share, comprising more than 14 per cent all told in 1910. Tea production was in European hands, the plantations being created from virgin jungle, not from the reallocation of land from peasant use. With respect to wheat exports, it is worth noting the influence of the Suez Canal, for before it was opened the grain became infested with weevils on the long voyage round the Cape to Europe.

What, then, were the goods which went to the various markets? Britain was the most important single destination for India's exports, and it comes as no surprise to find tea as the leading commodity, although wheat occasionally surpassed it in the new century. Indeed, the development of Indian wheat exports, mainly to Britain, was rapid after the opening of the Suez Canal, and was actively encouraged by the Government. Railway building aided the spread of wheat cultivation. Yet even though by 1904-13 India was supplying 18 per cent of Britain's wheat imports, only 13 per cent of the Indian crop was actually being exported, the rest being consumed at home. Britain was also the main consumer of Indian jute products, although Germany, France and the United States became important consumers, the United States being the leading purchaser of jute cloth and bags from the mid-1890s. At the beginning of the period Britian was the chief market for Indian raw cotton, but as Lancashire preferred the longer-staple, cleaner United States cotton, her share of the crop declined, and Indian cotton went increasingly to Europe. Hides and skins featured prominently in the British trade, particularly when dressed, but Germany and the United States were the more important buyers of raw hides and skins. Britain took linseed and castor seed, while the European countries took the rest of the seed market. Of other commodities, Britain took reasonable amounts of rice, but Germany, and particularly the Asian markets, were the leading buyers. Table 13 below shows the breakdown of Indian exports by region, and this reveals the relative decline in Britain as a consumer of Indian exports over the years. In part this was caused by

Table 13: Destination of Indian Exports, 1870-1910: Five-year averages (%)

	1870	1880	1890	1900	1910
UK	53.57	42.56	34.33	27.48	25.39
Europe	8.91	17.02	25.29	24.00	31.51
Africa	1.69	3.82	7.32	8.26	3.08
America	3.48	4.11	4.88	7.96	9.73
Asia	32.23	31.67	26.93	30.86	28.56
Australia	0.14	0.79	1.06	1.41	1.71

Source: *Statistical Abstracts for British India.*

the increased purchases by the United States and Europe as they industrialised, but it was also a result of the opening of the Suez Canal, which enabled France and Italy and other Mediterranean countries to be supplied direct from India rather than by way of the Cape and Britain.

As Britain's share of Indian exports declined, Europe's grew. Rice, cotton, wheat and jute were all important in the European trade, but oil seeds predominated. After 1900 Indian exports of these products, especially linseed, rape seed and groundnuts, increased rapidly in value. She became the world's leading exporter of rape seed and groundnuts, exporting three times as many of the latter as all the British West African colonies added together. France was the chief importer, although Europe in general took three-quarters of the total. Hides and skins were a substantial part of the European trade, raw hides going to Austria and also Germany, where they were made into heavy army boots.

Of the other regions to which India sent exports, the main part of the trade with America was jute and jute products; and to Africa and Australasia went miscellaneous items in which tea and rice presumably featured. But what of the Asian market, which took about a third of all Indian exports throughout the period, being the second most important market area after Britain overall, and indeed more important than Britain from the turn of the century? There is no doubt that at the beginning of the period opium was the major export to Asia, with China consuming most of it but with smaller quantities going to the Straits Settlements from where it was distributed throughout South East Asia. However, Chinese imports stopped increasing, and after the turn of the century were very much reduced, and this largely accounted for the fact that Indian exports to Asia in general remained at a fairly stable proportion. The decline in opium was offset in the China trade by the development of a good business in Indian cotton manufactures, especially twist and yarn, and in fact Indian cotton manufactures ousted British goods there to a large extent. Elsewhere in Asia Indian cotton manufactures were successful, with Japan emerging as the largest consumer of Indian raw cotton exports. Rice also was a major item in the Asian trade, and the growth of these rice exports from Burma marks the development of an intra-Asian rice trade of great significance. Most of the Indian rice went to Ceylon to feed the immigrant plantations workers there, but the Straits Settlements were a considerable purchaser, and Japan took increasing quantities towards the end of the period. As in the case of wheat, only a small proportion of the crop was exported, never more than 10 per cent, and in times of famine and scarcity the rice was diverted to other provinces of India.

Indian imports were mainly of manufactured goods, as table 14 (p.78) reveals. Cotton manufactured goods were the major category, although their share of the total fell from 44 per cent in 1870 to 32 per cent in 1910, as cotton manufacturing advanced in India itself. Cotton twist and yarn fell from second place to seventh for the same reason. The rest of the imports comprised a vast array of miscellaneous goods few of which amounted to more than 1 per cent of the total. This pattern of imports fits the general import pattern of many of the countries of the undeveloped world at this time. Categories which do stand out, however, are iron and steel, which rose to 7 per cent in 1910; railway plant and rolling stock which accounted for about 4 per cent throughout; and machinery and millwork which increased its share to 4 per cent at the end of the period. Brass and copper imports declined, silk and wool manufactures remained constant, and coal imports fell away as the Indian coal industry developed. Probably the most significant increase is shown by sugar, which rose from less than 2 per cent of imports in 1870 to over 9 per cent by 1910. This may well support the view that incomes were rising in India, causing increased demand for this luxury foodstuff. Salt, oils and hardware also figured, but the mass of miscellaneous items is shown by the very high proportion of 'other goods' in the table.

Table 14: Indian Imports, 1870-1910: Five-year Averages

	1870		1880		1890		1900		1910	
	%	Rank	%	Rank	%	Rank	%	Rank	%	Rank
Coal, etc.	1.83	–	2.48	6	2.15	10	0.70	–	0.56	–
Cotton: twist, yarn	8.28	2	7.18	2	5.24	2	3.31	6	2.74	7
Cotton: manufactures	44.69	1	43.22	1	39.08	1	36.58	1	32.11	1
Hardware	–	–	1.16	–	1.76	–	2.28	9	2.17	8
Machinery, millwork	1.93	7	2.02	10	3.40	6	3.63	5	4.06	5
Metals: iron, steel	3.72	5	3.52	4	4.29	3	5.65	3	7.32	3
Metals: brass, copper	4.64	3	3.64	3	2.65	7	1.58	–	2.16	10
Railway plant, stock	4.30	4	2.43	7	2.66	6	2.68	7	4.18	4
Oils	0.13	–	1.08	–	3.89	4	4.96	4	2.91	6
Salt	2.24	6	1.40	–	1.13	–	0.86	–	0.58	–
Sugar	1.88	–	2.91	5	3.79	5	6.36	2	9.26	2
Silk, manufactures	1.35	–	2.40	8	2.53	8	1.93	–	1.95	–
Wool, manufactures	1.81	–	2.35	9	2.45	9	2.33	8	2.16	9
Others	23.20		24.21		24.98		27.15		27.84	

Source: *Statistical Abstracts for British India.*

Table 15: Origin of Indian Imports, 1870-1910: Five-year Averages (%)

	1870	1880	1890	1900	1910
UK	83.70	81.26	74.60	66.36	62.40
Europe	1.81	2.97	7.69	17.24	15.02
Africa	2.00	3.07	3.29	3.33	2.61
America	0.29	1.01	2.00	1.67	3.14
Asia	11.21	11.38	11.94	10.66	16.02
Australasia	0.84	0.47	0.44	0.72	0.77

Source: *Statistical Abstract for British India.*

Table 15 (page 78) analyses Indian imports into the regions from which they came, and the overwhelming position of Britain as a supplier is obvious, with 83 per cent of the total in 1870 and 62 per cent in 1910. Lancashire cottons made up a large part of this, but it was this section which suffered most from the emergence of cotton manufacturing in India. Up to the mid-1880s imports from Britain had been cheap plain cottons, but after this Indian mills produced these stuffs. Although Britain led in every category of substance, European competition made itself felt in many trades, with Belgium being prominent in the metal trades, particularly iron and steel, after the 1880s. Belgium also was the major supplier of some minor items, such as dyeing and tanning materials, and Belgium, Austria and Germany sent glassware. Germany competed vigorously for an increased share in wool imports, and after the turn of the century Germany and Austria established re-eminence in the household utensil market. Despite German and United States' competition in the metal trades, Britain kept her hold of the biggest single class of metal imports, galvanised sheets and plates. Clearly, however, Europe's share of Indian imports increased at Britain's expense, and by 1910 was accounting for 15 per cent of imports. As for Asia, her share of India's imports grew a little, from 11 per cent to 16 per cent, partly because Japan took over from Britain as a supplier of silk goods, and also because of the rapid rise in sugar imports from Java, one of the most interesting facets of Indian trade in these years. China continued to send silk and silk manufactures, and the Straits Settlements supplied a whole range of minor items gathered from all over South East Asia and redistributed via Singapore, including drugs, medicines, matches, tin, oil, fish, silk, betelnuts and sugar.[5]

So how then did Indian trade balance with the various regions she traded with? As was discussed earlier, India had a very considerable surplus on her merchandise trade, while at the same time having a very substantial overall debit on her business with Britain. Graph 6 (page 80) traces India's trade balances with different regions, and demonstrates that India's increasing trade deficit with Britain was much more than offset by her increasing surpluses with Europe, America and especially Asia. Africa and Australasia also yielded surpluses but they were too small to include on the graph. The European surplus is easy to explain, for Europe's purchases of oilseeds, rice, hides and skins, raw cotton and other primary produce far outweighed her sales to India of manufactured goods. Similarly, the smaller American surplus was a result of the fact that the United States bought more jute and jute products, and hides and skins, than she sold mineral oil and manufac-

Graph 6: Indian Trade Balances with Major Countries, 1868-1914

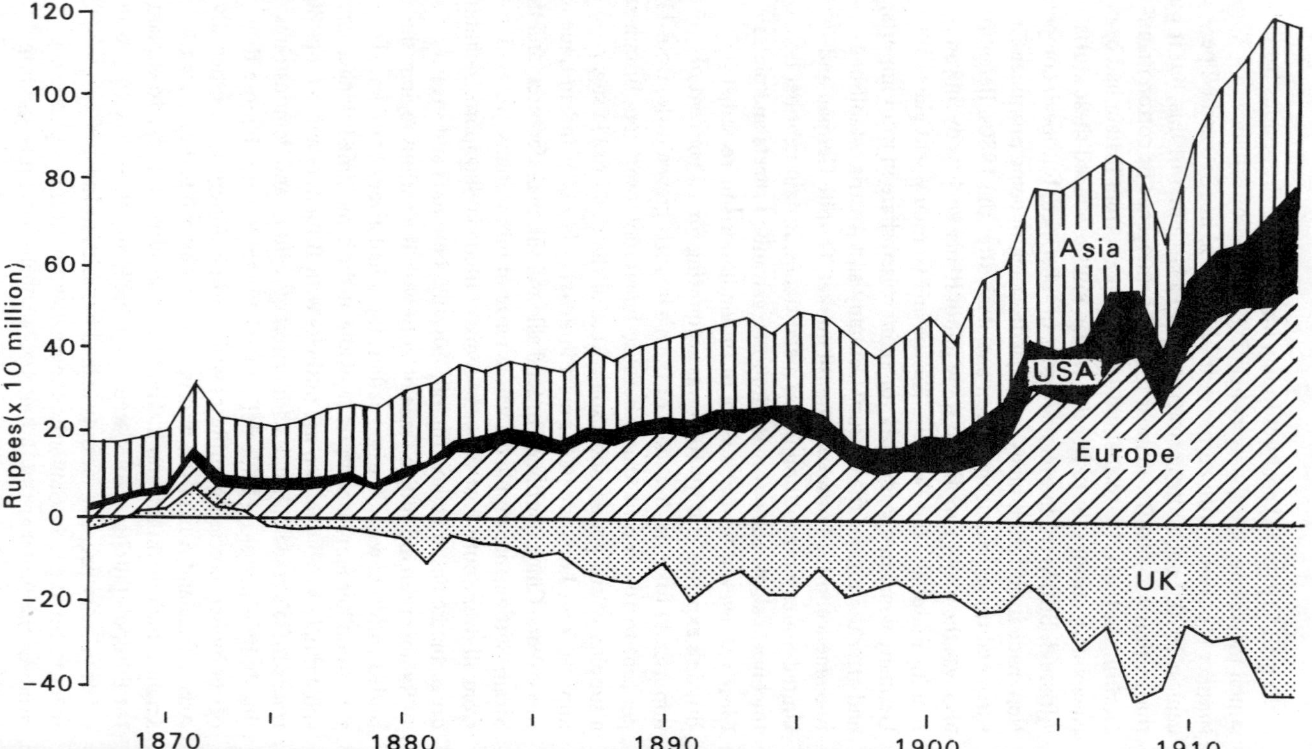

tured goods to India. But what of the Asian market, where by far the largest surpluses originated? Because this region was the most important source of the trade surplus with which India was able to sustain her debit with Britain, the very spinal cord of the international economy, it is worth examining in more detail. Graph 7 (page 82) gives a breakdown of India's surplus with Asia into the separate balances with the main countries there; as one might expect, the surplus on the China trade was of overwhelming importance. This was because of the opium trade to begin with, but it was subsequently owing to Indian exports of cotton yarn. Japan yielded a rapidly growing surplus after 1880, as she raced through her path of industrialisation, importing raw cotton, yarn and rice from India. Ceylon also provided a useful surplus, on account of Burmese rice imports, to feed the immigrant Indian workers employed on the coffee and tea plantations. Only with Java in the Dutch East Indies was there any substantial deficit, and this grew very rapidly after the turn of the century, as Indians pandered to their 'sweet tooths' with the luxury of sugar. Elsewhere in Asia, both with the Straits Settlements and other countries, India was in surplus, with rice and cotton being largely responsible. It is worth emphasising, therefore, that if India's ability to sustain a payments deficit with Britain was essential to the entire development of the international economy, then this was possible only because of the surplus India herself earned in Asia. Thus Asia was a vital integral part of the international system.

Having noted this, it is now worth looking at China, because China was the source of such a large part of India's Asian surplus. Besides this, Britain herself earned a substantial surplus on her trade with China, as has already been noted. So China, directly through Britain and indirectly through India, enabled Britain to sustain her deficits with the United States and Europe on which those countries depended for export stimulus and, in the case of the United States, capital inflow to some degree. The outstanding point about China's foreign trade in this period is her consistent and growing overall deficit, shown on Graph 8 (page 83). Moreover, China, like India, had few earnings of any importance outside trade other than the repatriation of money by emigrants, although in China's case this amounted to a sizeable sum. There are complexities involved in the use of Chinese trade statistics, because Hong Kong is classed as a foreign country in the Chinese accounts, although in reality it was a major port for Southern China. What is more, no trade figures were kept for Hong Kong, by which the situation might have been rectified. Nonetheless, China's trade can be seen to grow significantly in the period 1868/70 to 1911/13; exports

Graph 7: Indian Trade Balances with Asia, 1868-1914

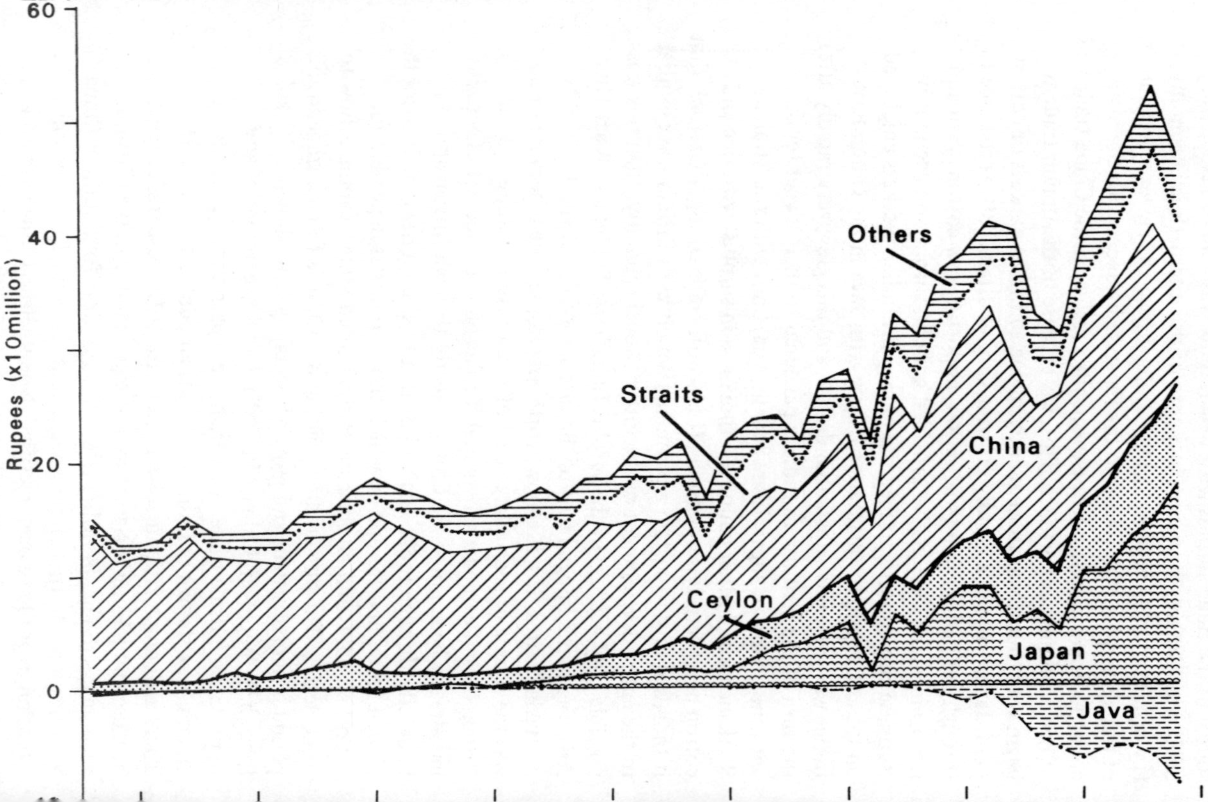

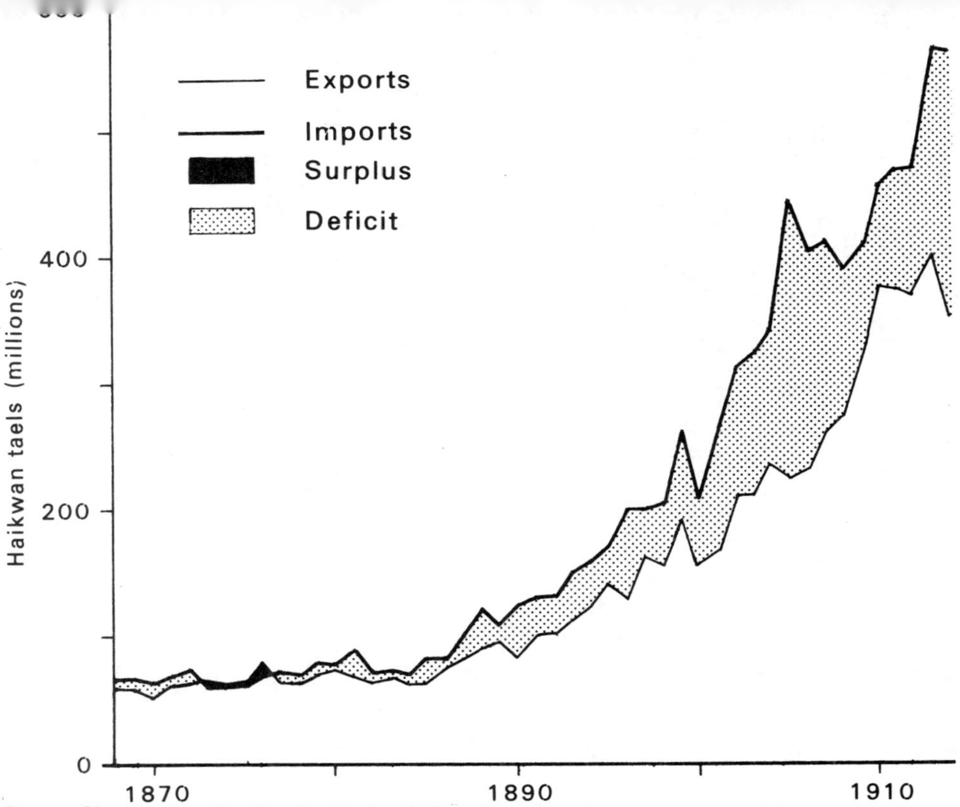

Source: Ping-Yin Ho, *The Foreign Trade of China* (Shanghai: Commercial Press, 1935), pp.15-16, 20-2; see Appendix 7.

rising by 4.4 per cent annually and imports by 4.8 per cent. Three sub periods are apparent, the first 1868/70 to 1883/5 when there was little growth of trade, exports growing annually at 0.8 per cent per year and imports by 1.2 per cent; this despite the improvements in communication by sea both to India and Europe and the establishment of telegraph links to world markets. The second period, 1883/5 to 1894/6 saw a rapid increase in China's trade, with exports rising by 6.4 per cent and imports 7.8 per cent annually. This period began with the Sino-French war of 1885 and ended with the Sino-Japanese war in 1895. The third period was from 1894/6 to 1911/13, in which trade continued to expand, exports rising by 6.3 per cent each year and imports by 6.2 per cent. This was the period after the Sino-Japanese war in which foreigners were allowed to open factories in China, and in which there was rapid railway building. After the Russo-Japanese war of 1904-5 Manchuria developed as a leading exporting region. As in the case of India, these calculations are based on the domestic currency unit, in this case the haikwan tael, and if these values had been calculated in terms of pounds or dollars, the growth would have appeared less, as the tael depreciated with silver right up to 1913. But what is particularly interesting is that over the period as a whole imports increased faster than exports, once again contradicting theoretical expectations for a country with a falling exchange rate. Only at the very end of the period did exports exceed imports in annual growth, and then only slightly. Remer investigated this problem, and found that only in the periods of the sharpest fall in the gold price of silver, 1891-4 and 1903-6, did the effects on trade conform with theory. Over the long period he thought the evidence was inconclusive, and argues that the failure of exports to increase as fast as imports was a result of Chinese middlemen not passing on the benefit of increased export prices to the peasants. Imports, on the other hand, rose so quickly because most of the goods were new and therefore purchasers had no yardstick of a previous price to deter them from buying, or they were goods such as opium, consumption of which was undeterred by price rises. Perhaps Remer might have also considered the possibility that as exports were only a very small proportion of total production, changes in their external price would have only a very small effect on each individual producer. The tendency for imports to increase, particularly rice, was related to population and demand growth in China itself. Indeed this in itself might have held back exports, as goods previously exported were consumed at home. Remer ends by noting that the crucial point about China's trade in this period was not connected with the price of silver, but with the fact that emigration was so large, and that Chinese foreign trade was so small, observations which seem to suggest a population outstripping its resources.

As already noted, the main point about China's trade in these years was her persistent and large trade deficit, which became worse as time went on. Foreign loans helped to partly offset this, but after the turn of the century repayments of principal and interest exceeded the inflow. Foreign investment after 1896 also helped, and China had favourable balances with her small overland trade. But remittances from Chinese emigrants were the major source of funds by which she was able to meet her obligations. Unfortunately there are no records of treasure movements before 1888, and there is the usual problem with Hong Kong, but such information as there is is shown on Graph 9 (page 86), which suggests that in most years there was an outflow of both gold and silver. However, the net figures show a small surplus over the period, a result of the surpluses of the middle 1890s and in the last years. Remer also believes there to have been an unrecorded inflow of silver both by returning emigrants taking their savings home and by smuggling. It is possible that the practice of the expatriate Chinese of returning their dead to China provided an excellent cover for the transshipment of these remittances. It is obvious, however, that the Chinese payments situation was nowhere near as healthy as that of India, and if it had not been for emigrant remittances there would have been a substantial net outflow of precious metals.

What then were the commodities in which China traded? Table 16 (p.87) shows her principal exports, with tea and raw silk far and away the most important items. In percentage terms there is then a big drop to the third item, silk goods. Other exports varied in importance from year to year, with sugar quite important until 1888 and then disappearing from the top eight commodities, perhaps because of increasing domestic consumption. Cereals appeared every year from 1898, and rose steeply in importance, reflecting the export of soya beans from Manchuria. Other goods were cotton, hairs, leather and hides, skins and furs, oils, pottery, paper and seeds, all of which appeared from time to time in the first eight items.

Table 17 (p.88) shows the main countries to which China exported. At the beginning of the period Britain was the chief destination, taking 61 per cent of exports, but by 1913 her share had dropped to 4 per cent. One reason for this was the taste shift in Britain away from Chinese tea to tea from Ceylon and India. Hong Kong was of increasing importance, and it is true that many of the exports there found their

Graph 9: Chinese Treasure Balances, 1888-1913

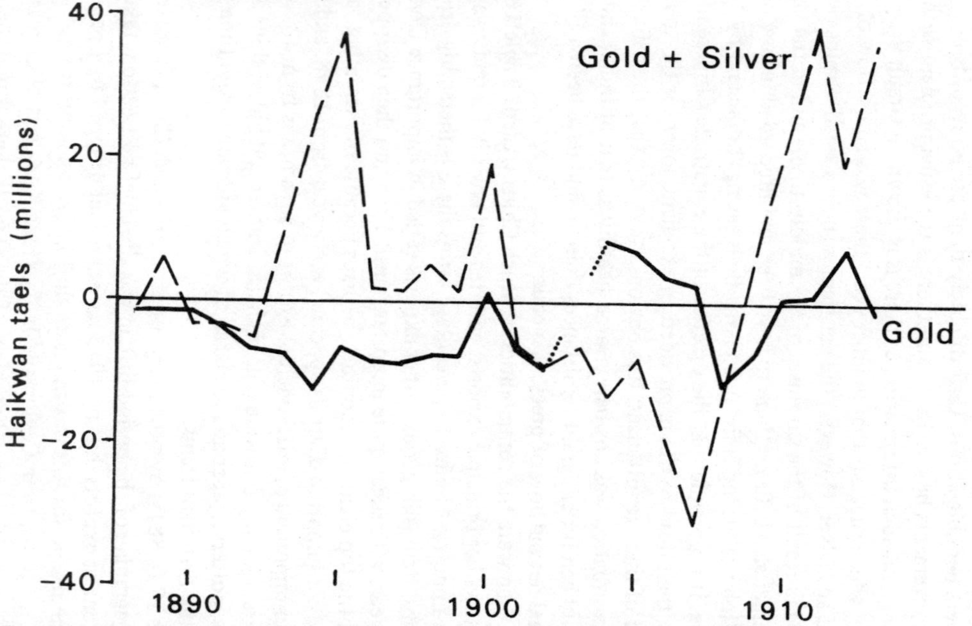

Source: C.F. Remer, 'International Trade between Gold and Silver Countries: China 1885-1913', *Quarterly Journal of Economics,* 40 (1926), p.630; see Appendix 8.

Table 16: Chinese Exports, 1868-1913

	1868		1878		1888		1898		1908		1913	
	%	Rank	%	Rank	%	Rank	%	Rank	%	Rank	%	Rank
Cereals	—	—	—	—	—	—	3.04	4	3.28	7	5.81	3
Cotton, raw	0.84	4	—	—	2.40	5	—	—	3.79	4	4.10	6
Hairs	—	—	0.43	8	1.14	8	—	—	—	—	—	—
Leather, hides	—	—	—	—	—	—	2.11	8	—	—	—	—
Oils	—	—	—	—	—	—	2.15	7	2.69	8	3.68	8
Paper	0.38	7	0.92	5	1.78	6	—	—	—	—	—	—
Pottery	0.42	6	0.80	6	1.17	7	—	—	—	—	—	—
Seeds	—	—	—	—	—	—	—	—	3.43	5	4.06	7
Silk, raw	36.84	2	30.13	2	25.17	2	27.99	1	23.98	1	19.88	1
Silk goods	3.00	3	7.05	3	9.10	3	6.72	3	5.27	3	5.40	4
Sugar	0.64	5	2.76	4	2.68	4	—	—	—	—	—	—
Skins, furs	—	—	0.52	7	—	—	2.35	6	3.37	6	4.90	5
Tea	55.41	1	47.65	1	32.78	1	18.15	2	11.88	2	8.41	2
Tobacco	—	—	—	—	—	—	2.40	5	—	—	—	—
Others	2.47		9.74		23.28		35.09		42.31		43.76	

Source: Ping-Yin Ho, *The Foreign Trade of China* (Shanghai: Commercial Press, 1935), pp.15-16, 37-39.

Table 17: Destination of Chinese Exports, 1868-1913 (%)

	1868	1878	1888	1898	1908	1913
UK	61.75	41.10	18.07	6.73	4.53	4.05
France	–	–	–	–	2.56	4.22
Germany	–	–	–	–	11.61	10.10
Hong Kong	12.98	22.29	36.31	39.03	33.29	29.04
India	0.38	0.55	1.12	0.83	1.47	1.53
Japan	1.34	2.50	3.85	10.11	13.41	16.25
Russia	1.15	4.96	5.85	11.19	10.68	11.13
United States	9.52	9.79	9.69	7.53	8.61	9.33
Others	12.88	18.81	25.11	24.59	13.84	14.35

Source: Ho, *Foreign Trade of China*, pp.55-6.

way to Britain. But Hong Kong was also the distribution centre for Asia in general, and many of the goods going to Hong Kong will have passed on to other parts of Asia, with India, and later Japan, taking much. The rise of Japan is demonstrated, with exports rising from 1 per cent in 1868 to 16 per cent in 1913. The United States took about 9 per cent of Chinese exports throughout, mainly in silk and silk products, and France also took a lot of silk goods. Russia was an increasing consumer of Chinese products, but India took hardly any, which perhaps is not surprising in view of the large surplus she enjoyed on her trade with China.

As for imports, opium was the main item until the turn of the century, but the statistics do not differentiate opium from some other miscellaneous items, so that on Table 18 (p.89) which shows Chinese imports, the figures for opium etc. have been excluded from the rank ordering. The situation with opium is that it declined as a percentage of total imports during the late nineteenth century, and in 1907 an agreement was reached with Britain restricting the import of opium from India. In 1911 increased duties were placed on opium, and imports rapidly fell, until 1917 when the Government banned opium imports. Apart from opium, cotton manufactures and yarn stand out amongst the imports, manufactures alone heading the list in all but one of the years examined, that being the year when yarn came first. This dominance of cotton goods follows the pattern of imports not only for India but for most of the rest of the undeveloped world. After cottons, there was a variety of commodities, only fish appearing in the first

Table 18: Chinese Imports, 1868-1913

	1868		1878		1888		1898		1908		1913	
	%	Rank	%	Rank	%	Rank	%	Rank	%	Rank	%	Rank
Cereals	—	—	—	—	7.71	3	4.98	4	6.73	4	3.26	5
Cotton, raw	6.08	3	1.37	7	—	—	—	—	—	—	—	—
Cotton, manufactures	29.20	1	19.06	1	24.79	1	18.28	2	16.40	1	19.27	1
Cotton, yarn	2.51	4	3.55	3	10.81	2	18.74	1	11.70	2	12.72	2
Dyes, pigments	—	—	—	—	—	—	—	—	—	—	3.10	6
Fish	1.32	6	2.89	4	3.02	5	2.22	7	2.39	7	2.59	8
Fuel, liquid	—	—	—	—	1.77	7	5.68	3	6.94	3	4.49	4
Fuel, solid	2.14	5	1.61	5	1.32	8	2.55	6	2.20	8	—	—
Iron, steel	0.11	7	1.39	6	1.84	6	2.05	8	—	—	—	—
Opium, etc.*	39.57	—	49.57	—	30.48	—	22.31	—	12.48	—	11.57	—
Railway materials	—	—	—	—	—	—	—	—	3.43	6	—	—
Sugar	0.80	8	—	—	—	—	4.29	5	4.97	5	6.36	3
Timber	—	—	1.28	8	—	—	—	—	—	—	—	—
Tobacco	—	—	—	—	—	—	—	—	—	—	2.91	7
Wool, manufactures	9.11	2	6.87	2	4.07	4	—	—	—	—	—	—
Others	9.16		12.41		14.19		18.90		32.76		33.73	

*Opium has not been placed in rank order, because the records include some miscellaneous items with opium. Clearly it would have ranked no.1 until about the turn of the century. Actual opium imports alone are estimated at: 1878, 45%; 1888, 25.9%; 1898, 14%.
Source: Ho, *Foreign Trade of China*, pp.15-16, 26-7, 30-2, 34-5.

eight in each of the years in question. Towards the end of the period cereals became important, and fuels (both solid and liquid) featured regularly. Cotton, sugar, iron and steel, timber, tobacco, dyes and pigments, and woollen manufactures appeared from time to time.

At the beginning of the period India was the leading source of imports, as Table 19 below indicates, and much of this was owing to the opium trade. Given the fact that India provided over 35 per cent of Chinese imports in 1868, and took less than 1 per cent of China's exports, it is not difficult to locate India's export surplus with China.

Table 19: Origin of Chinese Imports, 1868-1913 (%)

	1868	1878	1888	1898	1908	1913
UK	33.38	20.42	23.96	15.98	17.71	16.52
France	–	–	–	–	0.58	0.90
Germany	–	–	–	–	3.42	4.82
Hong Kong	21.37	37.49	55.06	44.44	36.68	29.28
India	35.59	28.79	5.22	8.74	7.44	8.23
Japan	3.65	5.53	4.55	12.51	12.81	20.35
Russia	0.12	0.20	0.36	0.80	2.11	3.79
United States	1.13	3.07	2.48	7.84	10.07	6.04
Others	4.76	4.50	8.37	9.96	9.18	10.07

Source: Ho, *Foreign Trade of China,* pp.56-7.

As the opium trade declined, India's share of China's imports decreased, although India increased her cotton yarn exports to China, which helped India to hold her share at about 8 per cent from 1898. Britain provided nearly as many imports as India in 1868, but her share halved to 16 per cent in 1913, particularly because of Japanese competition in the textile market, the Japanese share increasing by very much the amount that Britain's share dropped! This Japanese competition made its impact especially between 1888 and 1898 when Japan's victory in the Sino-Japanese war increased her commercial influence. Hong Kong was a major source of imports throughout, channelling into Southern China goods from all over the world. Other countries were relatively unimportant, the rise in the United States' share in the new century being accounted for by petroleum.

There now remains the problem of discovering with which countries China suffered trade deficits which accounted for her overall trade deficit. Graph 10 (page 91) reveals that in fact China moved into deficit

Graph 10: Chinese Trade Balances with Major Countries, 1868-1914

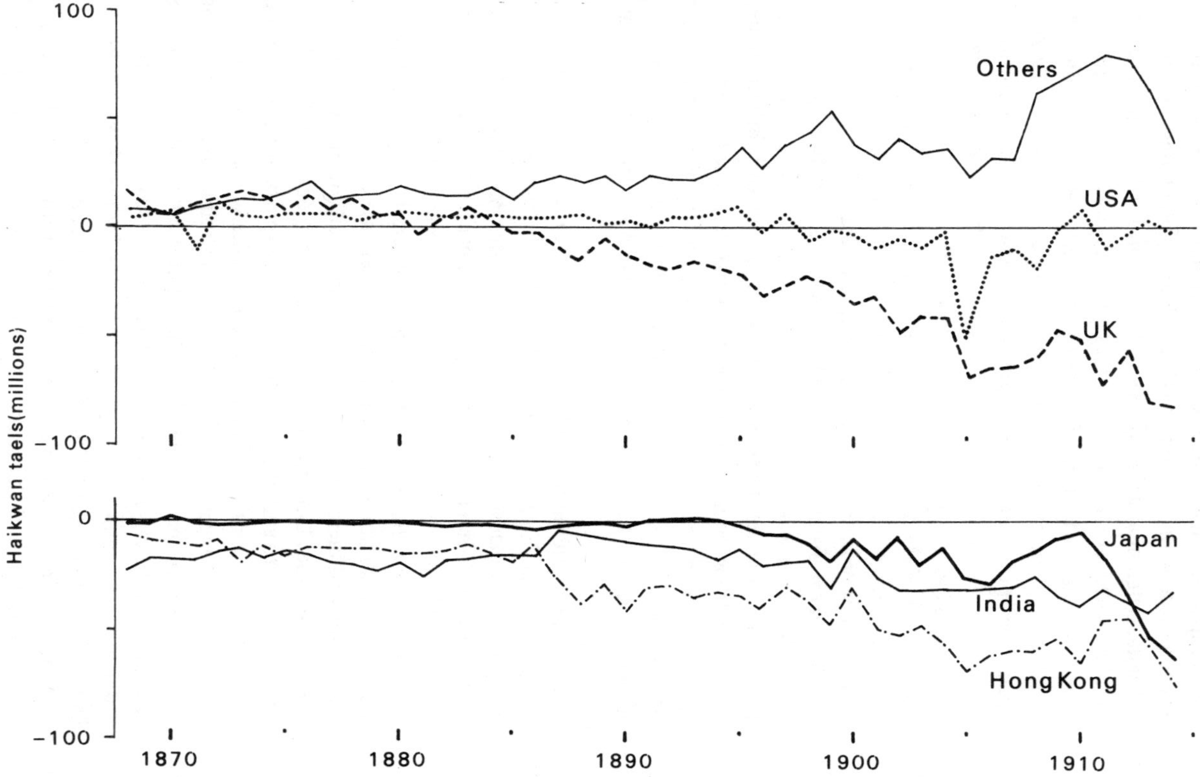

Source: Ho, *Foreign Trade of China*, pp.20-2, 70-1, 112, 162-3, 436-7, 632-3; *see* Appendix 9.

with most of her major trading partners over these years. Indeed, China's balances with the United Kingdom, Hong Kong, the United States, Japan, Germany and India were generally unfavourable; not to mention those with French Indo-China, Siam, Netherlands India, Australia, Belgium and Canada. Only those with Russia, Korea, France and Singapore were favourable and, as has been already discussed, they could not compensate for the unfavourable trade balances mentioned.[6]

India and China were of overwhelming importance in the trade of the undeveloped world, as is obvious from Table 8 (page 66) showing the exports of all the countries in question. So the remaining countries of Asia, and indeed of Africa, will be dealt with more briefly. Ceylon had a special relationship with both Britain and India, for the pattern of her development in these years is that she built up a plantation sector to supply Britain with coffee and, after that failed, tea. Workers were brought in from Southern India to work on the plantations and, to feed them, rice was imported from Bengal and Burma. Overall she tended to be in deficit on her trade account, as her surplus with Britain on her trade in coffee and tea was outweighed by her deficit with India resulting from her rice purchases. After rice, cotton manufactures were the next most important import, and towards the end of the period rubber added to her plantation exports. Copra was a significant peasant crop.[7]

The exports and imports of the Straits Settlements are rather difficult to interpret, because many goods passing through Singapore to and from other places often appear in the figures. Moreover, although her trade with different countries is recorded earlier, the quantities of goods traded is not given until 1901. However, she tended to be in deficit as a whole, like Ceylon importing large amounts of rice from India to feed her immigrant population, in her case the immigrants being mainly Chinese working in the tin mines, although there were some Indians too. Until the 1880s she was also in deficit with Britain, but this turned to surplus owing to her rising exports of tin and, at the end of the period, rubber. The Dutch East Indies was an important trading partner, as Singapore handled a lot of produce on its way to or from Java and Sumatra. Singapore's function as a distribution centre is evident from the large amounts of trade she carried on with Siam and China at the beginning of the period, added to by the Malay States, United States, Germany, Hong Kong and France, towards the end.[8]

Note has already been made of the big deficit that India had with Java after the turn of the century because of her substantial sugar imports from there. So it is not surprising to find the Dutch East Indies developing from a coffee exporter in 1870 to a sugar exporter by the beginning of the First World War. Petroleum followed sugar, developing rapidly from 1890, followed by tobacco, copra, tin, rubber, tea and cassava. These exports earned the Dutch East Indies a good surplus, as they exceeded her imports, which were made up of cottons, followed by rice for her plantation workers, machinery, iron and steel and fertiliser. Perhaps the outstanding feature of her foreign trade was a swing away from Europe and towards Asia in its orientation. This is particularly true of her export trade, with India and Japan taking a bigger share and the Dutch share falling. The Dutch remained the largest source of imports however, followed by the Straits Settlements and Britain.[9]

The story of Siam's international trade is marked by her phenomenal rise as a rice exporter, her success giving her a large trade surplus. These Siamese rice exports formed a vital part in the development of the intra-Asia rice trade in which Burmese rice also figured, along with exports from French Indo-China. Rice production became the major economic activity of her peasants, and from a mere 5 per cent in 1850 the proportion of the crop exported rose to just over 50 per cent by 1910. The major market for this rice was the Straits Settlements, where much was consumed by her immigrant mine and plantation workers, but considerable quantities were redistributed to the neighbouring Malay States and the Dutch East Indies for the same purpose. Most of the rest went to Hong Kong, and from there to China, with smaller quantities going to Europe. Apart from rice, Siam exported tin and teak, but they were much less significant. The rise in exports and the substantial surplus led to rising incomes and increased imports, in which British textiles feature strongly, along with sugar.[10]

As for French Indo-China, her foreign trade was dominated by her rice exports to China, so she too was part of the intra-Asian rice trade of these years. Exports of rice rose quickly after 1880, helped by the cutting of canals across central and western Cochin China, which enabled previously uncultivated areas to be brought into production. The quality of her rice, however, was inferior to Burmese and Siamese rice, as shipments tended to consist of a large number of varieties mixed up together. All France's rice came from here, and rice also went to the Dutch East Indies, Singapore and even British India on occasions. Fish products were the next export item, with China again taking the lion's share, and there were exports of corn, coal, hides, copper and rubber, but they were all comparatively unimportant, for in 1913 65 per cent of her exports were rice. Indo-China thus earned a substantial trade surplus in Asia, which paid for her deficit with France, where most of her imports originated. These consisted of cottons, followed by the paraphernalia of development; metal and metal products, machines and machinery, and iron and steel, most of these dating from the period of great development activity 1901-6. There were also small imports from China of noodles, vegetables, tea, tobacco, medicine, joss sticks, paper and silk fabrics.[11]

One feature that this examination of Asian trade has brought out is the development of the intra-Asian rice trade in these years. A map of the distribution of rice movements in Asia would show flows of rice from Burma, Siam and French Indo-China, to Ceylon, the Straits Settlements, the Dutch East Indies and also Hong Kong and China. This rice production was almost entirely in peasant hands, showing how peasant proprietors responded quickly to the market opportunities presented to them. With the exception of Hong Kong and China, most of the rice exports went to expanding plantation economies, where the immigrant labourers needed food. So a pattern emerges of plantations – or mines – producing for the European market, creating backward linkages to the peasant food producers. If dual economies appeared to be developing in the countries where the plantations or mines were, this was simply because the stimulus to peasant producers lay elsewhere. What is more, the demand for labour on the plantations or in the mines induced a flow of labour from areas where it was abundant, revealing the existence of an intra-Asian market not only for food but for labour as well. Each area contributed to the international economy whatever it was its comparative advantage to supply. If it was land, then the contribution was plantation agriculture, or peasant-produced rice. If it was labour, then it was plantation workers. In the case of the Straits Settlements and Malay States, Chinese entrepreneurs employed Chinese migrants in the tin mines, producing for the European market, but importing rice just like the plantation countries of Ceylon and Netherlands India.

Cottons are the other commodity requiring comment, for they were the major import item of nearly every Asian country, except those where rice or opium led, and there they came second. Cottons were equally important in Africa. Britain was the major supplier, but the Netherlands, France and Germany featured in their own colonies. Towards the end of the period, however, Japan made inroads in these markets, particularly in the new century, to some extent using yarn produced in India.

Turning to Africa, it is worth restating that Africa's contribution to world trade was extremely small, as was shown in Tables 9 and 10, page 67, providing in 1913 only 3.7 per cent of world exports and taking only 3.6 per cent of world imports. Asia's share was three times as large. If the countries dealt with here alone are examined, then Table 8 (page 66) showed that 77.8 per cent of the exports of the undeveloped world came from Asia in 1913 and only 22.1 per cent from Africa, this figure including South Africa. If South Africa is excluded, the figure drops to 6.5 per cent. In other words, Africa was really rather unimportant in world trade, particularly if South Africa is omitted. Nor did Africa make an important contribution to world settlements, for Saul has made it clear that the useful surplus which Britain earned on her business with West Africa was more than offset by her debits on her business with South Africa. So in its entirety Africa added up to another debit which had to be financed from her Asian surplus.[12]

Truly comparative details of African trade are not easy to find for this period, but Frankel has made a very useful breakdown of Africa's trade in the early twentieth century, and this is given in Table 20 (page 96). What is immediately apparent is the overwhelming importance of South Africa. In 1913 South Africa provided 63 per cent of the exports of these African countries, and received 50 per cent of their imports. Nigeria followed, a very long way behind, providing 6 per cent of exports and taking 7 per cent of imports. It makes sense therefore to begin with South Africa. Her development was tied to mineral discoveries, diamonds being the leading item until the discovery of gold on the Witwatersrand in the late 1880s. Thus in 1913, gold accounted for 56 per cent of exports and diamonds for 18 per cent, with wool contributing a further 8 per cent, and Britain taking nearly 90 per cent of the total. Her imports were made up of a mass of miscellaneous items: cottons, apparel, haberdashery and millinery, iron and steel, machinery, railway materials, wheat, none of which amounted to more than 7 per cent of the total. Mostly these came from Britain, but Germany and the United States also featured. Overall Britain's deficit on her trade with South Africa was £35.17 million that year, but South Africa herself enjoyed a substantial trade surplus, amounting to an annual average of £20.4 million in 1909-13.[13]

Nigeria, the second largest African trading country, exported mainly palm produce, both oil and kernels, importing in exchange cotton products, iron and steel goods, spirits, tobacco and sundries. Britain was the major supplier of her imports, and although the chief consumer of her exports, she took a smaller proportion than she provided imports,

Table 20: African Trade, 1907, 1913*

	1907				
	Exports		Imports		Balance
	£000	%	£000	%	£000
Gambia	280	0.42	285	0.59	–5
Sierra Leone	676	1.02	806	1.66	–130
Gold Coast	2,502	3.79	1,917	3.97	585
Nigeria	3,612	5.47	3,587	7.43	25
British West Africa total	7,070	10.71	6,595	13.66	475
Kenya	157	0.23)	897	1.85	–600
Uganda	140	0.21)			
Nyasaland	54	0.08	166	0.34	–112
Zanzibar	548	0.83	1,082	2.24	–534
British East Africa total	899	1.36	2,145	4.44	–1,246
N. Rhodesia	96	0.14	115	0.23	–19
S. Rhodesia	2,319	3.51	1,282	2.65	1,037
Rhodesia total	2,415	3.66	1,397	2.89	1,018
British Africa total (except S. Africa)	10,384	15.74	10,137	20.99	247
South Africa	45,485	68.96	25,691	53.22	19,794
British Africa total	55,869	84.70	35,828	74.21	20,041
French W. Africa	3,174	4.81	3,770	7.80	–596
French Equ. Africa	739	1.12	606	1.25	133
French Africa total	3,913	5.93	4,376	9.06	–463
Angola	961	1.45	1,366	2.82	–405
Guinea	122	0.18	187	0.38	–65
Mozambique	955	1.44	1,514	3.13	–559
Portuguese Africa total	2,038	3.08	3,067	6.35	–1,029
Belgian Congo total	2,340	3.54	993	2.05	1,347
Togo	296	0.44	334	0.69	–38
Cameroons	793	1.20	865	1.79	–72
South West Africa	81	0.12	1,620	3.35	–1,539
Tanganyika	625	0.94	1,190	2.46	–565
German Africa total	1,795	2.72	4,009	8.30	–2,214
Non-British Africa total	10,086	15.29	12,445	25.78	–2,359
Total	65,955		48,273		17,682

* The percentage figures do not add up exactly due to the rounding of decimal points.

Table 20: African Trade, 1907, 1913 (continued)

	1913				
	Exports		Imports		Balance
	£000	%	£000	%	£000
Gambia	655	0.64	611	0.76	44
Sierra Leone	1,376	1.34	1,324	1.66	52
Gold Coast	5,014	4.90	3,500	4.39	1,514
Nigeria	6,779	6.62	6,006	7.54	773
British W. Africa total	13,824	13.51	11,441	14.37	2,383
Kenya	444	0.43)	2,742	3.44	–1,734
Uganda	564	0.55)			
Nyasaland	201	0.19	192	0.24	9
Zanzibar	604	0.59	717	0.90	–113
British E. Africa total	1,813	1.77	3,651	4.58	–1,838
N. Rhodesia	195	0.19	247	0.31	–52
S. Rhodesia	3,297	3.22	2,782	3.49	515
Rhodesia total	3,492	3.41	3,029	3.80	463
British Africa total (except S. Africa)	19,129	18.70	18,121	22.77	1,008
South Africa	64,565	63.13	40,374	50.74	24,191
British Africa total	83,694	81.84	58,495	73.51	25,199
French W. Africa	5,000	4.88	6,030	7.57	–1,030
French Equa. Africa	1,468	1.43	834	1.04	634
French Africa total	6,468	6.32	6,864	8.62	–396
Angola	1,068	1.04	1,697	2.13	–629
Guinea	310	0.30	323	0.40	–13
Mozambique	1,678	1.64	2,341	2.94	–663
Portuguese Africa total	3,056	2.98	4,361	5.48	–1,305
Belgian Congo total	2,190	2.14	2,850	3.58	–660
Togo	457	0.44	532	0.66	–75
Cameroons	1,103	1.07	1,629	2.04	–526
South West Africa	3,515	3.43	2,171	2.72	1,344
Tanganyika	1,778	1.73	2,668	3.35	–890
German Africa total	6,853	6.70	7,000	8.79	–147
Non-British Africa total	18,567	18.15	21,075	26.48	–2,508
Total	102,261		79,570		22,691

Source: S.H. Frankel, *Capital Investment in Africa, Its Course and Effects* (London: Oxford University Press, 1938), pp.194-5, 196-7.

and thus gained a handy surplus. Germany and France were big consumers of Nigeria's exports, and so Nigeria was able to meet her deficit with Britain by way of her surplus with France and Germany. The position in the Gold Coast, the third African trading country, was somewhat different. Until after the turn of the century palm produce accounted for most of her exports, but then cocoa rapidly became the chief item, produced by peasant proprietors. Gold dust was in second place. The United Kingdom was the chief destination of the exports throughout, Germany trailing a long way behind in second place. Britain also was far and away the leading source of imports, which comprised the usual assortment of cotton goods, hardware, cutlery, galvanised iron, machinery, spirits, rice and tobacco. Unlike Nigeria, she tended to have a small surplus with Britain, and she had one with Germany too, giving her a comfortable overall surplus. Britain's other two West African colonies, Sierra Leone and the Gambia, were relatively insignificant international traders, Sierra Leone supplying palm produce and kolanuts, and the Gambia groundnuts, all products of African enterprise. Their imports were the usual miscellany of cotton goods, hardware, spirits, tobacco, etc.[14]

East Africa was much more backward as a trading area than West Africa. Kenya and Uganda were small participants in the international economic system even in the early years of the twentieth century, although in the last few years they became exporters of cotton, followed by coffee and sisal, the cotton crop being a product of peasant cultivation. Nyasaland also began its export development in the first decade of the new century, with cotton and tobacco the leading crops. Africans produced most of the tobacco and cotton, but tea was entirely a European product.[15]

Of the French West African Colonies, the groundnut production of Senegal in French West Africa was the leading export commodity before the First World War. Exports rose from the 1850s, although there was a setback after the opening of the Suez Canal, owing to competition from the Near East. With the opening of the 'groundnut railway' from Saint Louis to Dakar in 1885 exports recovered and expansion continued up to the war, when they made up 78 per cent of Senegal's total exports. Mahogany, rubber and palm produce each accounted for about a third of the Ivory Coast's exports at this time, and in Dahomey, palm produce made up some 87 per cent of the total. As for French Guinea, wild rubber comprised 72 per cent of total exports between 1900 and 1914. France herself was the major recipient of her colonies' exports from West Africa, although Germany took the biggest proportion from

Dahomey. France was also the main source of imports, but Britain came a close second in each territory, her cottons being particularly important. The remaining French territory was French Equatorial Africa, whose exports were principally of forest rubber, with some timber, whale oil and ivory. France was the leading trading partner, but Britain again came second as a source of imports. The imports were the usual mixture of cottons, hardware, spirits, tobacco, etc.[16]

Let us turn now to the German colonies. Togo exported chiefly palm produce, plus some rubber and cotton, Germany consuming most of this. Germany also was the major source of imports, which consisted as usual of cotton textiles, hardware and spirits. Britain, as in the French colonies, was the next most important source of imports. The Cameroons also exported palm produce, but wild rubber was the main product, and there was also some cocoa. Germany was again the main trading partner, but once more Britain was the second largest source of imports. South West Africa was rather different, as it owed its economic significance to the development of diamond mining. After 1902 there had been some copper mining, but the rapid exploitation of the diamond fields in 1909-13 was the crucial feature of her commerce. By 1912 diamonds accounted for 77 per cent of exports, with Germany taking most of them and also the greater part of the copper. Germany was the main source of imports too, but South Africa had a useful trade in mining machinery and accessories. The remaining German colony was Tanganyika, whose main exports were rubber and sisal, with some hides and cotton, the two major crops being plantation produce. Germany was the main trading partner, with India the second source of imports.[17]

In the early years of the twentieth century forest rubber and ivory accounted for almost all the exports of the Belgian Congo, in what Frankel calls the era of despoliation. It was not until after the war that minerals were exploited, and the substantial oil-palm plantations of Lever Bros' Société des Huileries du Congo Belge were established.[18]

There remains the situation in Portuguese Africa. Mozambique was comparatively neglected before the First World War, its economic importance lying in the two main railway lines which passed through it to Rhodesia and Nyasaland. Her exports were made up of many minor items, sugar being the leader, but even so providing less than 10 per cent. As for Angola, forest rubber was the main export item in 1913, followed by wild coffee. Portugal was the main trading partner of her African colonies, but as with the French and German possessions, Britain was the second most important source of imports, with cottons and machinery figuring strongly in her share of the market.[19]

Notes:

1. S.B. Saul, *Studies in British Overseas Trade, 1870-1914* (Liverpool: Liverpool University Press, 1960), pp.43-64.
2. Parimal Ray, *India's Foreign Trade Since 1870* (London, G. Routledge & Sons, 1934), pp.48-53, 67-88; J.B. Nugent, 'Exchange-Rate Movements and Economic Development in the Late Nineteenth Century', *Journal of Political Economy,* 81 (1973), pp.1114-17.
3. Saul, *British Overseas Trade,* p.236; Y.S. Pandit, *India's Balance of Indebtedness 1898-1913* (London: George Allen & Unwin, 1937), pp.46-7, Table VI.
4. Donald N. McCloskey and J. Richard Zecher, 'How the Gold Standard Worked', in *The Monetary Approach to the Balance of Payments,* ed. Jacob A. Frankel and Harry C. Johnson (London: Allen & Unwin, 1976), pp.368, 385; C.J. Daniell, *The Gold Treasure of India* (London: Kegan Paul, Trench & Co., 1884), pp.53-55; Vera Anstey, *The Economic Development of India,* 3rd ed. (London: Longmans, Green & Co., 1949), p.331 fn.
5. Saul, *British Overseas Trade,* pp.188-207; J.Q. Adams III, 'Economic Change, Exports and Imports: The Case of India, 1870-1960', University of Texas Ph D, 1966, pp.101-32, 167-185, 207-14; Anstey, *Economic Development of India,* pp.329-35; C.P. Wright, 'India as a Producer and Exporter of Wheat', *Wheat Studies,* 3 (1926-7), pp.317-412.
6. Ping-Yin Ho, *The Foreign Trade of China* (Shanghai: The Commercial Press, 1935), pp.10-58; C.F. Remer, *The Foreign Trade of China* (Shanghai: Commercial Press, 1926), pp.32-169, 204-26; C.F. Remer, 'International Trade between Gold and Silver Countries: China 1885-1913', *Quarterly Journal of Economics,* Vol.40, 1926, pp.597-643; Yu-Kwei Cheng, *Foreign Trade and Industrial Development of China, An Historical and Integrated Analysis through 1948* (Washington: University Press of Washington, 1956), pp.18-23; H.B. Morse, *The Trade and Administration of the Chinese Empire* (Shanghai: Kelly & Walsh Ltd., 1908), pp.270-301.
7. *Statistical Abstracts for the British Colonies;* D.R. Snodgrass, *Ceylon: An Export Economy in Transition* (Homewood, Illinois: Irwin, 1966), pp.1-55.
8. *Statistical Abstracts for the British Colonies;* Chong-Yah, *Economic Development of Modern Malaya,* pp.37-57, 97-113; Wong Lin Ken, 'Western Enterprise and the Development of the Malayan Tin Industry to 1914', in C.D. Cowan, ed., *The Economic Development of South-East Asia, Studies in Economic History and Political Economy* (London: George Allen & Unwin, 1964), pp.127-53.
9. J.S. Furnivall, *Netherlands India* (Cambridge: Cambridge University Press, 1944), pp.207-8, 336-9, 430-1; J.A.M. Caldwell, 'Indonesian Export and Production from the Decline of the Culture System to the First World War', in *The Economic Development of South East Asia,* pp.72-101.
10. J.C. Ingram, *Economic Change in Thailand* (Stanford: Stanford University Press, 1971), pp.36-74, 93-132, 331-5, Appendix C; J.C. Ingram, 'Thailand's Rice Trade and the Allocation of Resources', in *The Economic Development of South East Asia,* ed. C.D. Cowan, pp.102-126.
11. C. Robequain, *The Economic Development of French Indo-China* (London: Oxford University Press, 1944), pp.305-43.
12. See pages 67 to 70 above.
13. *Statistical Abstract for the British Colonies.*
14. *Statistical Abstract for the British Colonies.*
15. Frankel, *Capital Investment in Africa,* pp.260-75, 282-9; R.M.A. van Zwanenburg with Anne King, *An Economic History of Kenya and Uganda,*

1800-1970 (London: Macmillan, 1975) pp.38-40, 50-54, 187-96; Cyril Ehrlich, 'The Uganda Economy, 1903-1945', in V. Harlow and E.M. Chilver, ed., *History of East Africa:* Vol.2 (Oxford: Clarendon Press, 1965), pp.397-422.

16. Foreign Office, *Peace Handbooks:* Vol.XVII, *French African Possessions,* No.102, *Senegal,* pp.26, 35, 46-7; No.103, *French Guinea,* pp.27-8, 59-60; No. 104, *Ivory Coast,* pp.30-3; No.105, *Dahomey,* pp.32-5; No.108, *French Equatorial Africa,* pp.54-7; A.G. Hopkins, *An Economic History of West Africa,* (London: Longmans, 1973), pp.218-9, 221; Frankel, *Capital Investments in Africa,* pp.331-51.

17. Foreign Office, *Peace Handbooks:* Vol.XVIII, *German African Possessions (Late),* No.110, *Togoland,* pp.44-7; No.111, *Cameroon,* pp.66-8; No.112, *South West Africa,* pp.90-4; No.113, *Tanganyika,* pp.94-7; Frankel, *Capital Investment in Africa,* pp.216-27, 276-82, 352-4; W.O. Henderson, *Studies in German Colonial History* (London: Frank Cass, 1962), pp.38-9, 50-2.

18. Frankel, *Capital Investment in Africa,* pp.289-301; Foreign Office, *Peace Handbooks;* Vol.XVI, *British Possessions II, The Congo,* No.99, Belgian Congo, pp.94-5.

19. Foreign Office, *Peace Handbooks:* Vol.XIX, *Portuguese Possessions,* No.121, *Mozambique,* pp.84-7, 102-3; No.120, *Angola,* pp.78-9, 88-9; Frankel, *Capital Investment in Africa,* pp.367-73.

4 POPULATION AND MIGRATION

During the last chapter reference was made to migration by both Chinese and Indian labourers to work in the new plantations in Ceylon, the Straits Settlements and the Dutch East Indies, and also in the tin mines of the Malayan peninsula. This chapter will discuss in more detail the population changes of Asia and Africa, and the migration movements which took place in response to the demands of the international market.

It is not surprising to find that accurate census information does not exist for Africa and most of Asia during the nineteenth century, but this has not prevented guesstimates being made by population specialists. The figures, which are for world population, are given in Table 21 (page 104). The alternative estimates differ most for Africa and Asia, Asia being the area of biggest doubt because of the situation in regard to China. There were in the past many statistical surveys of the Chinese population, but they were usually incomplete and mutually contradictory, so little use can be made of them. The most obvious conclusion to be drawn from these figures, notwithstanding the differences in the estimates, is the overwhelming dominance of world population by Asia, which made up about 60-63 per cent of the world population in 1850, and 53-56 per cent in the early twentieth century. Africa was relatively insignificant, with 8-9 per cent in 1850 and 7-9 per cent at the turn of the century. As regards annual rate of increase, the estimates vary so much as to be rather meaningless, especially for Africa, although they do suggest that substantial population growth did take place during the period. It must be noted that of course the terms Asia and Africa, as used in these figures, include various countries not included in the present study, such as Japan, the Philippines and Egypt. Even so, it is clear that about half the world's population lived in the areas being discussed.[1]

Turning now to examine the situation in the individual countries under consideration, it is sensible to start with India, as she is better provided with population estimates than most countries of the undeveloped world. A census was carried out there between 1867 and 1872, which is usually taken to represent 1871, and thereafter a census was taken every ten years. Although Burma was included in the original censuses, it will be shown both separately here and also as part of the

Table 21: Estimated World Population, 1800-1920 (millions)

	1800		1850		1900		1920
	(a)	(b)	(a)	(b)	(a)	(b)	(c)
Africa	90	100	95	100	120	141	140
North America	6	6	26	26	81	81	117
Latin America	19	23	33	33	63	63	91
Asia	597	595	741	656	915	857	966
Europe & USSR	192	193	274	274	423	423	487
Oceania	2	2	2	2	6	6	9
Total	906	919	1,171	1,091	1,608	1,571	1,810

DISTRIBUTION OF WORLD POPULATION, 1800-1920 (%)

	1800		1850		1900		1920
	(a)	(b)	(a)	(b)	(a)	(b)	(c)
Africa	9.9	10.9	8.1	9.2	7.5	9.0	7.7
North America	0.7	0.7	2.2	2.4	5.0	5.2	6.5
Latin America	2.1	2.5	2.8	3.0	3.9	4.0	5.0
Asia	65.9	64.7	63.3	60.1	56.9	54.6	53.4
Europe & USSR	21.2	21.0	23.1	25.1	26.3	26.9	26.9
Oceania	0.2	0.2	0.2	0.2	0.4	0.4	0.5
Total	100.0	100.0	100.0	100.0	100.0	100.0	100.0

ANNUAL RATE OF INCREASE OF WORLD POPULATION, 1800-1920 (per 1000)

	1800-50		1850-1900		1900-20	
	(a)	(b)	(a)	(b)	(a)	(b)
Africa	1.1	0.0	4.7	6.9	7.7	–0.4
North America	29.8	29.8	23.0	23.0	18.6	18.6
Latin America	11.1	7.2	13.0	13.0	18.6	18.6
Asia	4.3	2.0	4.2	5.4	2.8	6.1
Europe & USSR	7.1	7.0	8.7	8.7	7.0	7.0
Oceania	—	—	—	—	—	—
Total	5.1	3.4	6.4	7.3	5.9	7.1

(a) A.M. Carr-Saunders, *World Population* (London: Royal Institute of International Affairs, 1936), pp.30-45.

(b) W.F. Willcox, 'Population of the World and Its Modern Increase', in *Studies in American Demography* (Ithaca: Cornell University Press, 1940) pp.22-51, 511-40.

Source: D.V. Glass and E. Grebenik, World Population, 1800-1950, in *The Cambridge Economic History of Europe,* eds H.J. Habakkuk and M. Postan (Cambridge: University Press, 1965), Vol.6, p.58.

total because Burma was such an important area of internal migration as she developed as a rice exporter to Ceylon. Ceylon is not included in the figures, and will be dealt with separately. Several points emerge from the figures shown in Table 22 (page 105). The population of British India as a whole appears to have increased by about 20 per cent between 1871 and 1911, and it did so by sudden bursts of growth. In

Table 22: Estimate of Population of British India, 1871-1911 (000)

	India	% growth over 10 years	Burma	% growth over 10 years	British India	% growth over 10 years
1871	255,166		8,007		263,173	
		0.86		14.01		1.26
1881	257,380		9,129		266,509	
		9.61		7.10		9.53
1891	282,134		9,778		291,912	
		1.11		11.12		1.45
1901	285,288		10,866		296,154	
		6.20		13.08		6.45
1911	302,985		12,288		315,273	
% increase over 40 years						
	India	18.74	Burma	53.46	British India	19.79

Source: Kingsley Davis, *The Population of India and Pakistan* (Princeton, New Jersey: Princeton University Press, 1951), pp.27, 236.

the 1870s growth was slow, owing to the famine of 1876-8, but in the 1880s growth was much more rapid, only to fall away again drastically in the 1890s as, once more, famine took hold. If the figures for Burma are extracted, it is clear that the population fluctuations were restricted to the Indian peninsula, for the population there grew by only about 19 per cent between 1871 and 1911, whereas in Burma it grew by over 53 per cent in the same period. There was substantial immigration to Burma from India, as the delta became a great commercial rice-producing area. The greater part of the immigrants were Indian coolies employed in the rice mills and elsewhere, but there were also money-lenders and traders, some of them Chinese, of whom there were 122,000 in 1911. Although the figures do not show it, there was also substantial internal immigration in India to Assam, the north-eastern tea-plantation zone, and also to Bombay, where cotton mills and other commercial enterprises flourished.[2]

There was also migration from India, and this was very important for the development of the international economy. The figures for Indian emigration for 1866-1915 are shown on Table 23 (p.106),

Table 23: Estimated Total Migration from India,* 1866-1915 (000)

	Emigrants	Returned migrants	Net**
1866-70	976	778	197
1871-75	1,235	958	277
1876-80	1,505	1,233	272
1881-85	1,545	1,208	337
1886-90	1,461	1,204	256
1891-95	2,326	1,536	790
1896-1900	1,962	1,268	694
1901-05	1,428	957	471
1906-10	1,864	1,482	383
1911-15	2,483	1,868	615
Total	16,785	12,492	4,292

* Burma not included.

** The figures for net emigration do not always equal the difference between emigrants and returned migrants, because of rounding.

Source: Kingsley Davis, *The Population of India and Pakistan* (Princeton, New Jersey: Princeton University Press, 1951), pp.115-16.

although it should be noted that emigration from India dates back to 1834 when the abolition of slavery in the British Empire created a new demand for labour in the tropics. A very high proportion of migrants eventually returned to India, so that net migration, especially when considered against the size of the Indian population, was very small. At the same time, the contribution of Indian labour to the development of tropical plantations was much greater than might be supposed from the net migration figures. Ceylon and the Straits Settlements were major destinations for Indian emigrants, and East and South Africa also received them, besides countries beyond the scope of this study: Mauritius, Fiji and the Caribbean. In the early days most labourers went abroad on a five-year indentured contract, after which they became free labourers and could return to India. But towards the end of the nineteenth century the short-term contract became more important, particularly for nearby areas like Ceylon. Called the *kangani* contract, it derived its name from the *kangani* or ganger who was both recruiter and field foreman. Usually of only 30 days duration, the contract was generally verbal rather than written. The system spread to British Malaya from the 1890s and almost completely ousted indenture during the first decade of the new century. Not all the Indians who migrated were field hands, however. Moneylenders and traders followed them, catering for the particular needs of their countrymen, and although their numbers were small in proportion to the labourers, their economic importance was great.[3]

Ceylon, a major destination for Indian emigrants, seemed to esçape the ravages of famine and disease which so greatly afflicted India in the late nineteenth century, as the figures in Table 24 (page 107) indicate. The overall population increase between 1871 and 1911 was about 70 per cent. Immigration clearly played a substantial part in this, as Table 25 (page 107) shows. The Tamil immigrants were from Madras Province, as shown in Map 4 (page 108). They came over on indenture to work on

Table 24: Population of Ceylon, 1871-1911

	000	% growth over 10 years	% growth over 40 years
1871	2,417		
		14.02	
1881	2,756		
		9.65	
1891	3,022		70.50
		18.56	
1901	3,583		
		15.01	
1911	4,121		

D.R. Snodgrass, *Ceylon: An Export Economy in Transition* (Homewood, Illinois: Richard D. Irwin Inc., 1966), pp.305-6.

Table 25: Net Immigration to Ceylon, 1871-1915 (000)

	(000)
1871-75	88.6
1876-80	193.3
1881-85	36.5
1886-90	97.1
1891-5	172.4
1896-1900	218.5
1901-05	157.5
1906-10	117.5
1911-15	194.3
Total	1,275.7

Source: D.R. Snodgrass, *Ceylon*, p.308.

Map 4: Origin of Tamil Labourers to Ceylon and British Malaya

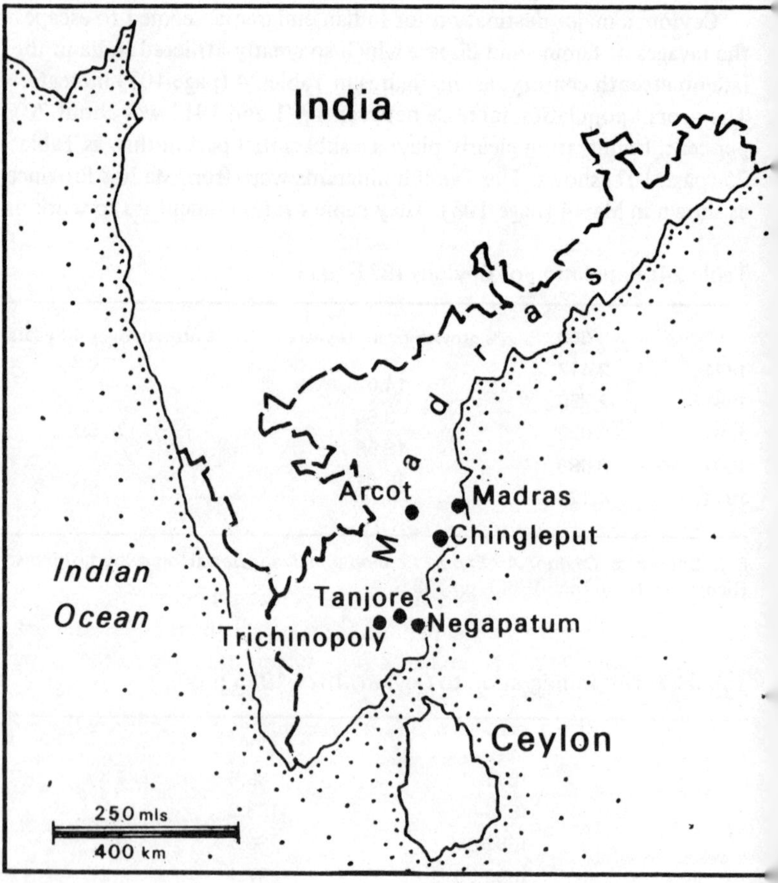

Source: J.N. Parmer, *Colonial Labour Policy and Administration, A History of Labour in the Rubber Plantation Industry in Malaya c.1910-1941* (New York: I.J. Augustin, 1960), p.53.

the coffee plantations, being driven to seek an alternative means of making a livelihood when their weaving industry was destroyed by competition from Lancashire. In the early 1880s immigration faltered when disease led to the collapse of coffee growing, but it revived when in the late 1880s tea growing restored the prosperity of the plantations.[4]

There are no adequate population figures for British Malaya until 1911, the figures for that year being given in Table 26 (page 109). Clearly it was in British Malaya that the flow of Indian emigrants east met the stream of Chinese emigrants coming west, both attracted by the demand for labour there. Such was the shortage of labour in British

Table 26: Population of British Malaya by Ethnic Group, 1911

	000	%
Malaysians	1,370	58.57
Chinese	693	29.62
Indians	239	10.21
Others	27	1.15
Total	2,329	99.55

Source: Lim Chong-Yah, *Economic Development of Modern Malaya* (Kuala Lumpur: Oxford University Press, 1967), p.344.

Malaya, particularly on the coffee and, later, the rubber plantations, that the Government and the plantation owners deliberately promoted migration from India. They raised wage levels to those prevailing in Ceylon, subsidised steam-ship fares, and from 1907 provided a centralised administrative machinery to bring the Indians over. Besides the labourers, clerks for the government service, teachers, lawyers and doctors came from India, along with the moneylenders and traders who seemed to follow the labourers wherever in the world they went. As in Ceylon, most of the immigrants were Tamils from Madras Province, although some were from the Central Provinces. Mostly the labourers were in Malay only on a temporary basis, as was the case with Ceylon, and this is reflected in the figures for Indian arrivals and departures shown in Table 27 (page 110). Thus as with Ceylon, the contribution of Indians to the development of Malayan plantations was greater than might be deduced from net immigration, or indeed from the number of Indians in Malaya shown in the 1911 census. At the same time, a considerable permanent Indian community did establish itself there.[5]

Before turning to examine Chinese immigration to Malaya, it must

Table 27: Arrivals and Departures of Indians in British Malaya, 1905-1913

	Arrivals	Departures	Net
1905	39,539	19,754	19,785
1906	52,041	21,878	30,163
1907	60,542	30,522	30,020
1908	54,522	30,920	23,602
1909	49,817	31,374	18,443
1910	83,723	39,080	44,643
1911	108,471	48,103	60,368
1912	106,928	63,885	43,043
1913	118,583	70,090	48,493
Total	674,166	355,606	318,560

Source: R.N. Jackson, *Immigrant Labour and the Development of Malaya, 1786-1920* (Kuala Lumpur: Government Press, 1961), p.139.

be noted that the term 'Malaysians' in the census figures for 1911 obscures the fact that there was some immigration of Malays from Java and Sumatra. Although the numbers were never as great as for Indians or Chinese, small-time traders and planters were coming from Java as early as the 1880s, and so were labourers. Some planters preferred Javanese or Sumatrans, because they felt they would assimilate with the local people more easily than Indians or Chinese whose cultural pattern was more foreign. But there were constraints on the supply of labourers from Java and Sumatra, because of the demand for their services by planters and public-works employers in their own territories. Nevertheless, in 1912 there were 10,897 Javanese labourers at work on estates in the Federated Malay States, of whom 6,368 were on three-year contracts.[6]

The Chinese were the biggest immigrant group in Malaya, as the 1911 census makes plain, for by that time they constituted nearly 30 per cent of the population, while the Indians mustered only just over 10 per cent. Unlike the Indians, however, the Chinese tended not to work for European plantation owners but for entrepreneurs of their own race, either tin-mine proprietors or planters. Of the two fields of enterprise, tin mining was by far the most important, with nearly all the mine owners and workers being Chinese in the thirty years before the turn of the century. Although the capital and enterprise came from Chinese already established in Penang and Malacca, rather than from China direct, it seems that the original miners had been peasant rice farmers in

Kwantung and Fukien provinces, and had adapted their farm implements to the needs of tin mining. This essentially involved scraping up buckets full of tin-bearing earth, which was then washed, leaving the tin ore behind. Thus their hoes, bamboo buckets on poles, bamboo pipes, and wooden chain pumps were easily adapted to their new task. If the proprietors of the mines came from Chinese families already established in Malaya by the middle of the century, they could not have succeeded without the newcomers they recruited from the provinces from which they themselves originated. As tin mining boomed, a highly organised system of recruiting built up, by which returned immigrants, known as *kheh thaus,* acted as professional recruiters in their home villages. Then they brought the *sin kehs,* or newcomers, to the mines in Malaya for which they were recruiting, and became the newcomers' gangers. As time went on, the system became more sophisticated, and recruiters sent their men to lodging houses in Chinese ports, from where they were transported to similar lodging houses in Malaya, which in effect acted as brokers to the employers, who then bid for the newcomers. The Hokkien from Fukien province, the Kwong-Fu and Hakkas from Kwantung and the Teochius from northern Kwantung were all channelled to Malaya via lodging-house networks dealing with their own separate communities. That the system led to the newcomers being herded like animals is indicated by the fact that it was known amongst those who operated it as the 'pig trade'. As to plantations, the Chinese were active in growing gambier, pepper, tapioca, sugar cane and coffee, and as rubber increased in importance at the turn of the century, they moved into this as well, recruiting labour from the lodging houses.[7]

Migration from Java to Malaya was relatively small, as has been noted, because of the demand for labour in the Dutch East Indies. This was despite the apparently considerable population growth in these islands. The figures for the population growth of Netherlands India are given in Table 28 (p.112). Looking at the decennial growth rates derived from these figures, it is immediately apparent that the figures for the islands other than Java are extremely erratic and cannot be relied upon. Even the figures for Java may be unreliable, for the growth of over 20 per cent in each of the ten-year periods from 1870 is far above that in Burma, where growth was high, and even above Ceylon, with the exception of the 1890s when growth exceeded 18 per cent. It is known that returns in the Javanese censuses were often far from complete. Yet, notwithstanding recent criticism, it seems inescapable that there was substantial population growth in Java in these years.

Table 28: Population of Netherlands India, 1870-1905 (000)

	Java	% growth over 10 yrs	Other islands	% growth over 10 yrs	Total
1870	16,452		4,285		20,737
		20.31		46.64	
1880	19,794		6,284		26,078
		20.81		7.69	
1890	23,914		6,767		30,682
		20.20		−2.83	
1900	28,746		6,575		35,322
		4.70*		11.08*	
1905	30,098		7,304		37,402

% increase over 35 years: Java 82.94%

* % growth over 5 years.

Source: Nitisastro Widjojo, *Population Trends in Indonesia* (Ithaca: Cornell University Press, 1970), pp.5-6, 60.

Much of this population growth was among the indigenous people, but this did not prevent the Chinese flocking in, in increasing numbers, as shown in Table 29 (p.113). Although again there must be reservations in accepting these figures at their face value, obviously an extensive Chinese community had established itself by the beginning of the twentieth century. They came from the same clans as the Chinese in Malaya, the Hokkien and Hakka mainly merchants, the Kwong-Fu craftsmen and the Teochius farmers. The coolies in the mines and on the estates were temporary immigrants, as repatriation was a condition of their employment, but many of them managed to find work outside the mines and plantations when their time was up, and they settled down and prospered. Numerous Chinese were busy in petty trading, connecting small producers and consumers up-country with the world market, and Chinese were active as carpenters, shoemakers, tailors, bakers and washermen. At the turn of the century most of the Chinese wealth accrued from opium shops, pawnshops and money lending.[8]

The Chinese were also present in Siam in large numbers. In 1884 when the population was guesstimated at 5.9 million, about 25 per cent of the inhabitants were said to be Chinese, and another guess (probably less accurate than the previous one) for 1890 mentions a population of 10 million, with 30 per cent being Chinese. More recent

Table 29: Growth of Chinese Population in Dutch East Indies 1860-1905 (000)

	Java	% growth over 10 yrs	Dutch East Indies	% growth over 10 yrs
1860	149		221	
		17.44		17.64
1870	175		260	
		18.28		32.30
1880	207		344	
		16.90		34.01
1890	242		461	
		14.46		16.48
1900	277		537	
		6.49*		4.84*
1905	295		563	

* growth over 5 years

Sources: J.S. Furnivall, *Netherlands India* (Cambridge: University Press, 1944), p.408; V. Purcell, *The Chinese in South-East Asia* (London: Oxford University Press, 1952), p.443.

estimates, still highly conjectural, suggest 7 million in 1909, with 10 per cent Chinese. What is certain is that there was a large Chinese community in Siam, which was concentrated around Bangkok and along the coast of Southern Siam. The usual Chinese tribes were evident, and there were also Hailams from Hainan, who were chiefly pedlars and fishermen, the poorest of all the groups. The Chinese played a crucial role in the commercial rice industry, Siam's chief export commodity. Although the rice was actually grown by the Siamese, it was the Chinese who purchased it from the growers and moved it by canal to the mills, which were also owned by Chinese and operated by Chinese workers. Of the 23 steam rice mills in Bangkok in 1889, 17 were owned by Chinese. The Chinese were even active as moneylenders to the tenant farmers who grew the rice, as were the Siamese. As in Malaya, the Chinese worked the tin mines in the Siamese portion of the Malay peninsula, the Government participating only through the royalty on tin production and the mining licence. The main centre was the island of Phuket, although there were a large number of small mines worked by the Chinese throughout southern Siam. The Chinese even operated crude smelters to process the ore. The other industry in which the

Chinese operated was the teak industry, but from the 1880s this increasingly fell into European hands, although the Chinese still provided workers.[9]

There are no accurate population estimates for French Indo-China in the nineteenth century, and the best guesses put the population at around 16 million in 1900. The rise of the rice export industry prompted substantial internal migration. As canals were cut to drain the mangrove swamps between Saigon and Mekong, Annamites migrated south to begin rice cultivation. They also moved south to work on coffee plantations, which prospered on the rich 'red land' of south Annam. To the north, in Tonkin, the French coal, zinc and tin mines also required Annamite migration. The Chinese were also present in large numbers: Kwong-Fu, Hokkien, Hakka, Teochiu and Hailams. Between 1889 and 1906 the Chinese population of Cochin China increased from 57,000 to 120,000 and, despite increased opposition from the French colonial authorities, their numbers continued to increase, although less quickly than before. Most of the Chinese clustered in southern Indo-China, principally in Cochin China and Cambodia. As in Siam, they were greatly involved in the rice trade, purchasing from the producers and transporting the rice to their mills to be prepared for export. Only some Hakkas were actually rice growers. Another agricultural activity in which the Chinese participated was pepper growing, the Hailams having a monopoly in this cultivation even before the French came and retaining it afterwards, for they had mastered the intricate skills needed. They would probably have taken an interest in rubber too, but were excluded from grants of the suitable land by the Government. They were also excluded from mining, but they ran sugar mills and saw mills. Chinese labourers were rarely found on European estates, as Annamites were preferred, but they were used on the construction of the Yunnan railway, where many died from malaria in 1904-5. Trade was their real metier, and they were prominent in the export trade not only of rice but also of fish and hides.[10]

The emigration of Chinese to other parts of South East Asia marks a population movement of great importance in international economic activity. Besides which, Chinese also went to the United States, Australia and other parts. So the population history of China is a matter of great interest. Unfortunately, as was mentioned earlier in this chapter, the dynastic statistics which were collected in China in the past cannot be relied upon and their scope and reliability is uncertain. Even the direct censuses of 1909-11 and 1912 were inaccurate and incomplete. While it is probably safe to assume that the Chinese population was greater than the 315 million of British India in 1911, any more definite figure would be misleading. However, Durand has recently provided estimates which give a population of 417 million for 1851 and 518 million for 1953, which would give an estimated population of 414 million for 1860, 443 million for 1880, 462 million for 1900 and 474 million for 1913, assuming a steady growth of 0.21 per cent per annum. These are somewhat lower than the figures guesstimated by Zimmerman in his study, which will be referred to in Chapter 5. Nor are there reliable figures for the numbers of Chinese who emigrated, although it is clear that the majority of emigrants were from Kwantung and Fukien Provinces, as shown on Map 5 below. This mass migration of people from these southern Chinese provinces suggests population pressure upon the resources in this area, something which is indicated by the rice imports which China made during this period. However, even in the 1920s imports amounted to less than 4 per cent of rice production.

Map 5: Origin of Chinese Migrants from Southern China

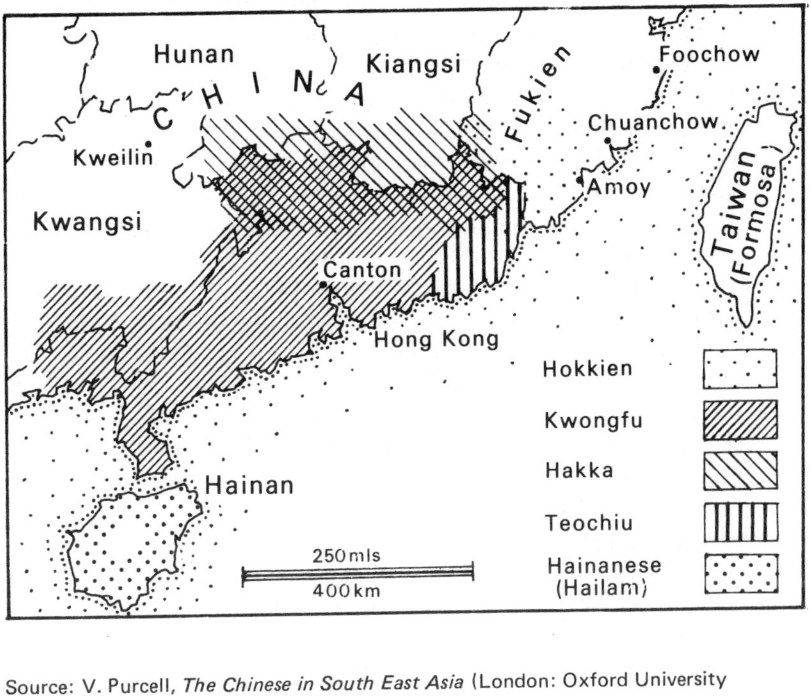

Source: V. Purcell, *The Chinese in South East Asia* (London: Oxford University Press, 1952), p.9.

Five tribes provided the majority of the emigrants. There were the Kwong-Fu, or Cantonese, from north-west Kwantung Province, who were chiefly engaged in commerce, although they did provide labourers, craftsmen and boatmen; the Hokkien from Fukien, especially from around Amoy, who were less numerous than the Kwong-Fu, but were similarly active in commerce; the Teochiu from the Swatow region of Kwantung, who were farmers, boatmen and coolies; and the Hakkas from north-east Kwantung, who were also cultivators and coolies. Lastly there were the Hailams from the island of Hainan, who became pepper planters and domestic servants in Indochina. Their migration was obviously a direct response to the demand for labour overseas, a demand which they met with considerable acumen and alacrity, providing the late nineteenth century and early twentieth century with one of its major migration flows.[11]

There remains the question of population growth and migration in Africa, and at the beginning of the chapter were presented the best estimates of Africa's population during this period. Frankly, these can only be guesses because of the complete inadequacy of the data. The figures for the rate of increase bring out how widely the various estimates vary. Perhaps the most important implication of the figures is that Africa harboured a very much smaller population than Asia, the African population apparently being 13-17 per cent of the size of the Asian population in 1900. This rough proportion was true in both 1850 and at the end of the second decade of the twentieth century. Put another way, Asia accounted for 85-89 per cent of the population of Africa and Asia at this time, Africa for a mere 11-15 per cent. As for world population, Africa seems to have supported less than a tenth, while Asia supported substantially more than half, as was noted earlier.

Of the African countries, the British African territories are best supplied with figures, and in Table 30 (p.117) are given the figures for the censuses of 1891, 1901 and 1911. None of these figures can be taken to be anything like exact, especially the 1891 census. For example, the figures for Nigeria are merely the figures for Lagos in this census, and the figures for Sierra Leone and the Gambia are for smaller areas than in subsequent censuses. Taking the 1911 figures simply as a very rough approximation, what emerges is that Nigeria was by far the largest British possession in population terms, holding half the population of all British African territories. Her population of over 17 million in 1911 was far ahead of the next largest country, the Union of South Africa, which had a population of nearly 6 million. Uganda and the East African Protectorate, subsequently Kenya, both had

Table 30: Population of British African Territories, 1891-1911

	Census 1891	Census 1901	Census 1911
West Africa			
Nigeria	85,607	13,606,093	17,126,983
Gold Coast	1,473,882	1,486,433	1,501,793
Sierra Leone	74,835	1,024,178	1,403,132
Gambia	14,266	90,354	146,101
Total	1,648,590	16,207,058	20,178,009
Southern Africa			
Union of South Africa	–	5,175,824	5,973,394
Swaziland	–	85,491	99,959
Basutoland	218,902	348,848	404,507
Bechunaland Prot.	190,000	120,776	125,350
Rhodesia:			
Southern	500,000	503,065	771,077
Northern	–	746,000	822,482
Total	908,902	6,980,004	8,196,769
East Africa			
Nyasaland Prot.	–	706,000	970,430
Uganda Prot.	–	3,500,000	2,843,325
East Africa Prot. (Kenya)	–	4,000,000	2,402,863
Zanzibar Prot.	200,000	250,000	197,200
Total	200,000	8,456,000	6,413,818
Grand total	2,757,492	31,643,062	34,788,596

Source: *Statistical Abstract for British Colonies*

populations of over 2 million, apart from which only the Gold Coast and Sierra Leone exceeded 1 million. But taking British Africa as a whole, their population of approximately 35 million was still paltry in comparison with the 315 million in British India in 1911. Calculation of population growth rates at this time would really be meaningless, although it is probable that the population of most of the territories was growing.

Immigration was important only in Southern and Eastern Africa, which received both European and Indian migrants. In 1902-11 inclusive, 698,115 immigrants landed at the ports of Natal and the Cape, while 576,624 left, giving a net immigration by sea of 121,491. Included in these figures were 66,547 indentured Indian labourers to Natal, but the absence of figures for them leaving on completing their time makes it impossible to obtain a net immigration figure. What can be said is that approximately one in ten of the migrants to the Cape and Natal at this time were Indians going to Natal, where the white settlers had been bringing them since the 1860s as a more reliable source of cheap regular labour than the indigenous Africans. Many Indians settled after completing their indentures, some receiving Crown land, others buying or renting land. Following these labourers came a flow of Indian traders on their own initiative, arriving to supply their countrymen with their special needs. Besides working on the farms, Indian labourers were employed on the railways and in the coal mines, and even as domestic servants. Some later took to fishing. However, the importation of Indian indentured labourers ended in 1911. Indians were not the only non-European immigrants, for in 1905-7, 59,296 Chinese were brought into the Transvaal on indenture, to work in the gold mines as they were rehabilitated at the end of the Boer War. Their numbers were not included in the immigration figures quoted above. Unlike most migrants who left China in this period, they were not Southern Chinese from Kwantung and Fukien, but Northern Chinese excluded from Manchuria by the Russo-Japanese war, and recruited via Chifu and Chinwangtao. They had all been repatriated by 1912.[12]

Indians also came to East Africa. In the East African Protectorate (Kenya) the census of 1911 gives the number of Asiatics as 20,986. Many of these had been brought in to build the railway, but the establishment of an Indian community there derived not from these labourers, most of whom returned to India, but from Indian families long resident on the East African coast. Together with new private immigrants from India, they moved into the interior to seize opportunities made available by the new railway and obtain clerical jobs in the British administration as it was consolidated. Indian traders set themselves up in business not only around the railway stations but also in the furthest African settlements, connecting them as buyers and sellers to the international market. They also moved into Uganda, where there were 2,216 of them in 1911, almost all of them traders. Like their relations in Kenya, they were for the most part Gujerati-speaking Muslims and Hindus from Bombay Presidency and Kathiawar, traditionally trading people. So Indian immigration to East Africa in general was greater than European, but the Indians still formed a minute proportion of the total population. Their economic importance was far greater than their numbers.[13]

In the non-British African territories, information on population is, if anything, worse than in the British areas. In French West Africa, the population of Senegal in 1911 was said to be 1,247,301 and that of French Guinea, in 1916, was estimated at 1,808,893. In the Ivory Coast, the indigenous population was given as 1,365,425 in 1911, and in Dahomey at the same time as 'about 900,000'. As for French Equatorial Africa, the figures are said to be unreliable, but estimated at 9,000,000 in 1915. So the French African territories may be supposed, very, very roughly, to have had a population of around 14 million on the eve of the First World War.[14]

The situation was similar in the German possessions, with the population of Togo in 1913 said to be 'partly by estimate and partly by enumeration, somewhat over 1,000,000'. In the Cameroons the figure for 1915 was 'estimated' 'at over 2,649,000'. In South West Africa the population was said to be 239,000 in 1912. As for Tanganyika, the indigenous population was estimated at around 7,641,800 with some 5,336 Europeans, in 1913. It was noted that 'a large number' of Asiatics, presumably Indians, had entered the territory as small traders and artisans. In 1912 the non-indigenous population, exclusive of Europeans, amounted to 14,933, of whom most were British Indians, but Goanese, Arabs and Levantines were also numerous. So a rough figure for the German territories would be 11,500,000 at the end of the period.[15]

In the Portuguese territories, the situation was actually worse. In Portuguese Guinea, the population at the end of the second decade of the new century was officially put at 400,000 but other estimates varied from 100,000 to 800,000. In Angola the position was as bad, with a census of 1914 giving an indigenous population of 2,124,000 but other estimates suggesting nearer 4,000,000. As for Mozambique, the suggested totals in 1920 were 10,500 whites, rather more Asiatics and half-castes, and about 2,800,000 Africans. Thus the overall figure for Portuguese Africa would perhaps be 10,000,000.[16]

There remains the situation in the Belgian Congo, but there are no estimates for it for this period.[17]

The population of the non-British territories which have been examined may then have been said to be in the region of 35 million just before the First World War, or roughly equivalent to the population of all the British territories, giving a total of some 70 million in all. Even this was small in comparison with British India alone, and emphasises again the relative unimportance of Africa.

Notes

1. D.V. Glass and E. Grebenik, 'World Population 1800-1950', in *The Cambridge Economic History of Europe,* eds H.J. Habakkuk and M. Postan (Cambridge University Press, 1965), Vol.6, pp.56-60, 63-5.

2. Kingsley Davis, *The Population of India and Pakistan* (Princeton, New Jersey: Princeton University Press, 1951), pp.115-16; J.S. Furnivall, *Colonial Policy and Practice: A Comparative Study of Burma and Netherlands India* (Cambridge: Cambridge University Press, 1948), pp.79-98; K.C. Zachariah, *A Historical Study of Internal Migration in the Indian Sub-Continent 1901-1931* (Bombay: Asia Publishing House, 1969), pp.44-135, 168-242; V. Purcell, *The Chinese in South East Asia* (London: Oxford University Press, 1952), pp.58, 94.

3. Davis, *Population of India,* pp.98-106.

4. D.R. Snodgrass, *Ceylon: An Export Economy in Transition* (Homewood, Illinois: Richard D. Irwin Inc., 1966), pp.16-38; N.K. Sarkar, *The Demography of Ceylon* (Colombo: Ceylon Government Press, 1957), pp.174-82; S. Rajaratnam, 'The Ceylon Tea Industry 1886-1931', *Ceylon Journal of Historical and Social Studies,* July-Dec (1961), pp.169-202; S. Rajaratnam, 'The Growth of Plantation Agriculture in Ceylon, 1886-1931', *Ceylon Journal of Historical and Social Studies,* Jan-June (1961), pp.1-19.

5. K.S. Sandhu, 'Some Preliminary Observations of the Origins and Characteristics of the Indian Migration to Malaya, 1786-1957', in *Papers on Malayan History,* ed. K.G. Tregonning (Singapore: *Journal of South East Asian History,* 1962), pp.40-72; S. Arasaratnam, *Indians in Malaysia and Singapore* (Bombay and Kuala Lumpur: Oxford University Press, 1970), pp.10-39, 49-96; R.N. Jackson, *Immigrant Labour and the Development of Malaya,* 1786-1920 (Kuala Lumpur: Government Press, 1961), pp.57-69, 96-108, 109-26, 132-40; J.N. Parmer, *Colonial Labour Policy and Administration: A History of Labour in the Rubber Plantation Industry in Malaya c.1910-1941* (New York: J.J. Augustin, 1960), pp.19-27, 38-78.

6. Parmer, *Colonial Labour Policy,* pp.108-13; Jackson, *Immigrant Labour,* pp.127-31.

7. Jackson, *Immigrant Labour,* pp.30-41, 42-56, 70-8, 79-90, 141-46, 147-57; Parmer, *Colonial Labour Policy,* pp.27-37, 79-85; W.L. Blythe, 'Historical Sketch of Chinese Labour in Malaya', *Journal of the Malayan Branch of the Royal Asiatic Society,* 20 (1947), pp.64-114; V. Purcell, *The Chinese in Malaya* (London: Oxford University Press, 1948), pp.97-117, 194-99; P.C. Campbell, *Chinese Coolie Emigration to Countries within the British Empire,* 2nd edn. (London: Frank Cass, 1971), pp.1-25; Lim Chong-Yah, *Economic Development of Modern Malaya* (Kuala Lumpur: Oxford University Press, 1967), pp.44-7, 115-16, 186-7.

8. Furnivall, *Netherlands India,* pp.408-13; Purcell, *Chinese in South East Asia,* pp.498-505, 534-46.

9. J.C. Ingram, *Economic Change in Thailand, 1850-1970* (Stanford: Stanford University Press, 1971), pp.70-2, 98-101; Purcell, *Chinese in Southeast Asia,* pp.105-8; K.P. Landon, *The Chinese in Thailand* (New York: Russell & Russell, 1941), p.10.

10. Purcell, *Chinese in Southeast Asia,* pp.213-15, 218-19; C. Robequain, *The Economic Development of French Indo-China* (London: Oxford University Press, 1944), pp.32-9, 53-5, 61.

11. Purcell, *Chinese in Southeast Asia,* pp.31, 213-14; Glass and Grebenik, 'World Population 1850-1950', in *Cambridge Economic History of Europe,* Vol.6, pp.64-5; Ping-Ti Ho, *Studies on the Population of China* (Cambridge, Mass.: Harvard University Press, 1959), pp.167-8, 192; John D. Durand, 'The Population

Statistics of China AD 2-1953', *Population Studies,* 13 (1959-60), pp.209-56.

12. Leo Kuper, 'African Nationalism in South Africa, 1910-1964', in *The Oxford History of South Africa,* eds. Monica Wilson and Leonard Thompson, Vol.2, *South Africa 1870-1966* (Oxford: Clarendon Press, 1971), p.430; Hilda Kuper, *Indian People in Natal* (Pietermaritzburg: Natal University Press, 1960), pp.1-17; Mabel Palmer, *The History of the Indians in Natal* (Cape Town: Oxford University Press, 1957), pp.9-29, 30-48; D.H. Houghton, 'Economic Development 1865-1965', in *The Oxford History of South Africa,* Vol.2, pp.15, 19; P.C. Campbell, *Chinese Coolie Emigration,* pp.161-216; Joseph Boute, *La Démographie de la Branche Indo-Pakistanaise d'Afrique* (Louvain-Paris: Editione Nauwelaerts, 1965), p.27.

13. R.R. Kuczynski, *Demographic Survey of the British Colonial Empire: Vol.2, East Africa* (London: Oxford University Press, 1949), pp.147, 251; C.C. Wrigley, 'Kenya: The Patterns of Economic Life, 1902-1945', in *History of East Africa, II,* eds. Harlow and Chilver (Oxford: Clarendon Press, 1965), pp.225-6; Cyril Ehrlich, 'The Uganda Economy, 1903-45', in *History of East Africa,* Vol.2, pp.398, 406-8; Boute, *Démographie de la Branche Indo-Pakistanaise d'Afrique,* p.30.

14. Foreign Office, *Peace Handbooks:* Vol.XVII, *French African Possessions,* No.102, *Senegal,* pp.6-7, No.103, *French Guinea,* p.6, No.104, *Ivory Coast,* p.5, No.105, *Dahomey,* p.7, No.108, *French Equatorial Africa,* p.17.

15. Foreign Office, *Peace Handbooks;* Vol.XVIII, *German African Possessions (Late),* No.110, *Togoland,* pp.11-12, No.111, *Cameroon,* p.11, No.112, *South West Africa,* p.8, No.113, *Tanganyika,* pp.9, 22.

16. Foreign Office, *Peace Handbooks:* Vol.XIX, *Portuguese Possessions,* No.118, *Portuguese Guinea,* p.7, No.120, *Angola,* p.10, No.121, *Mozambique,* pp.18-19.

17. Foreign Office, *Peace Handbooks:* Vol.XVI, *British Possessions, II, The Congo,* No.99, *The Belgian Congo,* p.17.

5 GROWTH AND FLUCTUATIONS

Previous chapters have examined the changes in communications which took place in the fifty years before the First World War, together with the expansion of trade and movements of capital and labour which accompanied this market widening. Now it is necessary to compare the economic growth which was taking place in the undeveloped world with that in the rest of the international economy, and also to consider the part which Asia and Africa played in the fluctuations which were such a prominent feature of international economic activity in these years.

Economic Growth

Even for the developed world of the West, the measurement of national income, and its derivative per capita income, poses immense problems for the late nineteenth century, as information is defective and the margin of error wide. For Asia and Africa the situation is even worse, and any estimates are at best highly speculative. L.J. Zimmerman braved the obvious difficulties and from what fragments of information he could collect constructed figures for the world's major areas. For the Far East he had to make his own guesstimates, based on trends found in other areas, and for China, both population and income had to be assessed on the basis of twentieth-century figures. As for Central Africa, he admitted defeat, and made no suggestions. His final estimates are given in Table 31 (p.123). While admitting that really very little reliance can be put upon these figures, it is interesting to note the intimation that despite considerable population increase in British India, per capita incomes in South East Asia, an area made up of British India and Siam, grew over the period at a rate of 0.25 per cent per annum. So progress was made despite two severe famines. In the Far East, the Philippines, Malaya and the Netherlands Indies, Zimmerman believes per capita incomes grew more quickly, at 1.12 per cent each year, again notwithstanding substantial population growth. As for China, a growth in per capita income of 0.13 per cent annually is put forward, although income per head was the lowest of all the areas in 1913.

The author then goes on to give estimates for the distribution of world income in 1860, as in Table 32 (p.123). The most interesting implication of these figures for 1860 is not that North America and

Table 31: World Per Capita Incomes, 1860-1913 ($ of 1952-54)

	1860	1913	Annual % change 1860-1913
North America	420	1,000	1.65
Oceania	440	580	0.52
North West Europe	230	460	1.31
Soviet Union	95	160	1.00
South East Europe	110	200	1.14
Latin America	100	160	0.89
Japan	40	90	1.54
Near East	–	–	–
Far East	50	90	1.12
Central Africa	–	–	–
South East Asia	48	65	0.52
China	44	47	0.13
Average	90	200	1.52

Source: L.J. Zimmerman, 'The Distribution of World Income 1860-1960', in *Essays on Unbalanced Growth,* ed. Egbert De Vries ('S-Gravenhage: Mouton & Co., 1962), p.35.

Table 32: Distribution of World Income in 1860

	Population (millions)	%	Aggregate income ($ millions)*	%
North America	34.6	3.1	14,400	14.8
Oceania	1.2	0.1	500	0.5
North West Europe	122.1	11.1	28,500	29.4
Soviet Union	74.0	6.8	7,000	7.0
South East Europe	86.9	7.9	9,500	9.7
Latin America	37.2	3.3	3,700	4.0
Japan	32.0	2.9	1,300	1.6
Near East	–	–	–	–
Far East	26.0	2.3	1,300	1.4
Central Africa	–	–	–	–
Far East	26.0	2.3	1,300	1.4
Central Africa	–	–	–	–
South East Asia	247.0	22.3	11,500	11.8
China	443.4	40.2	19,500	19.8
Total	1,104.4	100.0	95,900	100.0

* $ of 1952-4.

Source: Zimmerman, 'Distribution of World Income', p.36.

North West Europe had 14.2 per cent of the population and 44.2 per cent of world income, but that the Far East, South East Asia and China had 64.8 per cent of the population and 33 per cent of world income. When the situation in 1860 is compared with the situation in 1913, shown in Table 33 below, what emerges is that North America and North West Europe are held to have increased their share of world population to 17.8 per cent and their share of world income to 60.4 per cent. But the undeveloped world's share of world population had decreased to 56.7 per cent, and its share of world income to 16.7 per cent. Yet overall income in the Far East was four times as great, in South-East Asia nearly twice as great, and even in China it had risen by nearly a quarter. Per capita incomes had also increased, notwithstanding the vast population increase. Stagnation or regression did not occur, even in China.

In his Appendix, Zimmerman breaks down his figures into the individual countries which make up his major areas, with estimates given at twenty-year intervals. These are given in Table 34 (p.125), which deals with population, and Table 35 (p.126), which deals with National Incomes. What is immediately apparent is on how few countries

Table 33: Distribution of World Income in 1913

	Population (millions)	%	Aggregate income ($ millions)*	%
North America	99.8	6.3	100,300	32.9
Oceania	7.0	0.4	4,100	1.4
North West Europe	183.0	11.5	84,000	27.5
Soviet Union	139.0	8.7	22,500	7.4
South East Europe	130.4	8.2	26,000	8.5
Latin America	79.5	5.0	12,300	4.1
Japan	51.9	3.2	4,600	1.5
Near East	—	—	—	—
Far East	61.1	3.9	5,700	1.8
Central Africa	—	—	—	—
South East Asia	323.7	20.3	21,000	6.9
China	517.4	32.5	24,300	8.0
Total	1,593.8	100.0	304,800	100.0

* $ of 1952-4.

Source: Zimmerman, 'Distribution of World Income', p.37.

Table 34: Population of the Undeveloped World, 1860-1913

	1860		1880		1900		1913	
	millions	%	millions	%	millions	%	millions	%
Malaya	0.2	.01	0.2	.01	1.3	.09	2.7	0.16
Indonesia	21.0	1.90	28.0	2.24	40.0	2.79	49.0	3.07
India	233.0	21.09	257.0	20.63	282.0	19.70	303.0	19.01
Burma	8.0	0.72	9.0	0.72	10.0	0.69	12.4	0.77
Siam	6.0	0.54	6.8	0.54	7.6	0.53	8.3	0.52
China	443.4	40.14	470.0	37.72	498.2	34.81	517.4	32.46
Total	711.6	64.43	771.0	61.89	839.1	58.63	892.8	56.01
World total	1,104.4	100.00	1,245.7	100.00	1,431.0	100.00	1,593.8	100.00

Source: Zimmerman, 'Distribution of World Income', pp.48-9.

Table 35: National Incomes of Undeveloped World, 1860-1913

	1860		1880		1900		1913	
	millions $ *	%	millions $	%	millions $	%	millions $	%
Malaya	—	—	—	—	—	—	400	0.13
Indonesia	—	—	—	—	—	—	4,200	1.37
British India	11,100	11.57	14,300	10.14	15,800	6.94	19,700	6.46
Siam	—	—	—	—	—	—	—	—
China	19,500	20.33	20,700	14.69	23,000	10.10	24,300	7.97
Total	30,600	31.90	35,000	24.84	38,800	17.04	48,600	15.94
World total	95,900	100.00	140,900	100.00	227,600	100.00	304,800	100.00

* $ 1953.

Source: Zimmerman, 'Distribution of World Income', pp.50-1.

the figures are based. Yet as British India and China are covered, and they together supported 50-60 per cent of the world's population, a sufficient area of the undeveloped world may be said to have been covered. On the basis of these estimates, figures for per capita income were provided by Zimmerman in Table 36, figures being given for Indonesia, although there were no National Income figures for Indonesia. Once again the extremely tentative nature of these estimates is emphasised, but they do suggest per capita incomes were growing in all the countries, despite the population increase which made per capita income growth less than national income growth. If the gap in per capita income between these countries and the world average widened, per capita incomes still appear to have grown.[1]

Zimmerman's chief figures for the undeveloped world were for India and China, so it is worth considering the work of other scholars on these countries. Simon Kuznets in a recent study includes estimates of growth in India, as in Table 37. These figures do not exactly match Zimmerman's, and in any case they exclude Burma and Pakistan which were part of Zimmerman's calculations. But the implication is similar to some extent, in that both scholars agree that the early period of the 1860s and the decade of the 1880s were periods of high growth of population, per capita product and income, and total product and income. Kuznets, however, is more pessimistic than Zimmerman about per capita income towards the end of the period, reckoning a fall in per capita product of –3.1 per cent per annum from 1881-89 to 1901-09. To some extent this may be a consequence of excluding Burma, where rapid growth was taking place, and also of the fact that Kuznets

Table 36: Per Capita Incomes of Undeveloped World, 1860-1913

	1860 $*	1880 $	1900 $	1913 $
Malaya	—	—	—	140
Indonesia	50	60	65	85
British India	48	56	56	65
Siam	—	—	—	—
China	44	44	46	47
World per capita income	90	—	—	200

* $ 1953.

Source: Zimmerman, 'The Distribution of World Income', pp.52-3.

Table 37: Indian Rates of Growth per Decade, 1861-9 to 1901-9

	No. of years	Total product	Population	Product per capita	Derived GNP per capita in 1965 $ at 1st year
1861-69 to 1881-89	20	19.1	5.3	13.1	47
1881-89 to 1901-09	20	1.4	4.6	−3.1	60

Source: Simon Kuznets, *Economic Growth of Nations, Total Output and Production Structure* (Cambridge, Mass: Harvard University Press, 1971), p.31.

took 1909 as his final date, so that the famine and natural disasters of the late 1890s were not offset by the rapid growth of the last few years before 1913, which Zimmerman uses as his final year. This last point is borne out when Mukherjee's estimates are examined, these being the basis of Kuznets's calculations. They are given in Table 38 (p.129).

From Mukherjee's calculations, it would appear that per capita incomes in India, excluding the areas now in Pakistan and Burma, rose to a peak in the period centred on 1885 and then fell until the period centred on 1900. Then they once more began to rise and continued to do so through the period centred on 1910 to the period centred on 1915. In his summing up Mukherjee admits that it is difficult to tell to what extent his figures accurately represent the economic history of the area of the Indian Union in this period. But the progress which is suggested does fit with the improvement in railways and communications which is known to have taken place, the increased number of educational institutions, the increase in exports and imports, the growth of government revenue and the development of modern industry, particularly the cotton and coal industries. Where checks came in the growth of per capita incomes, known famines were largely responsible.[2]

K.G. Saini has roundly criticised Mukherjee's estimates, and states baldly that the available statistics make it impossible to construct such estimates for India for the period 1860-1913. In particular, he maintains that there is very little information on output or employment. He then examines manufacturing employment and output in the two major industries of British India, cotton and jute, and the two minor industries, paper and wool manufacture. His figures for employment and output in these industries are given in Table 39 (p.129).

Table 38: Average Per Capita National Income of Indian Union* at 1948-9 Prices for Overlapping Nine-year Periods, 1860-1914

Period	Centring	Per capita income in 1948-49 (Rs)
1857-1863	1860 (7 years)	169
1861-1869	1865	169
1866-1874	1870	172
1871-1879	1875	177
1876-1884	1880	197
1881-1889	1885	216
1886-1894	1890	204
1891-1899	1895	201
1896-1904	1900	199
1901-1909	1905	203
1906-1914	1910	220
1911-1919	1915	241

* Excludes Burma and Pakistan.

Source: M. Mukherjee, *National Income of India: Trends and Structure* (Calcutta: Statistical Publishing Society, 1969), p.61.

Table 39: Average Annual Per Cent Rates of Growth of Manufacturing Employment and Output in British India, 1880-1914

Period (year ended 31 March)	Manufacturing employment	Manufacturing output
1880-1881 to 1885-1886	9.3	13.0
1885-1886 to 1890-1891	8.2	16.7
1890-1891 to 1895-1896	5.9	5.8
1895-1896 to 1900-1901	4.1	–
1900-1901 to 1905-1906	7.6	6.0*
1905-1906 to 1910-1911	4.0	1.5
1910-1911 to 1913-1914	2.3	4.5

*Annual average per cent rate of growth here has been calculated at a ten-year interval because economic conditions were severely affected by plague and famine conditions which prevailed in India between 1898 and 1901. Production activity was particularly affected: a calculation of the rate of growth of manufacturing production between 1895-1896 and 1900-1901 yields a negative growth rate.

Source: K.G. Saini, 'The Growth of the Indian Economy: 1860-1960', *Review of Income and Wealth,* 15 (1969), p.260.

These figures seem to suggest that until about 1910 there was a relatively high rate of growth of manufacturing employment and manufacturing output. Then both slowed down, for reasons Saini finds difficult to explain. The famines in the late 1890s do not explain the slow rates of growth in the new century. Turning to agriculture, Saini quotes Blyn's production figures from 1891, as presented in Table 40. The implication here is that there was a high rate of growth of production of both food grains and crops in general from the early 1890s until the late 1890s and first years of the new century, when there was actually regression. Then the rate recovered sharply, only to fall away again after about 1910. Because Blyn's figures do not go back before 1890, Saini used an alternative method to try to examine agricultural trends prior to that time, using exports of agricultural products as a proxy for agricultural production. As the population increased in these years, and therefore ate more food, the resulting trends are likely to be underestimates rather than overestimates. Since wheat and rice were the main agricultural exports, Table 41 (p.131), shows the rate of growth of exports of these grains.

Saini believes that, on the basis of the figures for the growth of wheat and rice exports and those for agricultural production, a case can be made for arguing that productivity in the agricultural sector rose rapidly after 1860, reaching a ceiling in the late 1880s. This he thinks was probably owing to the fact that substantial investment was made in irrigation works after 1860, but that once the advance in productivity which these realised had taken place, no further investment in agricultural capital took place, and a new ceiling of productivity was

Table 40: Trends in Indian Agricultural Production, 1891-1914

Period (year ended 30 June)	Average annual per cent rate of growth of all-crop production	Average annual per cent rate of growth of food-grain production
1891-1892 to 1895-1896	5.3	5.0
1895-1896 to 1900-1901	0.9	0.8
1900-1901 to 1905-1906	−0.8	−1.2
1905-1906 to 1910-1911	5.1	5.8
1910-1911 to 1913-1914	−4.6	−5.5

Source: George Blyn, *Agricultural Trends in India, 1891-1947: Output, Availability and Productivity* (Philadelphia: University of Pennsylvania Press, 1966), p.349.

Table 41: Growth of Indian Wheat and Rice Exports, 1867-1891

Period (year ended 31 March)	Average annual per cent rate of growth of wheat exports	Average annual per cent rate of growth of rice exports
1867-1868 to 1875-1876	92.5	8.3
1875-1876 to 1880-1881	39.3	6.7
1880-1881 to 1885-1886	36.6	1.5
1885-1886 to 1890-1891	−6.4	4.8

Source: Saini, 'Growth of the Indian Economy', p.262.

reached. So although he disagrees with Mukherjee's methods, he also concludes there was stagnation in the 1890s.[3]

What all these studies seem to suggest and agree upon is that up to about the 1890s India prospered, with national and per capita income increasing. It was in the 1890s that things went wrong. However, what the studies seem to overlook, or perhaps simply underemphasise, is the extent of the recovery in the new century, which is revealed in Mukherjee's estimates, Blyn's figures for agricultural production and even the exports of wheat and rice to which Saini drew attention, as can be seen in Graph 11 (p.132).

One other feature of India's economic experience in this period is worth examining, and that is her terms of trade. Did adverse movements of her terms of trade tend to dampen the beneficial effects of her buoyant external trade at this time, hence lending support to the idea that the Indian economy stagnated from the 1890s onwards? Certainly Britain's terms of trade moved in her favour from the early 1880s, and it has often been assumed that a movement in the terms of trade in Britain's favour necessarily implied a movement against her trading partners who supplied her with primary goods. However, Bhatia has demonstrated that from 1864 to 1878 India's terms of trade improved, followed by a period of decline up to 1888. Then they recovered up to 1897, and sustained this recovery with fluctuations until the end of the period. This is shown clearly on Graph 12 (p.133), where movements in the British and Indian terms of trade are drawn. It is only in the short term that the terms of trade of the two countries moved in opposite directions; and the overall trend of both countries from the late 1880s was of improvement, the trend tending to level out in the new century. India's overall experience therefore tends to disprove the

Graph 11: Indian Exports of Rice and Wheat, 1868-1914

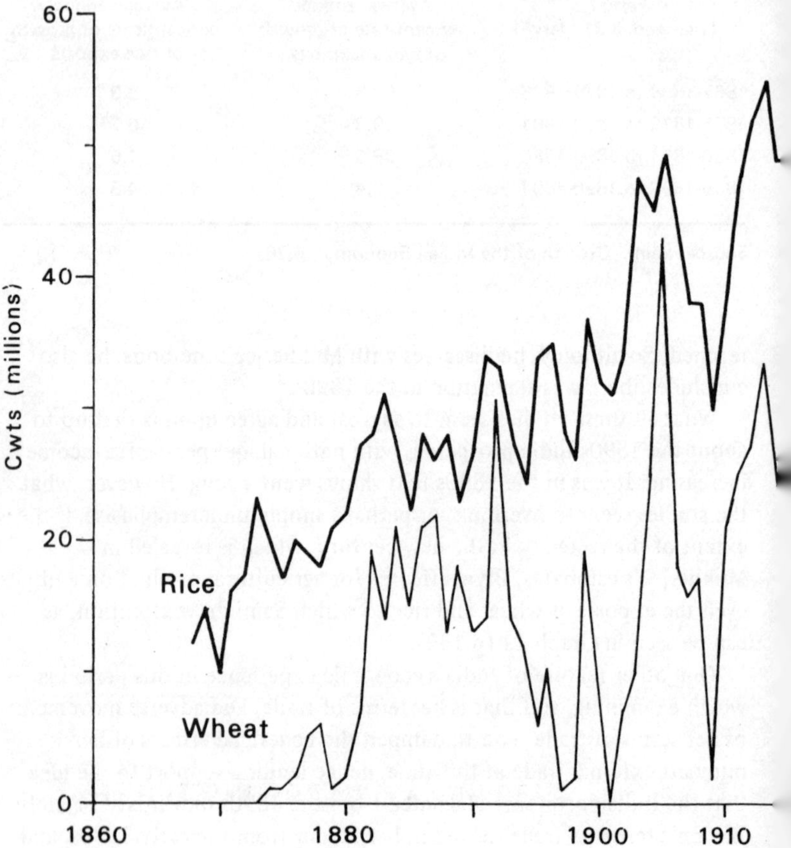

Source: *Statistical Abstracts for British India;* see Appendix 10.

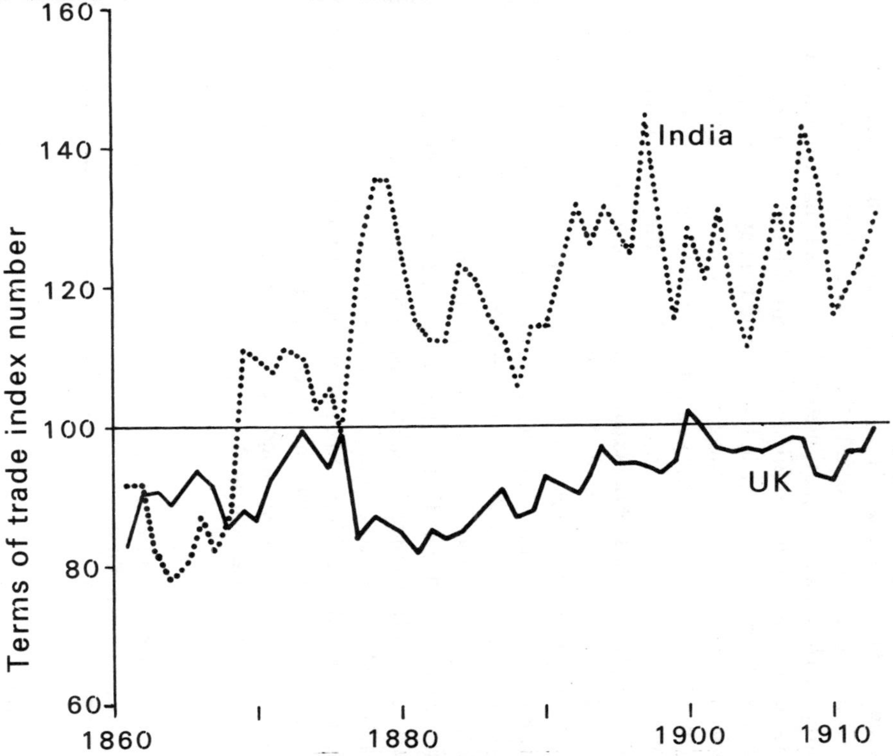

Sources: B.M. Bhatia, 'Terms of Trade and Economic Development: A Case Study of India 1861-1939', *Indian Economic Journal,* 14 (1969), pp.417-8; B.R. Mitchell and Phyllis Deane, *Abstract of British Historical Statistics* (Cambridge: University Press, 1971), pp.331-2; see Appendix 11.

common assumption that a movement in Britain's terms of trade implied an opposite movement in the terms of trade of her trading partners. The reason for this is presumably that as India exported more to Asia and Europe than to Britain, her terms of trade were more affected by price movements in these regions than by the prices paid in Britain for her goods. If anything, movements in her terms of trade helped to cushion India in her years of hardship, for they were more adverse in the prosperous years of the 1880s than they were in the difficult years of the 1890s. Certainly adverse terms of trade cannot be said to have been a cause of Indian stagnation.[4]

Turning to China, it has to be stated that the estimates of National Income in China are even more tentative than the highly speculative figures quoted for India. Apart from Zimmerman's guesstimates, the only other scholar who gives an estimate for this period is Feuerwerker. He suggests that Chinese GNP in the 1880s may have been in the region of 3,338,575 Haikwan taels, which converts to a sum between $4,716,681,590 and $3,819,007,980 in the dollars of the time. The value of this estimate is open to question, and it is probably far safer to accept his opening statement that precise quantitative information is not available and probably cannot be satisfactorily derived for prerepublican China. Feuerwerker's figures are given in Table 42 below.

Table 42: Estimated Gross National Product of China in the 1880s (Haikwan taels, 000)

Sector		Amount		Per cent
Agriculture		2,229,941		66.79
Non-agriculture		1,108,816		33.21
Mining	47,800		1.43	
Manufacturing	125,800		3.77	
Construction	30,000		0.90	
Transportation	30,000		0.90	
Trade	220,000		6.59	
Finance	74,645		2.24	
Residential housing	164,000		4.91	
Government services	164,000		4.91	
Professional, 'gentry' and other services	241,313		7.23	
Net income from abroad	11,258		0.34	
Total		3,338,757		100.00

Source: Albert Feuerwerker, *The Chinese Economy, c.1870-1911* (Ann Arbor, Michigan: Michigan University Press, 1969), p.2.

This work once again emphasises the extremely speculative nature of Zimmerman's estimates.[5]

The only other country in Asia and Africa for which there are national income estimates of any value appears to be Ghana, then the Gold Coast. Szereszewski constructed economic accounts for this country for 1891, 1901 and 1911, although he is at pains to point out that it is practically impossible to make up accounts which could claim to be orthodox estimates of Gross Domestic Product. However, his figures are given in Table 43 because they are the sole example for an African country. From them can be derived a figure of overall growth for the decade 1891-1901 of 20.29 per cent or 1.86 per cent per annum, and a growth of 45.15 per cent in the decade 1901-1911, at 3.77 per cent, principally the consequence of export growth and capital imports. For the entire period 1891-1911 the growth rate calculated on the basis of these figures is 2.82 per cent.[6]

Kuznets availed himself of Szereszewski's estimates, to produce the figures given in Table 44 (p.136). While these figures clearly infer a

Table 43: Gold Coast Estimated Expenditure on GDP, 1891, 1901, 1911 (1911 prices)

	1891	1901	1911
	£000	£000	£000
1. Export production	872	740	3,612
2. Private consumption of imported goods	1,595	2,741	4,310
3-4. Consumption of Government and public services	150	490	635
5. Gross capital formation	239	1,567	3,420
6. Traditional consumption	9,200	10,000	11,100
7. Imports of goods and non-factor services			
a. Imports of merchandise and non-factor services	−835	−1,870	−3,050
b. Net imports of specie	−73	−257	−560
Total (A) including 6	11,148	13,411	19,467
Total (B) excluding 6	1,948	3,411	8,367
Per capita (£)			
(A)	6.8	7.5	9.7
(B)	1.2	1.9	4.2

Source: R. Szereszewski, *Structural Changes in the Economy of Ghana 1891-1911* (London: Weidenfeld and Nicolson, 1965), p.149.

Table 44: Gold Coast Rates of Growth per Decade, 1891-1911

	No. of years	Total product	Population	Product per capita	Derived GNP per capita in 1965, $ at 1st year
1891-1911	20	32.1	10.1	20.0	107

Source: Simon Kuznets, *Economic Growth of Nations,* p.30.

more dynamic situation than in India, very little further conclusion can be drawn from them either in respect to Africa or elsewhere.

To conclude this section on economic growth in the undeveloped world, it must be said that the overwhelming impression is that the national income estimates for the undeveloped world are so speculative as to make calculations of growth, and of total income at particular times, little more than guesswork. Such attempts as have been made do maintain that there was some advance in total income of the various countries in general, and per capita incomes within them, despite the population growth which appears to have taken place. The undeveloped world seems to have been advancing, not retreating.

Fluctuations

Having considered the share of the world's income contributed by the undeveloped world, the next topic to be examined is the part the undeveloped world played in the fluctuations which the international economy experienced in these years. There were three basic kinds of cyclical fluctuation: the short 7-10 year cycle named after Juglar, who first noted it; the medium-term 18-20 year cycle now usually associated with Kuznets's name; and the long 40-50 year cycle, suggested by Kondratieff. Despite an enormous literature, Kuznets has to admit that the very profusion of terms used for some of these cycles – trend cycles, long swings, long cycles – is a reflection of the lack of assurance of their characteristics and causes, and he recognises that there is very little tested knowledge about them.[7] Elsewhere, in a recent survey of economic fluctuations, Aldcroft has noted that most studies of cyclic movements have dealt with a particular country, although they were a common feature of all the industrialising countries in the nineteenth century. While the pattern of fluctuations was not exactly the same in each, there was some similarity of phasing between these countries, as one might expect given their increasing interdependence. However, he maintains that the process by which fluctuations were transmitted from one country to another, along with the theory of international business cycles, has been very inadequately studied.[8] Thus there seems to have been a preoccupation with the experience of the industrial world by those studying cycles, as the work of Juglar, Kondratieff, Kuznets and Schumpeter will bear out. Even a recent teaching pamphlet by S.B. Saul on the great Victorian Depression of 1873-96, having dismissed the possibility of there actually being Kondratieff-type long swings, mentions little of the undeveloped world in the general discussion. He does, however, point out that the gradually worsening terms of trade of primary producers at this time would tend to impair their ability to import manufactured goods, and this would have affected the growth of at least Britain's exports to these areas. The snag with this point is that, as has already been shown, the terms of trade of India, Britain's largest market in the undeveloped world, did not deteriorate.[9]

Several questions emerge. Did the undeveloped world feel the fluctuations experienced by the developed world? And if they did, were the fluctuations transmitted from the developed world to the undeveloped world, or vice-versa? The first problem is to find some sort of indicator of economic fluctuations throughout the international economy, given the known difficulties about obtaining accurate statistical information on India, China and the rest of the undeveloped world. However, Britain, as the leading exporting nation for most of this period, exported to all the major regions of the world. It seems reasonable therefore to argue that British exports to a particular region rose and fell according to the level of economic activity in that region. When business activity was high, more British goods would be imported than when business activity was low. If this were so, then the rhythm of fluctuations of British exports to each region ought to reflect the rhythm of economic activity in each region, subject only to the modifying influence of tariff policy. Graph 13 (p.138), shows the pattern of British home-produced exports to the four crucial regions, Asia, Africa, the USA and industrial Europe, the latter consisting of Germany, Austria, Netherlands, Belgium, France and Switzerland. The influence of the short-term Juglar cycle is immediately obvious, working both in British exports to industrial Europe and to the USA. There were peaks in 1872, 1882-3, 1890, 1900 and 1907. Troughs came in 1878-9, 1885-6, 1894-5, 1901-2 and 1909. Clearly the pattern of British home-produced exports to these areas indicates that the rhythm of general business activity in industrial Europe and the United

Graph 13: British Home-produced Exports to Major Markets, 1865-1914

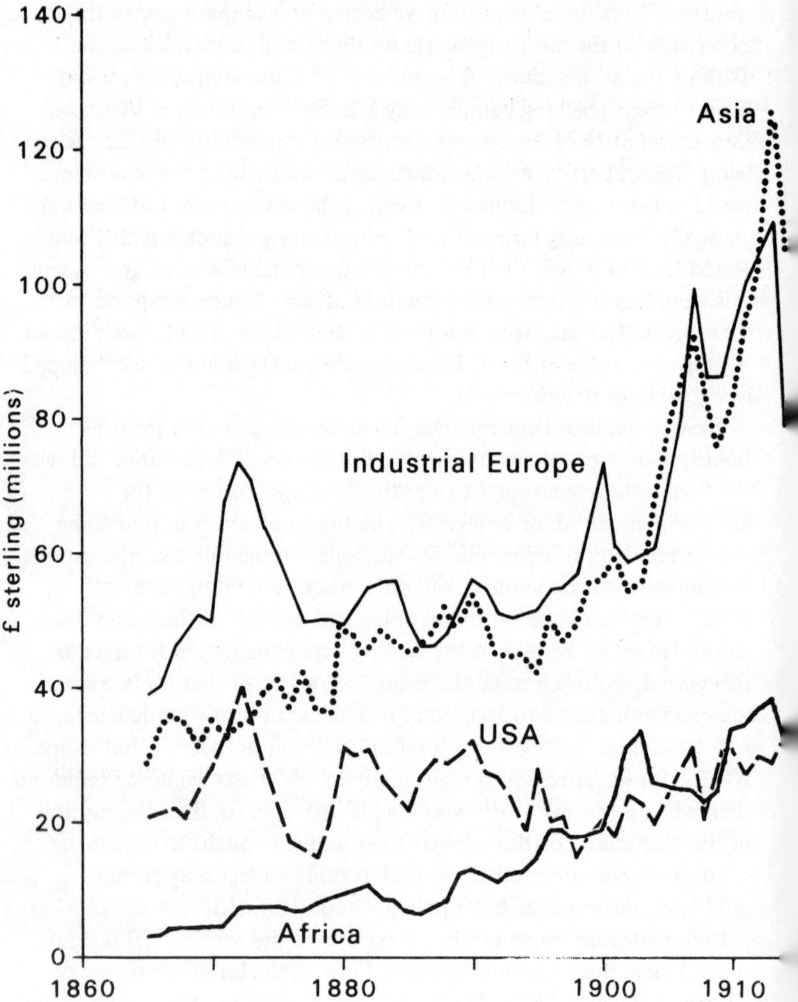

Source: B.R. Mitchell and Phyllis Deane, *Abstract of British Historical Statistics* (Cambridge: Cambridge University Press 1971), pp.315-27; see Appendix 12.

States coincided. This short cycle has often been explained in terms of the so-called multiplier-accelerator model, which provides a fairly satisfactory understanding of short-term business cycles in an advanced industrialised economy. But the surprising fact is that this cyclic pattern is also displayed in British exports to Asia. Exports to Asia experienced the same peak of exports as industrial Europe and the United States in 1882-3, and all three areas share the next peak of 1890. The peak in Asian exports in 1901 comes just a year after the peak to the other two areas in 1900. And all three areas enjoy the common peak of 1907. As for troughs, Asian exports share the troughs of exports to the industrial world of 1878-9, 1885-6, 1894-5, 1901-2 and 1908-9. Echoes of this pattern of exports can even be seen in British trade to Africa. One has therefore to ask why it should be that British exports to the vastly populated continent of Asia, with its essentially agricultural economy and its huge peasant communities, should be subject to the same ebbs and flows as exports to the increasingly industrialised world of Europe and the USA. The answer must surely lie outside any internal multiplier-accelerator model generating short-term cycles within the industrial world. The implication appears to be that some common factor was influencing economic activity generally in the world. That the cycles coincided more closely towards the end of the period might be explained by the introduction of the electric telegraph, which enabled shivers in confidence to be more rapidly transmitted across the network of international markets. It could of course be argued that the ebb and flow of business activity in the West induced a flow of imports from Asia, which in turn created the capacity to import from Britain. But this would suggest a lagged pattern of peaks and troughs, with British exports to Asia rising and falling a year or so after the pattern of exports to Europe and the USA. Such lags do not appear in the graphs.

A.G. Ford has investigated the rhythm of British exports, and in particular the relationship between fluctuations in British exports and British incomes and investment. He concluded that there was a strong positive correlation between fluctuations in exports, on the one hand, and incomes and employment on the other, while fluctuations in domestic investment showed no such relationship with incomes and employment. Moreover, the size of absolute fluctuations in export values was consistently 2 to 2½ times as great as that of home investment in this period, so that export values contributed more to multiplier influences on incomes than did domestic investment, and indeed were able to outweigh any opposite behaviour of investment.

He also investigated Britain's export trade to the major areas with which Britain traded and noted the point which has been made above, that there was considerable similarity in the incidence of cycles in the exports to these various areas, particularly at the times of major crisis, and with increasing agreement after 1890, the crisis of 1907 being especially marked. But of the various market areas, he maintains that the European market is the dominant force, exceeding the role of North and South America together. It was the European market which consumed the largest share of British exports, and hence it was fluctuations in exports to Europe which regulated fluctuations in incomes and employment in Britain. His emphasis on Europe effectively destroys the concept to which many have adhered, that there existed at this time an Atlantic economy in which essentially Britain and the United States were linked, cyclic tendencies in the United States being a dominant force on British economic activity and vice-versa. Certainly British exports to the United States were relatively unimportant, and indeed declined as the period progressed, to be overtaken by exports to Africa. However, a case can be made for suggesting that Ford himself overstated the importance of Europe. Europe in his definition included North and North East Europe, Western Europe, Central and South East Europe and Southern Europe. In other words, all the countries from Russia to Greece, including Morocco, Algeria, Tunis and Tripoli. This is an extremely wide definition, and it seems fair to argue that it is the relationship between Britain and industrial Europe which is important. It is for this reason that the graph showing British home-produced exports deals with exports to industrial Europe alone – Germany, Austria, Netherlands, Belgium, France and Switzerland. It is also true that Ford used total British exports for his calculations, re-exports being added to home-produced exports. But it is surely fluctuations in home-produced exports which are crucial, for it is they which determine employment and incomes in Britain rather than re-exports, which generate income and employment for only a small mercantile group. This being so, then a comparison of exports of British home-produced exports to industrial Europe and to Asia, shows that Asian exports were virtually as important as exports to industrial Europe, in terms of both absolute value and size of fluctuation. The great importance of Asia as a market for British home-produced exports is supported by Lars Sandberg's recent study of the Lancashire textile industry, in which he shows that by 1913 India accounted for 45 per cent of total yardage of cotton cloth exported from Britain, and that the increase in exports to India between any given year and 1913 is greater than the corresponding increase over the same period for any other market. China too was a very important market for Lancashire.[10] The conclusion is inescapable. Fluctuations in the Asian trade were almost as important as fluctuations in the trade to industrial Europe in determining fluctuations in British incomes and employment, and they were certainly much more important than fluctuations in the declining trade with the USA. Yet the question remains as to why fluctuations in exports to Asia and industrial Europe should coincide. In his study, Ford noted the possibility that fluctuations in British exports might be dependent on fluctuations in British capital exports, as they too showed a marked cyclical tendency, and fluctuations in overseas issues actually led fluctuations in British exports, and indeed world trade, by one or two years. The absolute size of the cyclical movements in overseas issues was only a little smaller than that of exports. The tempting hypothesis was that the capital exports put money into the hands of people abroad, who bought British goods with it, thereby pushing up British exports. However, he acknowledged the fact that as Britain exported relatively little capital to Europe at this time, fluctuations in capital exports there could hardly explain fluctuations in British exports to the area. A later study did not enable him to justify any closer explanation of the relationship between capital exports and exports.[11]

In order to investigate the possibility of some linkage between fluctuations in British capital exports to an area and British exports to the same area, the pattern of new British portfolio foreign investment in 1865-1914 has been drawn on Graph 14 (p.142). It is clear that there were substantial fluctuations, and that the rhythm of fluctuations to Europe, North America and Asia coincided to a marked degree. A careful comparison with Graph 13 (p.138), showing the cycle of British home-produced exports to these regions does not lend much support to the idea of fluctuations in capital exports to a region predating the rise of exports there. In the case of the United States, the investment peak to North America of 1872-4 if anything lagged behind the export peak of 1872, and the investment peak of 1882 coincided with the export peak in that year. In 1890 again both series peak simultaneously, and the minor export peak of 1900 is actually accompanied by a trough in investment. Only in 1907 is the export peak preceded by an earlier investment peak, that of 1905. As for Europe, where it must be admitted that the capital figures are for Europe as a whole but the export figures for industrial Europe alone, the pattern is similar. Both exports and investment peak together in 1872, although the 1881

Graph 14: New British Portfolio Foreign Investment to Major Areas, 1865-1914

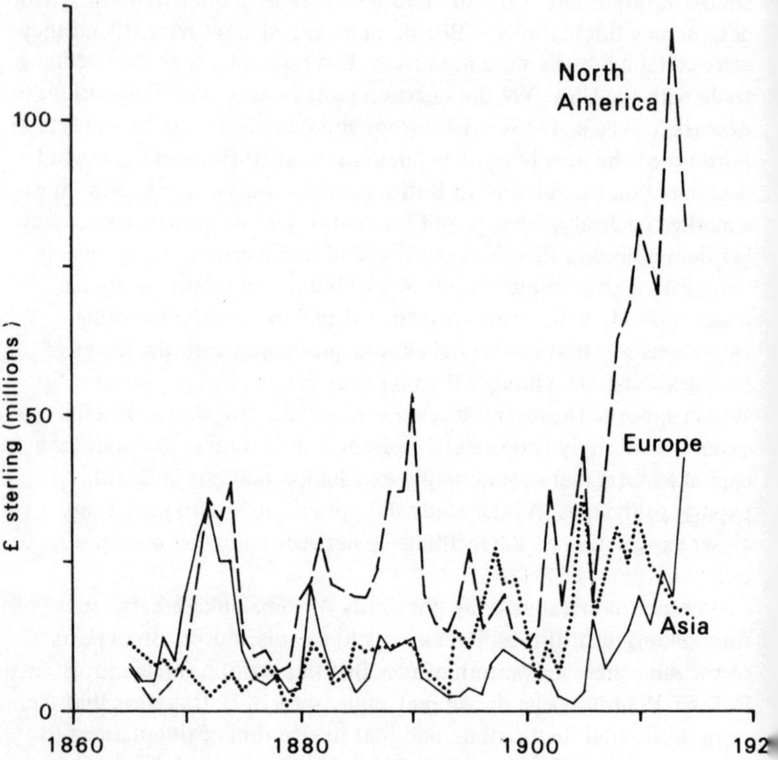

Source: Matthew Simon, 'The Pattern of New British Portfolio Foreign Investment', in *The Export of Capital from Britain 1870-1914*, ed. A.R. Hall (London: Methuen, 1968), p.39-40.

investment peak does precede the export peak of 1883. In 1890 both series again coincide, while the investment peak of 1898 does precede the export peak of 1900, as does the investment peak of 1906 precede the export peak of 1907. With Asia, the investment peak of 1877 coincides with the export peak that year, as did the investment peak of 1881 coincide with an export peak. The investment peak of 1889 preceded the export peak of 1890, and although the investment peak of 1897 preceded the small export peak of 1898, the main export peak here came in 1901. As was true with Europe, the investment peak of 1905 preceded the export peak of 1907. So there is some support for the idea that capital exports led exports, but not a great deal. The other problem, as Ford himself pointed out, is that the absolute magnitude of the capital flows to each region does not tally well with the exports to those regions. Capital flows to Europe and Asia were smaller, in relationship to the flow of exports to those regions, than was the case with the United States, which was the largest receiver of capital but a diminishing outlet for exports.

The fact that capital flows to North America, Europe and Asia fluctuated in unison raises another issue. As was noted earlier, the concept of an Atlantic economy was dealt a severe blow by the fact that British exports to Europe, and indeed to Asia as well, were far greater than exports to the United States. But Brinley Thomas has long maintained that the cycle of investment flows to the United States, as part of the Atlantic economy, was determined by the demographic cycles by which migrants from Britain created a demand for infrastructural investment in the United States at exactly the same time as their departure from Britain lowered the need for such investment in Britain. The surplus funds in Britain therefore flowed out to the United States to meet demand there. However, this attractive model does not explain why capital exports to Europe, from which migrants were also going to the United States, should increase at the same time as capital flows to the United States, nor why investment should also increase simultaneously to Asia, to where no British migrants were going. One can only assume, given both the low amount of British exports to the United States by comparison with Europe or Asia and the fact that the flows of capital to North America, Europe and Asia rose and fell together, that there was really no such thing as an Atlantic economy, but simply an international economy of which the Atlantic area formed merely a part.[12]

Ford was concerned with the short-term 7-10 year cycle, not the 18-20 year medium-term cycle, or the 40-50 year cycle. But the figures for home-produced exports do suggest the medium cycle, with peaks in the early 1870s, around 1890 and after 1910, and troughs in the late 1870s and in the mid-1890s, the pattern being clearly marked on the Asian series, just as on the series for industrial Europe and the United States. Similarly the trough of the Kondratieff long swing is apparent, running from the early 1870s to recovery at the end of the century through to the war. This is most clearly seen in the pattern of exports to industrial Europe, and to a lesser extent in the figures for the United States, whilst for Asia it is hidden to some extent by the sharply rising trend of exports to that region, the Kondratieff trough appearing there as a flattening of the trend. As for the African trade, the Kondratieff is only just discernible, but what is clear is that the strong upward trend in the African and Asian trades helped mitigate the downswing in British home-produced exports to both industrial Europe and the United States which the Kondratieff witnessed.

So far it has been noted that the short, medium and long cycles apparent in home-produced exports from Britain to industrial Europe, the United States and Asia tended to coincide, and these cycles may to a small degree have been influenced by the cycles in investment flows from Britain to these regions. Yet the evidence for this last assertion is weak, as the cycles of investment tended to coincide with the cycles in exports, whereas if investment cycles did directly cause export cycles a more obvious lag would be expected. So the peculiar fact remains that there were fluctuations in British home-produced exports to industrial regions, as well as to Asia, essentially a peasant agricultural region, containing more than half the world's population with low per capita income levels. As previously noted, most studies of fluctuations have concentrated on the advanced industrial nations, and assumed that cycles originated there. Yet the question must be asked, is it possible that fluctuations in British exports to Asia were caused by circumstances in Asia which affected Asia's capacity to consume British manufactured goods? Ashton maintained that in Britain in the eighteenth century, variations in the yield of the soil were the chief cause of economic instability, and it seems likely that in any mainly agricultural economy this will be so.[13] So the agriculturally based Asian economy must have been considerably influenced by variations in the supply of food, for climatic or other reasons. How one might test this assumption is another matter, given the vast range of roots, grains and pulses which formed the Asian diet. But an initial start to examining the matter would be to look at rice, the Asian food grain *par excellence.* Shortfalls in food production generally in Asia are likely to have affected the price of rice, even if rice production itself was not affected, because it was the obvious substitute food even in areas where it was not the mainstay. So it becomes necessary to find an appropriate series of rice prices during the period, to see if there is any relationship between fluctuations in the price of rice and fluctuations in the demand by Asians for British manufactured goods, chief of which were Lancashire cottons. Before checking the relationship, it is fair to assume that a rise in rice prices would cause a fall in British exports, as Asians would have to spend more of their incomes on rice, and therefore have less left over for buying British goods. Indeed the Giffen-good principle should operate, people buying more rice as the price of rice rose, because it was still the cheapest foodstuff, more expensive foods such as meat and vegetables being excluded. The rice series used, that based on the annual average price of rice imports to China, corrected for the fall of silver, is shown on Graph 15 (p.146). At first glance there seems to be no obvious relationship between the two series, and certainly no inverse relationship of the kind expected. British exports to Asia did not rise when the price of rice fell, or decrease when the price of rice rose. However, further observation suggests that there is a relationship between the two series, and this is that as rice prices increased in Asia, then British exports to Asia increased a year or so later. Thus the rice price peak of 1878 is followed by a peak in British exports to Asia in 1880, just as the rice price peak of 1886 is followed by a small peak of British exports in 1888, both rice prices and British exports sharing the peak of 1890. In 1899 rice prices peak and British exports follow in 1901; and in 1905 rice prices peak again, exports following two years later in 1907. The troughs in prices and exports also demonstrate a similar relationship. Both series experienced troughs in 1879, and in 1883 rice prices hit a low followed by exports in 1884. Similarly in 1894 rice prices collapsed, followed by exports in 1895. Yet again, in 1901 rice prices troughed, followed by exports in 1902. And the fall of rice prices in 1906 is succeeded by the export trough of 1908-9. Even the turndown at the end of the period is foreshadowed by the decline in rice prices after 1912. Besides this coincidence of fluctuations in rice prices and the value of British exports to Asia, albeit lagged by a year or so, it is fascinating to note that the rice price series follows the general pattern of the long Kondratieff cycle, with rice prices falling to 1894, then rising up to the end of the period, the turnround of 1894 preceding the upswing of British exports to Asia from 1895. While this is admittedly only a superficial examination of the relationship between

Graph 15: Rice Prices and British Exports to Asia

Sources: Hsaio Liang-lin, *China's Foreign Trade Statistics, 1864-1949* (Cambridge, Mass.: Harvard University Press, 1974), p.32; Mitchell and Deane, *British Historical Statistics*, pp.315-27, p.32; see Appendix 14.

these two series, the apparent relationship is interesting enough to justify further work, although this cannot be undertaken here. The fascinating question which remains is: why is the relationship between rises in rice prices and rises in British exports to Asia positive rather than negative? The answer to this may be that as incomes in Asia were in general extremely low, a fall in the price of rice would not mean that the ordinary peasant would purchase more British goods, but more meat, fish and vegetables. British goods were probably outside his reach whether the price of rice was high or low. But a rise in the price of rice would redistribute income away from the average peasant into the hands of farmers and merchants in the rice surplus areas, who supplied the Asian market. It is conceivable that these rice producers and dealers were at or beyond the threshold at which they had actually begun to buy British goods, and the redistribution of income in Asia to them when rice prices rose raised their incomes and hence their consumption of British cottons and other goods. In other words, income elasticity of demand for British goods operated only above a certain income level, which only those involved in supplying the rice market had reached. This can only be a suggestion until further research has been done, but it would explain the apparent paradox of British exports to Asia rising when rice prices rose. It is worth noting that a similar connection between wheat prices and demand for industrial goods during the early industrial revolution in Britain has been put forward by W.A. Cole.[14]

Some other points emerge from this discussion. If British exports to Asia were determined by fluctuations in the price of rice, then it can well be argued that, to a degree, the level of British incomes and employment was dependent upon the price of rice. As Britain was a major market for both the United States and industrial Europe, then it is conceivable that fluctuations were transmitted from Asia via Britain to the rest of the international system. It is also possible that if climatic conditions in the East were important in generating industrial demand in Britain, then these same climatic conditions may have also affected industrial demand elsewhere in the world via their effect on food prices and agricultural incomes. Again, this can only be a speculation until further research has been done. In conclusion, it must be said that the search for the origin of cycles in the industrial world alone is myopic. The undeveloped world may have exercised a crucial role in the generation of cycles, as has been suggested here. Certainly the possibility of a relationship between fluctuations in Asia and fluctuations in the international economy in general cannot be ignored.

Notes

1. L.J. Zimmerman, 'The Distribution of World Income, 1860-1960', in *Essays on Unbalanced Growth,* ed. Egbert de Vries ('S-Gravenhage: Mouton & Co., 1962), pp.28-55.
2. M. Mukherjee, *National Income of India: Trends and Structure* (Calcutta: Statistical Publishing Society, 1969), pp.37-122.
3. K.G. Saini, 'The Growth of the Indian Economy: 1860-1960', *Review of Income and Wealth,* 15 (1969), pp.247-63.
4. B.M. Bhatia, 'Terms of Trade and Economic Development: A Case Study of India, 1861-1939', *Indian Economic Journal,* 14 (1969), pp.414-33.
5. Albert Feuerwerker, *The Chinese Economy c.1870-1911* (Ann Arbor: Michigan: Michigan University Press, 1969), pp.1-2, 68.
6. R. Szereszewski, *Structural Changes in the Economy of Ghana, 1891-1911* (London: Weidenfeld and Nicolson, 1965), pp.128-9.
7. S. Kuznets, 'Long Swings in Population Growth and Related Economic Variables', in S. Kuznets, *Economic Growth and Structure: Selected Essays* (London: Heineman, 1965), p.353.
8. D.H. Aldcroft, 'Introduction', in *British Economic Fluctuations, 1790-1939,* ed. D.H. Aldcroft and Peter Fearon (London: Macmillan, 1972), p.14.
9. Clement Juglar, *Des crises commerciales et de leur retour périodique en France, en Angleterre et aux Etats-Unis,* 2nd ed (Paris: Guillaumin, 1889); N.D. Kondratieff, 'The Long Waves in Economic Life', *The Review of Economic Statistics,* 17 (1935), pp.105-15; J.A. Schumpeter, *Business Cycles, A Theoretical, Historical and Statistical Analysis of the Capitalist Process,* 2 vols (New York: McGraw-Hill, 1939); S.B. Saul, *The Myth of the Great Depression, 1873-1896* (London: Macmillan, 1969), p.30.
10. Lars G. Sandberg, *Lancashire in Decline. A Study in Entrepreneurship, Technology, and International Trade* (Columbus, Ohio: Ohio State University Press, 1974), pp.142, 165-70.
11. A.G. Ford, 'Notes on the Role of Exports in British Economic Fluctuations, 1870-1914', *Economic History Review,* 2nd series, 16 (1963), pp.332-7; A.G. Ford, 'Overseas Lending and Internal Fluctuations, 1870-1914', in *The Export of Capital from Britain, 1870-1914,* ed. A.R. Hall (London: Methuen, 1968), pp.84-102.
12. Brinley Thomas, *Migration and Urban Development. A Re-appraisal of British and American Long Cycles* (London: Methuen, 1972), pp.93-100.
13. T.S. Ashton, *An Economic History of England: The Eighteenth Century* (London: Methuen, 1955), p.62; Aldcroft, 'Introduction', in *British Economic Fluctuations,* eds. Aldcroft and Fearon, pp.38-43.
14. Phyllis Deane and W.A. Cole, *British Economic Growth, 1688-1959,* 2nd edn. (Cambridge: Cambridge University Press, 1967), pp.89-90.

6 SOCIAL RESPONSES

Asia and Africa came to form a vital integral part of the international economy which came into being during the second half of the nineteenth century. Yet society in Africa and Asia has often been characterised as 'traditional', its structure and attitudes locked in resistance to economic change. So how did society in the undeveloped world relate to the possibilities which were opening up? Did people there enthusiastically develop and seek out new opportunities, or were they reluctantly dragged into a harsh new world by materialistic Western interlopers?

India perhaps best fits the supposed archetypal traditional society, its social structure inflexibly constructed of tier upon tier of mutually exclusive occupational castes. Ties of kinship, caste and village are said to have bound people to the land of their birthplace, restricting them from finding new kinds of work in their own district and from going to other places to find work. Theoretically, at the top of the social pyramid were the brahmins, a caste of priests whose ritual purity was unsullied by manual work. Then came the warrior caste, followed by the traders, and beneath them the farmers. At the very bottom were the untouchable outcastes, who did the most menial and dirty work. But in practice, the situation was much more complicated, with about 200 occupational caste groups in each of India's main language regions, each of these caste groups being divided into equally exclusive occupational subcastes. It follows that the possibility of changing one's job was small. In a sense, this was the virtue of the system, for while it was difficult to leave the occupation of one's caste to take up a different livelihood, it did at least provide the guaranteed occupation one was born into. Thus the caste system was a very intricate and sophisticated work-sharing scheme. Members of different castes did not intermarry or even eat together, and kept apart in social life. Their dress, names and houses were distinctive, as were their diets, the highest groups being teetotal and vegetarian, the lowest eating pork and drinking local liquor. These differences not only made local social mobility difficult, they also made it hard for a man to move away from his home region. Because of the food restrictions, a man away from his own local caste could not eat or drink with strangers. He could not find a wife, and if he died there would be no one to perform his funeral rites, so the disposal of his body might be left to the local scavengers. Matters were made worse by the fact there were over 200 different languages in India and that in some parts local custom forbade the crossing of certain rivers.

Yet while the system seemed extremely inflexible, it was in fact less rigid than it appeared. While in the short run castes were fixed in their juxtaposition with each other, in the long run castes which became wealthy were able to improve their status by adopting the life style of a higher caste. So the long-term position of a caste in the system reflected the economic success of that particular caste. Clearly the structure of society was not inimical to economic progress. Not only was upward social movement by an entire social caste possible, but in practice people could move to a new region and take up a new occupation. The very substantial migration from Madras Province to Ceylon and Malaya has already been mentioned, these migrants initially being forced to look for a new means of livelihood by the collapse of their handloom weaving industry as a result of the competition from Lancashire. Later famine and epidemic added to their problems. In Malaya and Ceylon they became plantation workers. Indian migrants also went to Africa, some of them Tamils, especially to Natal, but there were also people from the United Provinces, Central Provinces and Western Bengal. Besides these there were Gujerati-speaking Muslims and Hindus from near Bombay, and also Parsees, who went to Africa as traders and merchants. Apart from migration abroad, there was considerable internal migration. Paralleling the movement of plantation workers to Ceylon and Malaya, large numbers travelled to the north-eastern estate regions of Assam and Eastern Bengal, the major tea-growing area, having been recruited in much the same way as the labourers going abroad. But quite apart from these plantations workers seeking new economic opportunities by selling their labour, Assam also saw from the turn of the century a mass movement of local farmers from one particular district of Bengal, seeking new land to break and cultivate along the Brahamputra valley. These men flocked to adopt this virgin territory of their own accord without any government help or the sponsorship of foreign proprietors. Nor were they the only Indian farmers who migrated to new lands, for in the Punjab the Government from the 1880s onwards built vast new irrigation projects, converting an arrid waste into fertile export-producing wheatlands. Under this irrigation scheme suitable settlers were encouraged to settle and work the land, promising men being picked to establish new villages there. The readiness of the peasantry to seize these new opportunities made the scheme one of the major successes of the British administration. Elsewhere in India modern factories were being set up, needing hands. In Bombay, one of the major industrial centres, most of the workers came from places over a hundred miles away. Moreover, although the workers came from different castes, it did not prevent them from working together on the factory floor, although untouchables were excluded from the weaving sheds. This may have been more a result of the desire of certain high caste groups to keep the best-paid jobs for themselves than a wish to avoid ritual defilement. In the coal mines of Bengal and Binar and Orissa, landless labourers from the lowest rung of the caste system and tribesmen outside the caste system altogether provided the labour, demonstrating the similar urge to work for wages by men both inside and outside the caste system. The factories of Bengal and the jute mills of Calcutta were equally successful in attracting labour.

Nor were those who were able to take new farmlands or sell their labour the only people who responded to the new opportunities. The Parsees, a people of Persian origin long settled in Gujerat above Bombay and who remained outside the caste system, played a crucial entrepreneurial role in the establishment of modern factory industry in India, particularly the cotton industry. Other similar but smaller groups, likewise long settled in India but outside the caste system, were active in the same way. Even Hindus and Muslims set up modern factories, but they were on the whole exceptions. So the point is established, that all the people of India were keen to take advantage of the new economic situation. If they were inside the caste system, then the caste system had to be bent to accommodate these aspirations, as in the Bombay cotton mills; and if they were outside the caste system there was no problem anyway, as with the Parsees. India's economic advance in these years bears witness to the desire of her people to seize new economic opportunities.[1]

British India also included Burma, which during this period became one of the world's major rice-exporting regions, a development which if anything overshadows the creation of the Punjab as a wheat-exporting territory. This substantial achievement was almost entirely the work of the Burmese, once again demonstrating the adaptability of the Asian peasant to new economic circumstances. Between 1872-3 and the end of the century rice exports nearly quadrupled to 2½ million tons. At the beginning of the 1870s lower Burma was mainly swamp and jungle, but as the market for rice increased small growers rapidly brought it into cultivation, men migrating from upper Burma to stake their claim.

They borrowed the necessary capital from Indian Chettiar moneylenders, who themselves obtained the money from European banks. As there was a tendency to overborrowing by the farmers, there was a high rate of bankruptcy, so that in time land ownership passed into the hands of the moneylenders, the farmers becoming an ever changing tenantry. At the same time, many steam rice mills were built to process the crop, which needed Indian coolie labour to work them, and hence a stream of new immigrants flowed in from Madras. The conditions under which the newcomers had to live were so foul that their arrival in the towns drove the indigenous Burmese labourers out to become hired hands in the rice fields. Immigrant Indian boatmen and dockers displaced other Burmese labourers who also went to become fieldhands. After 1900 the whole process was repeated in upper Burma. Thus an entirely revolutionary system of commercial rice farming came into being, financed by Indian moneylenders and operated by Burmese tenant farmers and labourers, the whole crop being transported and processed by immigrant labourers. It was a considerable success for Asian economic enterprise.[2]

In Ceylon, there was substantial immigration of plantation workers from Southern India, as the plantation economy there expanded. Indeed, it was to a large extent the need of these workers for rice which provided the incentive for the expansion of rice cultivation in the Burma delta. Yet the failure of the Sinhalese peasants to seek wage employment on the new plantations has been taken to imply that their immutable cultural traditions made them uninterested in the new chances for material gain. This is probably too simple an interpretation of the failure of the Sinhalese to become plantation wage earners. The fundamental difference lay in the economic situation of the Indian immigrants and the Sinhalese. No doubt both would have preferred to remain in their home villages were that economically possible. But the migrants from Southern India could no longer eke out a subsistence in their homelands, whereas the Sinhalese could still obtain a satisfactory living where they were. They could grow enough food to feed themselves and they could obtain desirable imported goods by selling small quantities of cash crops which were peripheral to their main food crops. In the early days coffee provided this handy cash income, for although the plantations grew the most and the best coffee, the peasantry still provided useful amounts. When coffee disease hit the bushes in the late 1870s, the peasants copied the estates and turned to cocoa or better, tea. From the turn of the century rubber was also grown by smallholders, and became more important to them than tea.

But the leading peasant crop, and perhaps the key to their contentment with their customary way of life, was copra, and coconut products in general. Long before plantations had ever intruded, the coconut had been a mainstay of the local economy, providing everything from food to building materials. Now it enabled the peasant to participate in the international economy without greatly changing his habits. Even though copra became an important export crop, production remained almost entirely in peasant hands. Exports of coconut produce increased from 2 million rupees in 1870 to 45½ million rupees in 1913 when plantation tea earned only 88 million rupees. So the explanation for the reluctance of the Sinhalese villagers to become plantation workers was not so much that they were unmoved by economic incentives as that the differential between what they could get living off their own lands and as working as labourers was too small to make it worth changing their entire way of life. Indeed, they may have been better off as they were, eating their home-grown food, and buying the occasional imported luxury with the profit obtained from selling the coconuts which grew naturally on their land.[3]

The position of the Malay peasant was in many respects similar to that of the Sinhalese. The story of the development of the tin mines in Malaya under Chinese enterprise and labour, and the establishment of rubber plantations using both Chinese and Indian workers, has already been related. But as in Ceylon, for the most part the Malays did not work on the plantations, but were content to remain in their villages, growing rice and fruit and supplementing their diet by what fish they could catch. However, towards the end of the period, many did add a few rubber trees to their holdings, to obtain a little ready money for the occasional imported luxury. But as in Ceylon, it was the coconut which was the key to the situation, for nearly all the copra produced in Malaya came from peasant plots, exports of coconut products rising from 9 million Straits dollars in 1906 to 17 million in 1912. So there was no reason for the Malayan peasantry to give up their comfortable way of life in their villages, and cease to be the masters of their own fields and gardens, to become wage drudges under the sometimes horrific conditions which obtained in the tin mines and on plantations. They had all they needed and could buy fancy foreign goods with the increasing returns they obtained for their copra. Far from being irrational, they were being extremely rational.[4]

The Dutch East Indies also became a plantation economy to a large extent in these years, with sugar being probably the most important crop, although coffee was very successful until the estates were decimated by disease in the late 1870s. Tea took its place, and in the new century rubber was also introduced. Tobacco too was an important crop. But the big difference between the plantation economy of the Dutch East Indies and that in Ceylon and Malaya was the fact that it did not depend on immigrant labour. Instead, the local people provided the necessary workforce. This was partly owing to the historic relationship between the Dutch authorities and the people. When sugar cultivation was introduced early in the century, villages were obliged to set aside land for sugar cultivation, to discharge land tax. Although workers were supposed to be freely recruited to harvest the crop, in practice headmen were often pressed to supply forced labour at low rates. So by the early 1870s production for export was intimately linked to the village communities. The owners of the sugar factories rented land from the villages for a period of a year and a half to put under sugar, after which it reverted to the village for their own crops. So there was a form of rotation between plantation sugar and village crops, which countered the exhaustive nature of sugar cane. By this time the practice of working for a wage when required was well established. Coffee production also began with an element of compulsion, chiefs being required to supply fixed quantities, but by the 1870s it was widely grown both on estates using local workers and by the peasants themselves. Indeed, after the coffee disease, estate production declined much more than peasant production. In tobacco growing the relationship between the proprietor and the village was intimate, particularly in East Java. There the proprietor leased land from the village, paid the land tax and supplied seedlings to the villagers. They contracted to supply him with leaf, which he bought. In east Sumatra the situation was rather different, as the local labour supply was inadequate and indentured Chinese labourers had to be brought in. Tea was very much an estate crop, using local workers, and so was rubber, although this was not produced in much quantity until after the First World War. So it is clear that in the Dutch East Indies, participation by the local people in the production of the major export crops was considerable, whether by renting land for the crops to be grown upon or by supplying labour for planting, harvesting and processing. At the same time, they produced export crops on their own account, particularly coffee, and later tea and rubber. They also grew tobacco, although most of this was for their own use. But the most important peasant crop, as in Ceylon and Malaya, was the coconut. Exports of copra became considerable in the last decade of the nineteenth century and trebled between 1900 and 1913, almost all from peasant growers. So in the Dutch East Indies the peasants took all the new opportunities open to them, by renting land to expatriate growers, by working for wages and by raising and selling copra and other coconut products, while at the same time maintaining their accustomed life style and the integrity of their villages. The worst problem they had to face was the increase in their own numbers.[5]

In Siam the response of the peasant to the new economic environment was astonishing. Like Burma, the economy was rapidly transformed from near self-sufficiency to a major commercial rice-growing area supplying the Asian market. Rice cultivation became the chief occupation of nearly nine-tenths of the people, and rice made up almost two-thirds of total exports. It was the growth of foreign demand which brought about this development, and exports rose from about 5 per cent of the total crop in 1850 to about 50 per cent in 1907. There was a vast increase in the area planted in rice, land which had previously been under cotton being turned to rice, or left idle in favour of land more suitable for rice. This represented a very real adaptation to the forces of the international market, as imported Lancashire cottons were destroying their own handicraft cotton industry. Indeed, much of the incentive to grow rice was to get the cash to buy Lancashire stuffs, rather than their own materials. The initiative for this huge expansion of rice growing came from the peasants themselves, although the Government did encourage them. During the last half of the nineteenth century the land of the Central Plain came under rice cultivation, the existing network of canals and streams providing easy transport for the crop to Bangkok. From the turn of the century the outer provinces too came under rice, as railway building improved communications. Uncultivated land was free to anyone who would clear and cultivate it, and this was usually the farmer himself, although agricultural wage labour grew in importance over the years. Although there were many Siamese moneylenders who provided the credit which financed this expansion, for the most part the Siamese concentrated their entrepreneurial energies on the actual growing of the rice, the remaining moneylenders, and virtually all the middlemen and millers, being Chinese. Few Chinese actually tilled the soil. Indeed, it might be suggested that the Chinese in Siam played the part the Indians played in the development of the rice economy in Burma. But it was the Siamese peasants who made this whole expansion feasible, acting on their own account in response to the opportunity of earning cash profits which they could spend on Manchester goods, by cultivating unused land.[6]

As in Siam, exports of rice from French Indo-China also increased rapidly, until they made up about two-thirds of total exports. The central area of Cochin China was marshy and covered in forest, but from 1870 canals were cut and the land was drained. As the work proceeded peasants from overcrowded Annam to the north east moved in, sailing up the new canals in their sampans, bringing their belongings, plus their pigs and chickens in crates. There they settled and began to grow rice, making the whole expansion of rice production possible. As in Siam, the Chinese were active as moneylenders, financing the whole process and having an almost complete monopoly as middlemen. Not that rice was the only peasant export crop, for both maize and copra were produced. But rice growing was not the sole incentive which attracted Annamites south, for in South Annam European-owned coffee plantations were established, the soil and climate being suitable, and later tea plantations were set up, with rubber appearing in the new century. To these plantations the Annamites came to find work, as they did to the coal, zinc and tin mines of Tonkin. Once more the Asian peasant was revealing his basic flexibility when offered the chance of material advance.[7]

As has been shown in Chapter 3, China's foreign trade position was extremely weak at this time, as her tea trade declined and her silk trade stagnated. None of the new plantation crops made much headway there, and far from being a rice exporter, she became increasingly dependent on rice imports. Yet this does not mean that her people refused to respond to market opportunities, for the migration from Kwantung and Fukien provinces marks a vital shift in the supply of labour to the international economy without which the development of Malaya and other parts of Asia would not have been possible. For there they were active as plantation and mine owners, moneylenders, merchants, millers and labourers, besides a host of other activities. The problem is to explain why this powerful enterprising energy was channelled out of China, rather than used within it to establish new lines of business there. If their migration is put down to population pressure, exactly how did this force the Southern Chinese abroad? A clue may be gathered from the experience of the other major group which migrated in the same period, the Tamils of south-west India. They were driven abroad by the collapse of their domestic handicraft cotton industry. Moreover, one of the reasons that the Siamese took to rice cultivation was the failure of their own cotton industry to compete with Lancashire. It may have been a similar force which drove the peasants of Kwantung and Fukien from their homelands. China, like other countries in Southern Asia, had a network of handicraft industries, such as potters, brassworkers, blacksmiths, basketmakers, brickmakers, jewellers, etc. Probably the most important of these was the handweaving and spinning of cotton. Although the major centre was in the Yangtze delta, the finished product being distributed the length and breadth of China, in other places spinning and weaving cotton was carried on in addition to growing the food on which the family was dependent. Yarn was sold to itinerant merchants, or bought from them to be woven. This extra income from spinning and weaving may have made the crucial difference between being above or below the subsistence level for many of the poorer farmers, whose plots were tiny after generations of subdivision. Thus when imported yarn flooded into Southern China in the 1870s and 1880s, those peasants who depended on growing and spinning yarn for the additional income which kept them above the subsistence level were ruined. It was Kwantung Province in particular which absorbed imported yarn in this period and it was that province from which the main stream of emigrants flowed. Thus the chances are that it was the force of the international cotton market which drove the Southern Chinese abroad, as it had already done the Indians of Madras Province. Whereas the Siamese, given similar circumstances, could turn to rice cultivation as an alternative means of gaining a living, the peasant of Kwantung and Fukien did not have spare land available, and so had no choice but to emigrate. By the 1880s cheap yarn from Bombay continued the process, and from the 1890s Japanese yarn took over.

If China did not take up the export of any of the new plantation crops, it is not true that there were no indications of change in the Chinese economy. Towards the end of the period oil seeds and bean products began to be exported from the north, and in the south modern manufacturing enterprises began to be set up, particularly around Shanghai and in Kwantung. Coal mining, ore mining and smelting, cotton manufacturing, silk reeling, flour milling and many other industries featured, all under Chinese ownership. There were also various foreign-owned enterprises. So the nascent Chinese entrepreneurial zeal was making itself felt on its home territory, even if the only alternative to many was emigration.[8]

Turning from Asia to Africa, it might be supposed that this less advanced continent might provide evidence to support the idea that the traditional structure and attitudes of society prevented the people from seizing the economic opportunities which were opening up. Nothing could be further from the truth. South Africa in particular, and Southern Africa in general, was the continent's main contributor to the international economy, the gold, diamonds and other minerals of the region being very much the product of European enterprise. It would be idle to suppose that Africans had much entrepreneurial role in this vast disgorgement of wealth. Yet the Africans had a part to play, in supplying the labour necessary to work the mines. The considerable migration of African workers to the mining centres of South Africa and Southern Rhodesia from within their borders, and from Mozambique, Nyasaland and neighbouring territories, demonstrates clearly the desire of Africans to earn cash incomes in this way. However, the demand for labour in the mines consistently ran ahead of the supply, which is why Chinese labourers were brought into the Rand mines in 1905-12, a factoı to which reference has already been made. This labour problem, which also affected the mines of Southern Rhodesia in the new century, has often been taken as proof of the unwillingness of Africans to respond to the demands of the labour market. Yet the situation is more complicated than this, for just as the Sinhalese and Malayan peasants were unwilling to give up their comfortable customary life to work on plantations or in mines in unpleasant conditions, so were the Africans. If a community has enough land to feed itself adequately, and enough left over for growing a surplus for cash to buy luxuries, an employer seeking labour has to provide a considerable incentive to persuade individuals to give up their rights to land in that community, to become dependent on wages which might disappear literally at a moment's notice. Africans could not only support themselves by their farming, but they had surplus cattle, grain, beer and vegetables to sell at a tidy profit. Thus the reason why the flow of labour to the mines was not as great as the mine owners would have liked was that they were not paying enough to encourage the African to give up the increasingly profitable farming he was doing. Unfortunately, merely raising wages might not have altered the situation much, as if food production did not rise it might simply have put up food prices still further, giving Africans even more reason to remain where they were. The alternative was to curb the returns Africans got from their farming, thereby increasing the differential gain to be obtained from wage earning without increasing wage rates. This appears to have been exactly what happened. Tax demands were made upon the Africans which took away the cash they earned from selling their surplus, and their access to land was restricted so that some were dispossessed and others left with the situation that population increase would slowly impoverish them with each generation. The inflow of cheap foreign grain as railways penetrated the interior was a final blow. The natural response by the Africans to this situation was to take up wage employment in the mines. Yet because there was still a return to be had from their rights to land in their home communities, they did not migrate permanently to the mineheads, but retained their rights at home and went to work for periods at the mines, returning home after doing their stint. This was a very rational solution, giving them the best of both worlds. No inhibiting social pressures prevented this.[9] It is worth noting that, in acting in this way, African workers were behaving in a similar manner to both Indian and Chinese indentured labourers who worked abroad for a period and then returned home. They too wished to retain their rights in their home communities and also earn wages.

In East Africa, Africans also responded to the new opportunities available to them, and were in fact more successful in producing new crops for export than were the European settlers. Here there was no mining, so the choice for the African was between his customary farming together with a new cash crop or being paid to work on the plantations which were being set up. Most settled for the former. The rapid development of African-grown cotton is the best example in East Africa of the local people's desire to make a profit. In the early years of the new century cotton was in short supply internationally and prices soared. The Government of Uganda brought in some cotton seed from Egypt and distributed it among the Chiefs in 1904, and by 1907-8 production had reached nearly 4,000 bales. As there were complaints made by buyers, official control was introduced to ensure a high quality, a policy which proved astoundingly successful. The growth of cotton exports enabled the total value of Ugandan exports to increase eight times between 1903 and 1910. While there seems little doubt that the Ganda chiefs had stood over their people to see that the cotton had grown, it was their eagerness to obtain the returns involved which made them so keen to drive on their men. By contrast, the European coffee and rubber plantations had not properly come to maturity by the outbreak of war. Africans also produced chillies, hides and skins, which were worth more when exported than the sum of rubber and coffee exports combined in 1913.[10]

In British East Africa, subsequently Kenya, European-directed agriculture was the first aim of government policy, and it was hoped that there would be mass colonisation by small working farmers from Europe. By 1908 it was clear that conditions were unsuitable and the policy was not going to work, while attempts to get the Africans to grow cotton had also failed. It has been said that the reason why the local people would not take to cotton cultivation was because they could earn good money on the rubber and coffee plantations which were coming into being, although the rubber plantations also failed as conditions were not suitable. But the most likely explanation is that the Africans were concentrating their attentions on maize, a very profitable crop at this time. As in Uganda, up to the First World War African agriculture and enterprise contributed more to the economy than did the settlers.[11]

In German East Africa, or Tanganyika, European plantations were little more successful, with rubber plantations being hit by the general collapse in rubber prices at the end of the period, just as they were coming into production. Sisal estates fared better. Both cotton and coffee did poorly as plantation crops, although the Africans grew coffee with some success. They also produced copra and groundnuts for export, proving themselves keen to grow crops for the market, as elsewhere in East Africa.[12]

But it was in West Africa that Africans scored the most spectacular successes in growing for the market. In Nigeria, there had been a steady expansion of exports of palm produce ever since the end of the slave trade early in the century, palm oil being joined by palm kernels from the late 1860s. Palm oil had long been an item of local diet, so the methods of collection and processing of the palm fruit were well understood. While the palm tree was not a cultivated crop in the normal sense, it was not a wild tree. It was associated with farming, proliferation of the tree being encouraged by the simple means of scattering palm nuts on the ground when a cultivated patch was allowed to return to bush fallow. This was the traditional form of shifting cultivation used in the main producing area between the Cross River and the Niger Delta. The steady expansion of palm produce exports during the century bears witness to the success of this policy of encouragement. There were no big plantations in this region, the crop belonging to the peasants on whose land the trees grew. The collection and transport of the crop remained in African hands until the turn of the century when European trading stations began to be built up-country at convenient points on the rivers. Further west, in the Lagos hinterland, leading chiefs actually established palm-oil plantations, as they did in neighbouring Dahomey. Thus the responsiveness of West Africans to external market pressures was clear. But palm trees grew successfully only in the tropical rain forest region, and Africans beyond these parts had to find other sources of cash income. In the region from Senegal to Sierra Leone, groundnuts were the answer, and from the 1830s production increased until they dominated the exports of the region in the last quarter of the nineteenth century. All the crop was grown by the local people, cultivation spreading inland as the railways were built, providing transport to the coast. Right at the end of the period production was just beginning in Northern Nigeria, where the railways had just arrived. Far from being resistant to cash cropping, even the Muslim sects became involved, and the Mourides, a Muslim group founded in 1886, began to make converts in Senegal, teaching the classic economic ethic that hard physical work in this world was a passport to salvation in the next. Initiates were taught how to grow groundnuts and, their novitiate complete, they went forth to set up farms of their own to train new converts to the faith of groundnut farming.

Because the history of palm production and groundnut farming has not been so well documented as that of cocoa, the development of the latter cash crop in the Gold Coast from 1892 has attracted attention as the most outstanding example of the willingness of African peasants to develop new crops when they could see the chance of profit. Although cocoa was not an indigenous tree, actually originating in South America, the plant became a major crop in the Gold Coast, shipments rising from nothing to 40,000 tons between 1892 and 1911, making the colony the largest cocoa exporter in the world. Migrant farmers in the south-east of the country moved to nearby virgin land suitable for cocoa, in order to grow the crop specifically to sell, for they had no use for it themselves. As some became specialists in cocoa, others specialised in food production to sell to the cocoa farmers. In the Ivory Coast a similar process took place in the period immediately before the Great War.[13]

So the success of West Africa in developing substantial exports of oilseeds and cocoa was very much the success of the African. In no way did the structure or attitudes of society there inhibit economic development. Of countries not mentioned, the German colonies of Togoland and the Cameroons were both peasant palm-oil producers, although there was some cocoa there, plus wild rubber, and the Germans had made some progress with plantations. As to the countries to the south, French Equatorial Africa and Angola, they were still in the era of wild rubber and ivory collection. This too of course was an example of African enterprise, as it was they who did the hunting and gathering! Even the Belgian Congo had not moved out of this stage of development before the First World War. As for German South West Africa, the pattern of development here was similar to that in Southern

Africa, being based on diamonds.[14]

Wherever one turns in the undeveloped world between 1865 and 1914, the ordinary people in the countries there are seen to be playing an active part in the development taking place. Where European enterprise and capital built mines and plantations, it was the Asians and Africans who provided the workforce, often migrating hundreds of miles to do so. Often they were taking up new occupations which the international market had created, at the same time as it had destroyed their old occupations, and they were making the rational response. Elsewhere they developed cash crops, in some places rice or maize, to feed the new plantation and mine workers; in others copra, palm produce, groundnuts, coffee, tea, cocoa and cotton for the international market. Sometimes they were entrepreneurs on a larger scale, as in the tin mines and rubber plantations in Malaya and the cotton industry in India. Indeed, it is possible to suggest that the seminal European role in Africa and Asia in these years was not so much the creation of mines and plantations but the provision of infrastructure with its lowering of transport costs. It was the market-widening effect of this which liberated the energies of Asians and Africans in the pursuit of economic gain. The structures and values of their societies did not prevent them from organising themselves to obtain increased material prosperity when they could see the chance of profit.

Notes

1. Angus Maddison, *Class Structure and Economic Growth: India and Pakistan since the Moghuls* (London: George Allen & Unwin, 1971), pp.24-30; M.N. Srinivas, *Social Change in Modern India* (Berkeley: University of California Press, 1969), p.91; M.N. Srinivas, *Caste in Modern India and Other Essays* (London: Asia Publishing House, 1962), pp.42-45, 58-9; M.D. Morris, *The Emergence of an Industrial Labor Force in India. A Study of the Bombay Cotton Mills, 1854-1947* (Berkeley: University of California Press, 1965), pp.71-82, 198-201; D.H. Buchanan, *The Development of Capitalistic Enterprise in India,* 2nd edn. (London: Cass, 1966), pp.143-8, 296-7; Kingsley Davis, *The Population of India and Pakistan* (New Jersey: Princeton University Press, 1951), pp.108, 115-20, 134-6; C.P. Wright, 'India as a Producer and Exporter of Wheat', *Wheat Studies,* 3 (1926-7), p.339; Hilda Kuper, *Indian People in Natal* (Pietermaritzburg: Natal University Press, 1960), pp.5-9; M.D. Morris, 'Towards a Re-interpretation of Nineteenth Century Indian History', *The Indian Economic and Social History Review,* 5 (1968), p.10.

2. J.S. Furnivall, *Colonial Policy and Practice: A Comparative Study of Burma and Netherlands India* (Cambridge: Cambridge University Press, 1948), pp.84-98.

3. D.R. Snodgrass, *Ceylon: An Export Economy in Transition* (Homewood,

Illinois: Irwin, 1966), pp.5-7, 21-67, Table A-52.

4. Lim Chong-Yah, *Economic Development of Modern Malaya* (Kuala Lumpur: Oxford University Press, 1967), pp.115-16, 120-2, 146, 153, 155, 184-5; G.C. Allen and A.C. Donnithorne, *Western Enterprise in Indonesia and Malaya, A Study in Economic Development* (London: George Allen & Unwin 1954), pp.115, 139-40.

5. Allen and Donnithorne, *Indonesia and Malaya,* pp.73-105, 118-20, 139-40, 172-3, 273; J.A.M. Caldwell, 'Indonesian Export and Production from the Decline of the Culture System to the First World War', in *The Economic Development of South-East Asia,* ed. C.D. Cowan (George Allen & Unwin, 1964), p.89; J.S. Furnivall, *Netherlands India* (Cambridge: Cambridge University Press, 1944), pp.214-16, 320-1; J.S. Furnivall, *Colonial Policy and Practice: A Comparative Study of Burma and Netherlands India* (Cambridge: Cambridge University Press, 1948), pp.256, 326; J.H. Boeke, *Economics and Economic Policy of Dual Societies, as Exemplified by Indonesia* (New York: Institute of Pacific Relations, 1953).

6. J.C. Ingram, *Economic Change in Thailand, 1850-1970* (Stanford: Stanford University Press, 1971), pp.36-74; J.C. Ingram, 'Thailand's Rice Trade and the Allocation of Resources', in *The Economic Development of South-East Asia* (London: George Allen & Unwin, 1964), pp.102-26.

7. C. Robequain, *The Economic Development of French Indo-China* (London: Oxford University Press, 1944), pp.44-59, 70-1, 168, 184-6, 190-99, 201-3, 213, 219-31, 243-51, 308-17.

8. Albert Feuerwerker, *The Chinese Economy c.1870-1911* (Ann Arbor, Michigan: Michigan University Press, 1969), pp.17-58; G.O. Allen and Audrey G. Donnithorne, *Western Enterprise in Far Eastern Economic Development: China and Japan* (London: George Allen & Unwin, 1954), pp.52-68, 69-74.

9. D.H. Houghton, 'Economic Development 1865-1965', in *The Oxford History of South Africa,* eds. Monica Wilson and Leonard Thompson, Vol.2 (Oxford: Clarendon Press, 1971), pp.21-2; J. Forbes Munro, *Africa and the International Economy, 1800-1969. An introduction to the Modern Economic History of Africa South of the Sahara* (London: J.M. Dent, 1976), pp.109-13; James Duffy, *Portuguese Africa* (Cambridge, Mass.: Harvard University Press, 1961), pp.169-70; Colin Bundy, 'The Emergence and Decline of a South African Peasantry', *African Affairs,* 71 (1972), pp.369-88; I.R. Phimister, 'Peasant Production and Underdevelopment in Southern Rhodesia, 1890-1914', *African Affairs,* 73 (1974), pp.217-28; G. Arrighi, 'Labour Supplies in Historical Perspective: A Study of the Proletarianisation of the African Peasantry in Rhodesia', *The Journal of Development Studies,* 6 (1970), pp.197-234.

10. Cyril Ehrlich, 'The Uganda Economy, 1903-1945', in *History of East Africa,* eds. V. Harlow and E.M. Chilver, Vol.2 (Oxford: Clarendon Press, 1965), pp.405-6.

11. C.C. Wrigley, 'Kenya: The Patterns of Economic Life, 1902-1945', in *History of East Africa,* eds. V. Harlow and E.M. Chilver, Vol.2 (Oxford: Clarendon Press, 1965), pp.214-32.

12. W.O. Henderson, 'German East Africa, 1884-1918', in *History of East Africa,* Vol.2, eds. Harlow and Chilver, pp.143-5, 152-3; O.F. Raum, II, 'German East Africa. Changes in African Life under German Administration, 1892-1914', in *History of East Africa,* Vol.2, eds. Harlow and Chilver, pp.187-92.

13. A.J.H. Latham, *Old Calabar, 1600-1891: The Impact of the International Economy upon a Traditional Society* (Oxford: Clarendon Press, 1973), pp.55-90; A.G. Hopkins, *An Economic History of West Africa* (London: Longmans, 1973), pp.128-9, 141, 210-11, 214, 217-21; Polly Hill, *The Migrant Cocoa Farmers of Southern Ghana, A Study in Rural Capitalism* (Cambridge: University Press, 1963).

14. Jean Suret-Canale, *French Colonialism in Tropical Africa 1900-1945* (London: C. Hurst & Co., 1971), pp.37-42; Duffy, *Portuguese Africa,* pp.154-55; A.B. Keith, *The Belgian Congo and the Berlin Act* (Oxford: Clarendon Press, 1919), pp.244-6; R. Anstey, *King Leopold's Legacy, The Congo under Belgian Rule, 1908-1960* (London: Oxford University Press, 1966), pp.5-8; H. Bley, *South-West Africa under German Rule, 1894-1914* (London: Heineman, 1971), pp.250-1, 196-8.

7 ECONOMIC DEVELOPMENT AND SOCIAL CHANGE

The previous chapter demonstrated how the people of Asia and Africa seized the new economic opportunities which opened to them after 1865. Whatever social restrictions existed in theory to prevent them doing this were disregarded in practice. Wherever the force of the market and the ethos of society were in conflict, the market won.

This raises a question which has provoked bitter controversy amongst the economic historians of West Africa, although overlooked or ignored by economic historians in general, to their shame.[1] Essentially the dispute is over the nature of the economy of pre-industrial society. One school of thought, led by the late Karl Polanyi, believed the economy of pre-industrial society was embedded in the fabric of society, the needs of society determining how the economy operated. But when the industrialised market economy of the modern world came into being, the situation was reversed, the needs of the market determining how society operated. Thus it held that in primitive society men produced goods because it was their obligation to society, not so as to make a personal profit from selling them. They shared these goods with their near and distant kinfolk, in the unspoken understanding that this favour would be returned. Society at large ensured that those with plenty provided for those without. This communal welfare system had no use for market exchange, and markets were of little importance, except for the provision of the minor items which the community could not provide for itself. Personal gain achieved by selling produce in the market was alien, as it would have been contrary to the general good, produce being transferred from the community which should have been shared within it. But the coming of the market economy tore apart this mutual-benefit organisation as individuals rejected their obligations to other members of society in order to produce and sell for their own profit. As the old fabric of society disintegrated, a new structure came into being based on the power of those who profited most, and which no longer cared for those in need. Communal responsibility was replaced by individual irresponsibility.[2]

Polanyi openly admitted that this understanding of primitive society was based upon the work of Malinowski and Thurnwald, but subsequent empirical work, for example by Polanyi on Dahomey and by his follower Paul Bohannan on the Tiv of Nigeria, was held to substantiate these views.[3] When Polanyi first expounded these ideas, he explicitly challenged the established beliefs of economic theorists, who witnessed the behaviour of men in the modern market economy, and assumed that man had always acted in this way in economic matters.[4] Thus, as a recent study has made clear, the conflict which Polanyi was provoking was between two differing methodologies. On the one hand, there was the method of economics, which began with a set of assumptions about economic behaviour and built upon these assumptions a logical framework deduced from them. On the other was the method of modern anthropology, which set about observing people in their economic activities, and then induced conclusions about economic behaviour from these observations. The challenge of the Polanyi school was the claim of empirical research to show that the general assumptions of economists about primitive man were wrong.[5] But the Polanyi school itself has been challenged in recent years by those who do not agree that the coming of the market economy marked a great transformation in society in the nineteenth century. This current challenge to the Polanyi school does not come from economists, who are uninterested in the debate, but from economic historians, themselves empirical and inductive in their methods. Their argument is that the empirical research of the Polanyi school does not stand up to investigation.

A central issue in the discussion has been the role of money in primitive society. For the impartial purchasing power which money confers is not necessary in a society whose production is based on the desire of men to contribute to the general welfare, and where the distribution of goods is done according to need. Money is not required where goods are not acquired through the market. As items in general were not bought and sold, there was no need for a unit of general purchasing power. However, in many societies of the kind Polanyi had in mind there did appear to be money-like objects. In his study of Dahomey, Polanyi explained this by arguing that money in these societies was used only for the exchange of those goods which conferred status upon the owner, and was therefore a powerful bond maintaining the structure of society. The elite groups exchanged these goods between themselves for money and were therefore marked out from the subordinate groups in society who did not have access to money, and so could not obtain status-conferring goods. He traced this status-coupon system in Africa back to the fourteenth century, where he believed the Arab geographer Ibn Battuta observed such a system operating in the Niger region. The currency system there consisted of copper wires, both thick and thin, and Polanyi maintains that thin wires, in which wages were paid, bought only firewood and coarse millet, while the thick ones bought anything, including elite goods. In this way limitations were placed upon the consumption of the poor, whilst the higher standard of life of the leisured classes was safeguarded. The snag with this interpretation is that the text Polanyi was quoting does not actually mention wage payments at all, and states that firewood and meat were obtainable with thin wires, not firewood and coarse millet. Millet, wheat, butter and slaves could be bought with the thick wires, and both thick and thin wires were exchangeable for gold, and therefore were interchangeable. Far from serving the limited purpose of exchanging status goods, these copper wires formed a true general-purpose money.[6] Polanyi's work on the cowrie has been shown to be equally full of shortcomings resulting from faulty research. Similarly grave doubts have been cast on Bohannan's widely quoted study of the Tiv brass-rod currency. So the West African currencies quoted by the Polanyi school as examples of currencies with the limited use of exchanging status goods appear in fact to be true general-purpose currencies which could purchase anything from grain to slaves. They functioned as means of exchange, units of account, standards of deferred payment and stores of wealth. West Africa used true money on a wide scale. This implies that the market operated widely in West Africa, for the prime requisite of a market economy is a means of exchange. Money and markets are synonymous. While goods were often shared amongst kinfolk according to their need, they nevertheless could be, and were, sold in the market.[7] In some respects it could be argued that it was more a market economy than our own, for slaves could be bought. In our own economy only a man's labour or a woman's services can be bought. But in West Africa, the man or woman in question was for sale.

In a recent publication dedicated to Polanyi and Bohannan, George Dalton, another disciple, seems to have shifted his ground, admitting significant differences between the type of society Polanyi was interested in and a peasant society such as that of the Gold Coast cocoa farmers.[8] In so doing he is surrendering the argument of his school, for such peasant societies were in the majority in West Africa. Communities of the kind Polanyi describes, if they existed at all, or even had existed, must have been very rare indeed. It was precisely because the peasants of West Africa were used to money and markets that they responded so easily and rapidly to the stimulus of market expansion in the late nineteenth century, providing palm produce, groundnuts and cocoa for export. Already the market enabled them to obtain specialities and luxuries in exchange for their surplus goods, and they simply produced a bigger surplus to channel through the market to satisfy international demand, allocating more land and labour to this end.

Polanyi had not meant his ideas to relate only to West Africa of course, but to have more universal application. That is why it is surprising that his ideas have not attracted more attention amongst economic historians in general. As regards the rest of Africa, money, that crucial indicator of the market economy, was evident everywhere before the introduction of colonial monetary systems at the end of the nineteenth century. In Kenya, Uganda and Tanganyika, cattle formed the basic monetary unit, with goats as subsidiary units, and cowrie shells came into use towards the end of the nineteenth century. In Southern and South West Africa, again cattle provided the basic currency. In fact one is tempted to speculate that cattle might have been the currency everywhere in Africa, as they were in early times in many parts of the world, had it not been for the tsetse fly! It would be difficult to explain the readiness of the Africans in Uganda to grow cotton for cash, or those in Kenya, Tanganyika and Southern Africa to grow food for cash at the turn of the century had they been accustomed only to the self-sufficient economy which Polanyi suggests. The existence of the monetary unit proves their understanding of market exchange. In the Belgian Congo, copper wires were the medium of exchange, and also iron bars and cowries were used, the latter being the medium of exchange in Angola, where cloth was also used. That cash crops did not develop in these last two regions in these years is presumably because the forests still held an abundance of wild rubber and ivory, which the Africans could collect and sell with the surplus labour not needed to produce their own food.[9]

If Polanyi's ideas do not apply to Africa, they are even less applicable to Asia. There money dated back many centuries, with some similarities to the African situation. As early as the twenty-fourth century BC, the Chinese invaders found cowries in use as money in China by the indigenous peoples. Cowries continued to be used in Yunnan Province adjoining Burma up to the seventeenth century AD, and probably later, as they were in Siam and French Indo-China in the late nineteenth century. In India too cowries were used from the third century BC, up to the eighteenth century AD. Cows had been used in India before this, dating back to the tenth century BC.[10] But coins had also been used in Asia for many centuries, and it is tempting to suggest that the sophistication of the monetary unit itself is an index of the sophistication of the economy and the society in which it operates. Thus a society which uses livestock as its currency unit may be assumed to be less complex than one using a coin minted to a specified weight and fineness and bearing a stamp of authority. Be that as it may, coins had been used in Asia for many centuries, but were not used in Africa before the colonial period. In China coins certainly date from the fourth century BC, and may go back to the fourteenth century BC, India using coins from the fifth century BC.[11]

So by the middle of the nineteenth century, most of Asia had been monetised for many centuries, India now having a system based on the silver rupee, which was also used in Ceylon and Malaya. Tin ingots and gold dust had previously been used in Malaya, as in the Netherlands Indies, where Dutch money was current. In Siam the silver baht or tical was introduced in the middle of the century, and in Indo-China the dollars of various nations circulated alongside cowries and iron and copper bars, immediately before the arrival of the French. In China the currency situation was chaotic, with the dollars of various nations and copper coins all circulating, although there was no minted Chinese silver currency unit.[12]

It is inconceivable that Asia, being so widely monetised, was not permeated by the force of the market. Indeed, it was precisely because the market was operating that the Lancashire cotton industry wrecked the Indian cotton industry early in the nineteenth century and did such damage to the Siamese and Chinese cotton industries later in the century. At the same time, the existence of this and other handicraft industries in Asia reveals the fact that the internal division of labour had already reached a considerable level. Again, it was because Asian peasants so fully understood the principle of the market that they moved so quickly to take up the new opportunities for wage employment and the growing of cash crops, from rice to copra.

That the market operated so widely in Asia and Africa, symbolised by the ubiquitous use of money, also suggests that the spirit of capitalism was everywhere present. For if the term capitalism is used in the sense of an economic system using capital for the production and exchange of goods and services, the existence of money clearly demonstrates that the economic system is capitalistic.[13] For money is the 'tool' by which exchange is facilitated, making greater division of labour and specialisation of task possible in society at large. The stock of money implies a considerable investment by society in general in its own distributive system. If the money is metal, then that metal is not being used for making implements or equipment. If the money is livestock, then food is being withheld from consumption. So society is saving and investing in its own distributive system. On this basis, the money-using societies of Asia and Africa, and that is the vast majority, were capitalistic.

However, if capitalism is taken to mean a system in which there is individual ownership of capital, the means of production, as opposed to communal ownership, then this too is implied by the existence of money.[14] For money gives access to the possession of the means of production, and money was owned individually. On this basis too the majority of societies in Asia and Africa at the beginning of the last quarter of the nineteenth century were capitalistic, with individual ownership of trees and crops and often of land too. Even Dalton accepts that peasant societies like the Gold Coast cocoa farmers were capitalist.[15]

But Schumpeter has suggested that the crucial measure of whether a system is capitalist or not is whether it uses credit. Here again the use of true general-purpose money implies that the system is capitalistic, as one of the features of true money is that it can be a standard for deferred payments, and a deferred payment clearly implies credit. There is plenty of evidence to show that credit, and interest payments, went back to the fourth century BC, in China, as it did in India, where the Chettiar caste were specialist moneylenders. Elsewhere in Asia there was credit, as there was in Africa.[16]

Yet another definition of capitalism, however, would hesitate to describe the economies of Asia and Africa in the nineteenth century as capitalist. This definition, used by Tawney, stresses that capitalism means the direction of industry by the owners of capital for their own pecuniary gain, together with the social relations which establish themselves between the owners and the wage earners they employ.[17] In other words, the presence of wage labour becomes the vital factor identifying capitalism. On this basis, it would appear difficult to describe Asia and Africa as capitalist in the nineteenth century, for although wage labour came to be used extensively in plantations and mines, these were obviously developments new to the nineteenth century for the most part. On the other hand, wage labour did exist in China before the nineteenth century, and elsewhere a labour market had existed in the form of slaves, in places as various as West Africa, India, Siam, Cambodia and Sumatra.[18] Some of course would argue that an economy using slave labour is entirely different from one using wage labour, and cannot be described as capitalist. This would mean, however, that the economy of the South of the United States prior to the civil war could not be described as capitalist, which seems absurd, as it supplied the raw material for the Lancashire cotton industry, which was capitalist by anyone's reckoning. Wage labour then does not appear to be necessary for a system to be capitalist, and capitalism exists wherever market economies exist. Thus capitalism was widespread in Asia and Africa throughout the nineteenth century, and it was because the ethos of capitalism was so widespread that Asians and Africans responded so rapidly to the increased market opportunities which came with cheaper international transport. As the capitalism of Europe expanded seeking new areas of investment in Asia and Africa, it created new openings for the indigenous capitalism in Asia and Africa. The capitalism of the West met the capitalism of the East to each other's mutual advantage.

The fact that the majority of people in Asia and Africa were small-time capitalists, eager for new opportunities of profit, throws new light on the views of those development economists who see the people of the undeveloped world as trapped in a vicious circle of poverty. This is usually expressed in terms of the low income of the people there making saving impossible and therefore preventing the capital formation necessary to create higher levels of income. The people were poor because they were poor.[19] This view has rightly been condemned by P.T. Bauer, on the basis that if such a poverty trap existed, no economic advance could ever have been made anywhere. For all mankind was at one time poor, and if the vicious circle of poverty operated it would have remained poor. As economic advance did take place, then the concept of a vicious circle of poverty is nonsense.[20] Moreover, as this book has shown, substantial economic advance was made all over the undeveloped world in the late nineteenth century, in India, Burma, Ceylon, Malaya, the Dutch East Indies, Siam, French Indo-China and in East, West and Southern Africa. Exports from these countries rose, whether it was peasant-produced rice, or peasant-produced copra, palm produce, groundnuts, maize, cocoa, coffee or rubber. Exports of Asian-produced tin also rose. There was no evidence of a vicious circle of poverty operating here, and on the contrary a virtuous circle operated by which rising incomes generated increased savings, which made possible increased investment in these crops and mines. If it was the new demand of the international market which triggered off the cultivation of these cash crops and products, it was the local population which did the work. This alacrity in responding to new opportunities effectively disposes of the myth that Africans and Asians do not respond to economic incentives, or are incapable of long-term investment decisions. They had surplus land and labour available and quickly brought these into use to meet the stimulus of world demand.[21]

As the peasantry of the undeveloped world took advantage of the opportunities available to them, it was inevitable that strains should arise within their communities. The more enterprising became wealthier than the less enterprising, regardless of what might have been their ascribed place in society. In West Africa, successful palm produce traders provided a challenge to traditional chiefs. In one area witchcraft activities broke out as men with traditional status used covert aggression against their relations who had acquired the new status of wealth, thus not offending the *mores* of society against open aggression to kinfolk.[22] In India, men had to break the local customs against leaving the village or crossing rivers, to seek employment elsewhere. In the cotton factories the castes had to abandon their traditional separateness to work together. The Chinese too had to break the bond with their village and homeland to seek work abroad. So tensions arose between attachment to the customary values of society and the pull of the market. But this conflict dates back long into history, in the West since the beginning of Christianity and probably before, and it still continues, as in twentieth-century Britain. It is the simple conflict between the philosophy that the members of society should take a communal responsibility for each other's needs and the fact that individuals will seek personal economic gain if the chance is presented to them. This clash has been present as long as there have been markets, money and capitalism, which is probably as long as man has lived in settled communities. Since then it has been the persistent victory of capitalism in this issue which has provided the mainspring for economic and social development.

Notes

1. George Dalton, Review of A.G. Hopkins, *An Economic History of West Africa,* in *African Economic History Review,* 1 (1976), pp.51-101.
2. Karl Polanyi, *The Great Transformation. The Political and Economic Origins of our Time,* 2nd edn. (Boston: Beacon Press, 1967), pp.46, 47-8, 57, 58, 68, 71, 75; *Primitive, Archaic and Modern Economies, Essays of Karl Polanyi,* ed. George Dalton (Boston: Beacon Press, 1968), pp.xii-xiii.
3. Karl Polanyi, *Dahomey and the Slave Trade. An Analysis of an Archaic Economy* (Seattle: University of Washington Press, 1966); Paul and Laura Bohannan, *Tiv Economy* (London: Longmans, 1968).
4. Polanyi, *Great Transformation,* pp.43-4.
5. Harold K. Schneider, *Economic Man. The Anthropology of Economics*

(New York: Free Press, 1974), pp.24-6.

6. Polanyi, *Dahomey,* pp.174-5; A.J.H. Latham, 'Currency, Credit and Capitalism on the Cross River in the Pre-Colonial Era', *Journal of African History,* 12 (1971), p.602.

7. Polanyi, *Dahomey,* pp.173-194; Marion Johnson, 'The Cowrie Currencies of West Africa', *Journal of African History,* 11 (1970), pp.17-49, 331-53; Marion Johnson, 'The Ounce in Eighteenth-Century West African Trade', *Journal of African History,* 7 (1966), pp.197-214; P. Bohannan, 'Some Principles of Exchange and Investment among the Tiv', *American Anthropologist,* 67 (1955), pp.60-70; P. Bohannan, 'The Impact of Money on an African Subsistence Economy', *Journal of Economic History,* 19 (1959), pp.491-503; Latham, 'Currency, Credit and Capitalism', pp.599-605; A.G.Hopkins, *An Economic History of West Africa* (London: Longmans, 1973), pp.68-71.

8. George Dalton, *Economic Anthropology and Development, Essays on Tribal and Peasant Economies* (New York: Basic Books, 1971), p.105.

9. Paul Einzig, *Primitive Money in its Ethnological, History and Economic Aspects* (London: Eyre & Spottiswoode, 1955), pp.160-71, 126-35.

10. Einzig, *Primitive Money,* pp.100-5, 250-1, 253-8, 285, 311; Len-sheng Yang, *Money and Credit in China. A Short History* (Cambridge, Mass.: Harvard University Press, 1965), pp.1-29.

11. Jacques Melitz, *Primitive and Modern Money: An Interdisciplinary Approach* (Reading, Mass.: Addison-Wesley Publishing Co., 1974), pp.84-9; Alexander Del Mar, *History of Monetary Systems. A History of Actual Experiments in Money Made by Various States of the Ancient and Modern World,* 2nd edn. (New York: Augustus M. Kelley, 1969), pp.1-7; Yang, *Money and Credit in China,* pp.20-9.

12. Einzig, *Primitive Money,* pp.100-5; Del Mar, *History of Currency Systems,* pp.16-17; see Chapter 2 above.

13. D.S. Landes, Introduction, in *The Rise of Capitalism,* ed. D.S. Landes (New York: Macmillan, 1966), p.1.

14. *The Concise Oxford Dictionary of Current English,* ed. H.W. Fowler and F.G. Fowler, 5th edn. (Oxford: Clarendon Press, 1964), p.177.

15. Dalton, *Economic Anthropology and Development,* p.95.

16. Yang, *Money and Credit in China,* pp.5-7; Einzig, *Primitive Money,* pp.101, 131, 251, 257; J.S. Furnivall, *Colonial Policy and Practice: A Comparative Study of Burma and Netherlands Indies* (Cambridge: Cambridge University Press, 1948), pp.86-7; Latham, 'Currency, Credit and Capitalism', pp.602-3; A.J.H. Latham, *Old Calabar, 1600-1891: The Impact of the International Economy upon a Traditional Society* (Oxford: Clarendon Press, 1973), pp.27-30, 38-9, 85-6; Hopkins, *West Africa,* pp.63-4, 70-1.

17. R.H. Tawney, *Religion and the Rise of Capitalism. A Historical Study* (London: Murray, 1926), p.84.

18. Yang, *Money and Credit in China,* pp.5-7; Srinivas, *Castes Old and New,* p.92; Ingram, *Economic Change in Thailand, 1850-1970* (Stanford: Stanford University Press, 1971), pp.13-4; Einzig, *Primitive Money,* pp.100, 115, 249-50; Hopkins, *West Africa,* p.104; C.G.F. Simkin, *The Traditional Trade of Asia* (London: Oxford University Press, 1968), pp.124, 333.

19. Ragnar Nurkse, *Problems of Capital Formation in Underdeveloped Countries* (Oxford: Blackwell, 1953), p.4; Gunnar Myrdal, *Asian Drama. An Enquiry into the Poverty of Nations,* Vol.3 (London: Allen Lane, The Penguin Press, 1968), pp.1843-7; H.W. Singer, 'Economic Progress in the Underdeveloped Countries', *Social Research,* 16 (1949).

20. P.T. Bauer, *Dissent on Development, Studies and Debates in Development Economics* (London: Weidenfeld and Nicolson, 1971), pp.31-4.

21. H. Myint, *The Economics of Developing Countries* (London: Hutchinson, 1967), pp.41-4.

22. A.J.H. Latham, 'Witchcraft Accusations and Economic Tension in Pre-Colonial Old Calabar', *Journal of African History,* 13 (1972), pp.249-60; Hopkins, *West Africa,* pp.142-7.

CONCLUSION

The fifty years from 1865 to 1914 saw a communications revolution in Asia and Africa. The Suez Canal was opened and steam ships churned through, drawing Europe more closely to the ports of the undeveloped world and interconnecting those ports with each other. From the ports, railways were constructed linking them to their hinterlands up-country. At the same time, the electric telegraph put markets from Dakar to Shanghai in direct contact with London, centre of the world's communications system and the world market. Western enterprise and capital were responsible for all this, Britain being particularly prominent. Meanwhile the countries of Asia and Africa completed their integration into the international economy by adopting the gold standard, only China, Hong Kong, French Indo-China and the Portuguese territories remaining outside the gold system at the end of the period.

As these developments took place, the trade of the undeveloped world grew quickly. Britain found her exports to Asia and Africa expanding more rapidly than her exports to the United States or industrial Europe, where tariff barriers had been set up against her. What is more, she earned a considerable surplus on her trade with Asia in general, and India in particular, which enabled her to settle the deficits she owed on her transactions with the United States and Europe. Without this surplus, she would have been unable to meet these debts, and would have had to abandon free trade by adopting reciprocal tariffs against the United States and Europe. This would have had severe repercussions upon their development, as Britain was a major export market for both regions. So the growth of the United States and Europe was dependent to a degree upon Britain's Asian surplus. India was the main source of this positive balance and she herself enjoyed a vast trade surplus, which was indicated by her heavy imports of gold and silver. Much of this surplus came from her own trade with Asia, particularly China. Britain also had a favourable balance with China, so that China's large trade deficit in these years was an important feature of the international economy. Africa was less important than Asia in this respect, for although Britain had a useful surplus with West Africa, her deficit with South Africa rendered her overall balance with Africa negative.

As Asia and Africa became more assimilated within the international system, increased investment from Britain and Europe was put into mines and plantations. This created a demand for labour, and set up a new international labour market in the undeveloped world. As the handicraft cotton industry of Southern India collapsed under the strain of competition from Lancashire, the people there were forced to seek a livelihood elsewhere, and seized the opportunity of going to work on plantations in Ceylon and Malaya for limited periods, returning home when their time was up. In Malaya, they met a stream of migrants from Southern China, also displaced from their homes by the products of Lancashire, this time cheap yarn which undercut the hand-spun yarn which maintained the delicate balance of their household economy. The Chinese owned and operated tin mines and plantations in Malaya, besides providing the workforce. All over South East Asia, from Siam to Sumatra, the Chinese were to be found seeking new opportunities for trade and work. Indians and Chinese were also brought to Africa, but the majority of the labourers in the plantations and mines there were Africans, many of whom migrated from distant regions to obtain employment. Like the Indians and many of the Chinese, they worked for a limited time and then returned home.

But wage earning was not the only opportunity which integration into world markets brought to Asians and Africans. For the new wage workers on the plantations and in the mines needed food, and a rapid expansion of peasant rice production took place in Burma, Siam and French Indo-China to supply this need. Peasants in other regions, who already had sufficient food for their own needs, developed cash crops to sell to obtain imported luxuries. Copra was especially important to Ceylon, the Dutch East Indies and Malaya, with some coffee, tea and rubber. In West Africa palm oil and kernels, groundnuts and cocoa became major cash crops and in East Africa cotton led the way, with smaller amounts of copra and maize. In Southern Africa, foodstuffs earned good returns. So successful was this commercial agriculture that in many places the peasants had no incentive to go and work as wage labourers, and in Southern Africa sufficient labour was recruited for the mines only when the new railways carried in cheap food from abroad which brought down local food prices and cut the profits to be made from growing provisions.

In consequence of these developments, considerable economic growth took place in the undeveloped world and, despite population increases, there appear to have been advances in per capita income levels, even in China, perhaps the most backward region. That interdependency between the developed world and the undeveloped world was growing is revealed by the fact that fluctuations in Britain's sales to Asia had as much effect on British incomes and employment as her sales to industrial Europe, and considerably more effect than her sales to the United States. These fluctuations in her Asian trade were apparently a result of circumstances operating in Asia, connected to variations in the price of rice, as British exports seem to have increased following rises in the price of rice. The extent to which these fluctuations were then transmitted onwards from Britain to those countries for whom Britain was a major market, to the United States and the countries of industrial Europe, is a matter for interesting conjecture.

Attention has been drawn to the alacrity with which Asians and Africans responded to the new economic opportunities which were presented to them, by taking wage employment or producing for the market. This runs contrary to the ideas of those who see these people as locked in inhibiting social constraints which prevented them from responding to economic incentives. In actual fact, wherever social obligations conflicted with the chance of personal profit, personal profit prevailed. Incomes rose, increasing savings and investment, which enabled surplus land and labour to be brought into production to supply the world market. In this, Asians and Africans were acting as true capitalists. Thus the overall pattern of development in these years is of the capitalism of the developed world expanding outwards, bringing new opportunities to the indigenous capitalism of the undeveloped world, to each other's mutual advantage.

BIBLIOGRAPHY

Books

Adams, J.Q. III, 'Economic Change, Exports and Imports: The Case of India, 1870-1960', University of Texas PhD, 1966

Aldcroft, D.H. and Peter Fearon, *British Economic Fluctuations, 1790-1939* (London: Macmillan, 1972)

Allen, Fawcett, *An Atlas of Commercial Geography* (Cambridge University Press, 1913)

Allen, G.C. and Donnithorne, A.G., *Western Enterprise in Far Eastern Economic Development: China and Japan* (London: George Allen & Unwin, 1954)

Allen, G.C. and Donnithorne, A.G., *Western Enterprise in Indonesia and Malaya, A Study in Economic Development* (London: George Allen & Unwin, 1957)

Ambedkar, B.R., *The Problem of the Rupee. Its Origin and its Solution* (London: P.S. King & Son, 1923)

Anstey, R., *King Leopold's Legacy. The Congo under Belgian Rule, 1908-1960* (London: Oxford University Press, 1966)

Anstey, Vera, *The Economic Development of India,* 3rd ed. (London: Longmans Green, 1949)

Arasaratnam, Sinnappah, *Indians in Malaysia and Singapore* (Bombay and Kuala Lumpur: Oxford University Press, 1970)

Arndt, E.H.D., *Banking and Currency Development in South Africa, 1652-1927* (Cape Town and Johannesburg: Juta & Co., 1928)

Ashton, T.S., *An Economic History of England: The Eighteenth Century* (London: Methuen, 1955)

Bauer, P.T., *Dissent on Development. Studies and Debates in Development Economics* (London: Weidenfeld and Nicolson, 1971)

Bley, H., *South-West Africa under German Rule, 1894-1914* (London: Heineman, 1971)

Blyn, George, *Agricultural Trends in India 1891-1947. Output, Availability and Productivity* (Philadelphia: University of Pennsylvania Press, 1966)

Boeke, J.H., *Economics and Economic Policy of Dual Societies as Exemplified by Indonesia* (New York: Institute of Pacific Relations, 1953)

Bohannan, Paul and Laura, *Tiv Economy,* (London: Longmans, 1968)

Bohm, Elemer, *La mise en valeur des Colonies Portugaises* (Paris: Les Presses Universitaires de France, 1938)

Boute, Joseph, *La Démographie de la Branche Indo-Pakistanaise d'Afrique* (Louvain-Paris: Editions Nauwelaerts, 1965)

Britain and Germany in Africa: Imperial Rivalry and Colonial Rule, eds Prosser Gifford and W.M. Roger Louis (New Haven: Yale University Press, 1967)

British Economic Fluctuations, 1790-1939, eds D.H. Aldcroft and Peter Fearon (London: Macmillan, 1972)

Brode, H., *British and German East Africa. Their Economic and Commercial Relations* (London: Edwin Arnold, 1911)

Buchanan, D.H., *The Development of Capitalistic Enterprise in India,* 2nd ed. (London: Cass, 1966)

Callis, H.G., *Foreign Capital in South East Asia* (New York: Institute of Pacific Relations, 1942)

Campbell, P.C., *Chinese Coolie Emigration to Countries within the British Empire* (London: P.S. King & Son, 1923)

de Cecco, Marcello, *Money and Empire: The International Gold Standard, 1890-1914* (Oxford: Basil Blackwell, 1974)

Chalmers, Robert, *A History of Currency in the British Colonies* (London: HMSO, 1893)

Chamberlain, M.E., *Britain and India: The Interaction of Two Peoples* (Newton Abbot: David & Charles, 1974)

Cheng, Yu-kwei, *Foreign Trade and Industrial Development of China An Historical and Integrated Analysis through 1948* (Washington, DC: University Press of Washington, 1956)

Chong-Yah, Lim, *Economic Development of Modern Malaya* (Kuala Lumpur: Oxford University Press, 1967)

Colonialism in Africa, 1870-1960, eds L.H. Gann and Peter Duigan, 5 vols (Cambridge: Cambridge University Press, 1969-75)

Dalton, George, *Economic Anthropology and Development. Essays on Tribal and Peasant Economies* (New York: Basic Books, 1971)

Daniell, C.J., *The Gold Treasure of India* (London: Kegan Paul, Trench & Co., 1884)

Das, M.N., *Studies in the Economic and Social Development of Modern India, 1848-1856* (Calcutta: Mukhopadhyay, 1959)

Davies, P.N., *The Trade Makers: Elder Dempster in West Africa, 1852-1972* (London: George Allen & Unwin, 1973)

Davis, Kingsley, *The Population of India and Pakistan* (New Jersey: Princeton University Press, 1951)

Deakin, B.M. and T. Seward, *Shipping Conferences: A Study of their*

Origins, Development and Economic Practices (Cambridge: Cambridge University Press, 1973)

Deane, Phyllis and W.A. Cole, *British Economic Growth, 1688-1959*, 2nd ed (Cambridge: Cambridge University Press, 1967)

Duffy, James, *Portuguese Africa* (Cambridge, Mass: Harvard University Press, 1961)

Einzig, Paul, *Primitive Money in its Ethnological, Historical and Economic Aspects* (London: Eyre & Spottiswoode, 1951)

Ekundare, R.O., *An Economic History of Nigeria, 1860-1960* (London: Methuen, 1973)

Essays in Money and Banking in Honour of R.S. Sayers, ed C.R. Whittlesey and J.S.G. Wilson (Oxford: Clarendon Press, 1968)

Essays on Unbalanced Growth, ed Egbert de Vries ('S-Gravenhage: Mouton & Co., 1962)

Farnie, D.A., *East and West of Suez. The Suez Canal in History* (Oxford: Clarendon Press, 1969)

Federated Malay States Railways, *Fifty Years of Railways in Malaya, 1885-1935* (Kuala Lumpur: Federated Malay States Railways, 1935)

Feis, Herbert, *Europe, the World's Banker, 1870-1914. An Account of European Foreign Investment and the Connection of World Finance with Diplomacy before the War,* 2nd ed (New York: Augustus M. Kelley, 1961)

Feuerwerker, Albert, *The Chinese Economy, c.1870-1911* (Ann Arbor, Michigan: Michigan University Press, 1969)

Garratt, G.R.M., *One Hundred Years of Submarine Cables* (London, HMSO 1950)

Foreign Office, *Peace Handbooks:* Vol.16, *British Possessions,* 2, *The Congo,* (London: HMSO, 1920)

Foreign Office, *Peace Handbooks:* Vol.17, *French African Possessions* (London: HMSO, 1920)

Foreign Office, *Peace Handbooks:* Vol.18, *German African Possessions (Late)* (London: HMSO, 1920)

Foreign Office, *Peace Handbooks:* Vol.19, *Portuguese Possessions* (London: HMSO, 1920)

Frankel, S. Herbert, *Capital Investment in Africa. Its Course and Effects* (London: Oxford University Press, 1938)

Friedman, Milton and Anna Jacobson Schwartz, *A Monetary History of the United States, 1867-1960* (Princeton: Princeton University Press, 1963)

Furnivall, J.S., *Netherlands India* (Cambridge: Cambridge University Press, 1944)

Furnivall, J.S., *Colonial Policy and Practice: A Comparative Study of Burma and Netherlands India* (Cambridge: Cambridge University Press, 1948)

Greaves, Ida, *Colonial Monetary Conditions* (London: HMSO, 1953)

Grey, Richard and David Birmingham, *Pre-Colonial African Trade: Essays on Trade in Central and Eastern Africa before 1900* (London: Oxford University Press, 1970)

Gunasekera, H.A. de S., *From Dependent Currency to Central Banking in Ceylon: An Analysis of Monetary Experience 1825-1957* (London: G. Bell & Sons, 1962)

Hammond, R.J., *Portugal and Africa 1815-1910. A Study in Uneconomic Imperialism* (Stanford, California: Stanford University Press, 1966)

Harlow, V., and E.M. Chilver, *History of East Africa,* 2 vols (Oxford: Clarendon Press, 1965)

Henderson, W.O., *Studies in German Colonial History* (London: Frank Cass, 1962)

Hieke, Ernst, *G.L. Gaiser: Hamburg-Westafrica, 100 Jahre Handel Mit Nigeria* (Hamburg: Hoffman und Campe Verlag, 1949)

Hill, M.F., *Permanent Way,* 2 vols (Nairobi: East African Railways & Harbours, 1961-2)

Hill, Polly, *The Migrant Cocoa Farmers of Southern Ghana. A Study in Rural Capitalism* (Cambridge: Cambridge University Press, 1963)

Ho, Ping-ti, *Studies on the Population of China, 1368-1953* (Cambridge, Mass: Harvard University Press, 1959)

Ho, Ping-yin, *The Foreign Trade of China* (Shanghai: Commercial Press, 1935)

Hopkins, A.G., *An Economic History of West Africa* (London: Longmans, 1973)

Hou, Chi-ming, *Foreign Investment and Economic Development in China, 1840-1937* (Cambridge, Mass: Harvard University Press, 1965)

Hsaio, Liang-lin, *China's Foreign Trade Statistics, 1864-1949* (Cambridge, Mass: Harvard University Press, 1974)

Hsu, Mongton Chih, *Railway Problems in China,* 2nd ed. (New York: Ams Press, 1968)

Huttenbach, August, *The Silver Standard and the Straits Currency Question* (Singapore: Fraser and Neave, 1903)

Huybrechts, Andre, *Transports et structures de développement au Congo: Etude du progrès économique de 1900 à 1970* (Paris: Mouton et IRES, 1970)

Hyde, F.E., *Blue Funnel. A History of Alfred Holt & Co., Liverpool, 1865-1914* (Liverpool: Liverpool University Press, 1957)
Hyde, F.E., *Shipping Enterprise and Management. Harrisons of Liverpool, 1830-1939* (Liverpool: Liverpool University Press, 1967)
Hyde, F.E., *Far Eastern Trade 1860-1914* (London: Black, 1973)
Iliffe, John, *Tanganyika under German Rule, 1905-12* (Cambridge: Cambridge University Press, 1969)
Ingram, J.C., *Economic Change in Thailand, 1850-1970* (Stanford: Stanford University Press, 1971)
Iyer, K.V., *Indian Railways* (Calcutta: Oxford University Press, 1924)
Jackson, R.N., *Immigrant Labour and the Development of Malaya, 1786-1920* (Kuala Lumpur: Government Press, 1961)
Jenks, L.H., *The Migration of British Capital to 1875* (London: Thos. Nelson & Sons, 1963)
Juglar, Clement, *Des crises commerciales et de leur retour périodique en France, en Angleterre et aux Etats-Unis,* 2nd ed (Paris: Guillaumin, 1889)
Katzenellenbogen, S.E., *Railways and the Copper Mines of Katanga* (Oxford: Clarendon Press, 1973)
Keith, A.B., *The Belgian Congo and the Berlin Act* (Oxford: Clarendon Press, 1919)
Kemmerer, E.W., *Modern Currency Reforms. A History and Discussion of Recent Currency Reforms in India, Porto Rico, Philippine Islands, Straits Settlements and Mexico* (New York: Macmillan, 1916)
Kent, P.H., *Railway Enterprise in China. An Account of its Origin and Development* (London: Edwin Arnold, 1907)
Kieve, J.W., *The Electrical Telegraph. A Social and Economic History* (Newton Abbot: David & Charles, 1973)
King, Frank H.H., *Money in British East Asia* (London: HMSO, 1957)
King, Frank H.H., *Money and Monetary Policy in China, 1845-1895* (Cambridge, Mass: Harvard University Press, 1965)
Kirkaldy, A.W., *British Shipping. Its History, Organisation and Importance* (London: Kegan Paul, Trench, Trubner & Co., 1914)
Kirkaldy, A.W. and A.D. Evans, *The History and Economics of Transport,* 3rd ed (London: Pitmans, 1924)
de Kock, M.H., *Selected Subjects in the Economic History of South Africa* (Cape Town and Johannesburg: Juta & Co., 1924)
de Kock, M.H., *The Economic Development of South Africa* (London: P.S. King & Son, 1936)
Kuczynski, R.R., *A Demographic Survey of the British Colonial Empire,* 3 vols (London: Oxford University Press, 1948-53)

Kuper, Hilda, *Indian People in Natal* (Pietermaritzburg: Natal University Press, 1960)

Kuznets, Simon, *Economic Growth and Structure: Selected Essays* (London: Heineman, 1965)

Kuznets, Simon, *Economic Growth of Nations. Total Output and Production Structure* (Cambridge, Mass: Harvard University Press, 1971)

de Laboulaye, E., *Les chemins de fer de Chine* (Paris: 1911)

Landon, K.P., *The Chinese in Thailand* (New York: Russell & Russell, 1941)

Latham, A.J.H., *Old Calabar 1600-1891: The Impact of the International Economy upon a Traditional Society* (Oxford: Clarendon Press, 1973)

Lawford, G.L., and L.R. Nicholson, *The Telecon Story* (London: Telegraph Construction and Maintenance Co., 1950)

Leavens, Dickson H., *Silver Money* (Bloomington, Indiana: Principia Press, 1939)

Leduc, Michel, *Les Institutions Monétaires Africaines des Pays Francophones* (Paris: Editions A. Pedone, 1965)

Lehfeldt, R.A., *Gold Prices and the Witwatersrand* (London: P.S. King & Co., 1919)

Leubuscher, Charlotte, *The West African Shipping Trade, 1909-1959* (Leyden: A.W. Sythoff, 1962)

Lin, Cheng, *The Chinese Railways. An Historical Survey* (Shanghai: China United Press, 1935)

Liverpool and Merseyside: Essays in the Economic and Social History of the Port and its Hinterland, ed J.R. Harris (London: Cass, 1969)

Loynes, J.B., *The West African Currency Board, 1912-1962* (London: West African Currency Board, 1962)

Maddison, Angus, *Class Structure and Economic Growth* (London: George Allen & Unwin, 1971)

Del Mar, Alexander, *History of Monetary Systems. A History of Actual Experiments in Money made by Various States of the Ancient and Modern World,* 2nd ed (New York: Augustus M. Kelley, 1969)

Masayoshi, Count Matsukata, *Report on the Adoption of the Gold Standard in Japan* (Tokyo: Government Press, 1899)

Melitz, Jacques, *Primitive and Modern Money: An Interdisciplinary Approach* (Reading, Mass.: Addison-Wealey Publishing Co., 1974)

Middleton, P.H., *Railways of Thirty Nations* (New York: Prentice-Hall, 1937)

Mitchell, B.R. and Phyllis Deane, *Abstract of British Historical Statistics*

(Cambridge: Cambridge University Press, 1962)
Morris, M.D., *The Emergence of an Industrial Labour Force in India. A Study of the Bombay Cotton Mills, 1854-1947* (Berkeley: University of California Press, 1965)
Morse, H.B., *The Trade and Administration of the Chinese Empire* (Shanghai: Kelly and Walsh, 1908)
Mukherjee, M., *National Income of India: Trends and Structure* (Calcutta: Statistical Publishing Society, 1969)
Munro, J. Forbes, *Africa and the International Economy, 1800-1969. An Introduction to the Modern Economic History of Africa South of the Sahara* (London: J.M. Dent, 1976)
Murray, Marischal, *Union Castle Chronicle, 1853-1953* (London: Longmans Green, 1953)
Myint, H., *The Economics of Developing Countries* (London: Hutchinson, 1967)
Myrdal, Gunnar, *Asian Drama. An Inquiry into the Poverty of Nations.* 3 vols (London: Allen Lane, The Penguin Press, 1968)
Newlyn, W.T. and D.C. Rowan, *Money and Banking in British Colonial Africa: A Study of the Monetary and Banking Systems of Eight British African Territories* (Oxford: Clarendon Press, 1954)
Nurkse, Ragnar, *Problems of Capital Formation in Underdeveloped Countries* (Oxford: Blackwell, 1953)
O'Connor, A.M., *Railways and Development in Uganda. A Study in Economic Geography* (Nairobi: Oxford University Press, 1965)
Palmer, Mabel, *The History of the Indians in Natal* (Cape Town: Oxford University Press, 1957)
Pandit, Y.S., *India's Balance of Indebtedness, 1898-1913* (London: George Allen & Unwin, 1937)
Papers on Malayan History, ed K.G. Tregonning (Singapore: *Journal of South East Asian History,* 1962)
Parmer, J.N., *Colonial Labour Policy and Administration. A History of Labour in the Rubber Plantation Industry in Malaya c.1910-1941* (New York: J.J. Augustin, 1960)
Perera, G.F., *The Ceylon Railway* (Colombo: Ceylon Observer, 1925)
Phillips, George, *Chamber of Commerce Atlas. A Graphic Survey of the World's Trade with a Commercial Compendium and Gazetteer Index* (London: Royal Geographical Institute, 1912)
Poel, J. Van Der, *Railway and Customs Policies in South Africa, 1885-1910* (London: Longmans Green, 1933)
Polanyi, Karl, *Dahomey and the Slave Trade, An Analysis of an Archaic Economy* (Seattle: University of Washington Press, 1966)

Polanyi, Karl, *The Great Transformation. The Political and Economic Origins of Our Time,* 2nd ed (Boston: Beacon Press, 1967)
Portuguese Africa: A Handbook, eds David M. Abshire and Michael A. Samuels (London: Pall Mall Press, 1969)
Primitive, Archaic and Modern Economies. Essays of Karl Polyani, ed. George Dalton (Boston: Beacon Press, 1968)
Purcell, Victor, *The Chinese in Malaya* (London: Oxford University Press, 1948)
Purcell, Victor, *The Chinese in South-East Asia* (London: Oxford University Press, 1952)
Ray, Parimal, *India's Foreign Trade since 1870* (London: G. Routledge & Sons, 1934)
Remer, C.F., *The Foreign Trade of China* (Shanghai: Commercial Press, 1926)
Remer, C.F., *Foreign Investments in China* (New York: Macmillan, 1933)
Robequain, C., *The Economic Development of French Indo-China* (London: Oxford University Press, 1944)
Rudin, Harry R., *Germans in the Cameroons, 1884-1914, A Case Study in Modern Imperialism* (London: Jonathan Cape, 1938)
Sahni, J.N., *Indian Railways. One Hundred Years 1853-1953* (New Delhi: Ministry of Railways, 1953)
Sandberg, Lars G., *Lancashire in Decline. A Study in Entrepreneurship, Technology and International Trade* (Columbus: Ohio State University Press, 1974)
Sanyal, N., *Development of Indian Railways* (Calcutta: University of Calcutta, 1930)
Sarkar, N.K., *The Demography of Ceylon* (Colombo: Ceylon Government Press, 1957)
Saul, S.B., *Studies in British Overseas Trade, 1870-1914* (Liverpool: Liverpool University Press, 1960)
Saul, S.B., *The Myth of the Great Depression, 1873-1896* (London: Macmillan, 1969)
Schneider, Harold K., *Economic Man. The Anthropology of Economics* (New York: Free Press, 1974)
Schumpeter, J.A., *Business Cycles. A Theoretical, Historical and Statistical Analysis of the Capitalist Process,* 2 vols (New York: McGraw-Hill, 1939)
Shirras, G. Findlay, *Indian Finance and Banking* (London: Macmillan, 1919)
Simkin, C.G.F., *The Traditional Trade of Asia* (London: Oxford Univer-

sity Press, 1968)
Snodgrass, D.R., *Ceylon: An Export Economy in Transition* (Homewood, Illinois: Irwin, 1966)
Srinivas, M.N., *Caste in Modern India and Other Essays* (London: Asia Publishing House, 1962)
Srinivas, M.N., *Social Change in Modern India* (Berkeley: University of California Press, 1966)
Sun, E-tu Zen, *Chinese Railways and British Interests, 1898-1911* (New York: Kings Crown Press, 1954)
Suret-Canale, Jean, *French Colonialism in Tropical Africa, 1900-1945* (London: C. Hurst, 1971)
Szereszewski, R., *Structural Changes in the Economy of Ghana, 1891-1911* (London: Weidenfeld & Nicholson, 1965)
Tawney, R.H., *Religion and the Rise of Capitalism. An Historical Study* (London: Murray, 1926)
The Cambridge Economic History of Europe, eds H.J. Habakkuk and M. Postan, Vol.6 (Cambridge: Cambridge University Press, 1965)
The Economic Development of South-East Asia. Studies in Economic History and Political Economy. ed C.D. Cowan (London: George Allen & Unwin, 1964)
The Export of Capital from Britain, 1870-1914, ed A.R. Hall (London: Methuen, 1968)
The Oxford History of South Africa, eds Monica Wilson and Leonard Thompson (Oxford: Clarendon Press, 1971)
The Monetary Approach to the Balance of Payments, eds Jacob A. Frenkel and Harry G. Johnson (London: Allen & Unwin, 1976)
The Monetary Problem. Gold and Silver: Final Report of the Royal Commission Appointed to Inquire Into the Recent Changes in the Relative Values of the Precious Metals, Presented to Both Houses of Parliament, 1888, ed R. Robey (New York: Colombia University Press, 1936)
The Rise of Capitalism, ed D.S. Landes (New York: Macmillan, 1966)
Thomas, Brinley, *Migration and Urban Development: A Re-appraisal of British and American Long Cycles* (London: Methuen, 1972)
Triffin, Robert, *The Evolution of the International Monetary System: Historical Re-appraisal and Future Perspectives* (Princeton: Princeton University Press, 1964)
Tropical Development 1880-1913. Studies in Economic Progress, ed W.A. Lewis (London: George Allen & Unwin, 1970)
Walker, F.A., *International Bimetallism* (London: Macmillan, 1896)
Westwood, J.N., *Railways of India* (Newton Abbot: David & Charles,

1974)
White, Benjamin, *Silver: Its History and Romance* (London: Hodder & Stoughton, 1917)
White, Benjamin, *Gold: Its Place in the Economy of Mankind* (London: Pitman, 1920)
Widjojo, Nitisastro, *Population Trends in Indonesia* (Ithaca: Cornell University Press, 1971)
Wiener, Lionel, *Les chemins de fer coloniaux de l'Afrique* (Bruxelles: Goemaere, 1931)
Willis, H.P., *A History of the Latin Monetary Union,* 2nd ed (New York: Greenwood Press, 1968)
Woodruff, William, *Impact of Western Man. A Study of Europe's Role in the World Economy, 1750-1960* (New York: St Martin's Press, 1966)
Yang, Lien-sheng, *Money and Credit in China. A Short History* (Cambridge, Mass: Harvard University Press, 1965)
Yates, P. Lamartine, *Forty Years of Foreign Trade. A Statistical Handbook with Special Reference to Primary Products and Under Developed Countries* (London: George Allen & Unwin, 1959)
Zachariah, K.C., *A Historical Study of Internal Migration in the Indian Sub-Continent 1901-1931* (Bombay: Asia Publishing House, 1964)
Zwanenburg, R.M.A. van with Anne King, *An Economic History of Kenya and Uganda, 1800-1970* (London: Macmillan, 1975)

Articles

Abshire, David M., 'From the Scramble for Africa to the "New State" ' in *Portuguese Africa: A Handbook,* David M. Abshire and Michael A. Samuels (eds), (London: Pall Mall Press, 1969), pp.60-90
Aldcroft, D.H., 'Introduction' in D.H. Aldcroft and Peter Fearon (eds), *British Economic Fluctuations* (London: Macmillan, 1972), pp.1-73
Arrighi, G., 'Labour Supplies in Historical Perspective: A Study of the Proletarianisation of the African Peasantry in Rhodesia', *The Journal of Development Studies,* 6 (1970), pp.197-234
Bhatia, B.M., 'Terms of Trade and Economic Development: A Case Study of India, 1861-1939', *Indian Economic Journal,* 14 (1969), pp.414-433
Blythe, W.L., 'Historical Sketch of Chinese Labour in Malaya,' *Journal of the Malayan Branch of the Royal Asiatic Society,* 20 (1947), pp.64-114
Bohannan, P., 'Some Principles of Exchange and Investment among the Tiv', *American Anthropologist,* 67 (1955), pp.60-70

Bohannan, P., 'The Impact of Money on an African Subsistence Economy', *Journal of Economic History,* 19 (1959), pp.491-503

Bundy, C., 'The Emergence and Decline of a South African Peasantry', *African Affairs,* 71 (1972), pp.369-388

Caldwell, J.A.M., 'Indonesian Export and Production from the Decline of the Culture System to the First World War', in C.D. Cowan (ed), *The Economic Development of South-East Asia* (London: George Allen & Unwin, 1964), pp.72-101

Clauson, G.L.M., 'The British Colonial Currency System', *The Economic Journal,* 54 (1944), pp.1-25

Dalton, George, Review of A.G. Hopkins, *An Economic History of West Africa, African Economic History Review,* 1 (1976), pp.51-101

Davies, P.N., 'The African Steam Ship Company', in J.R. Harris (ed), *Liverpool and Merseyside: Essays in the Economic and Social History of the Port and its Hinterland* (London: Cass, 1969), pp.212-238.

Durand, John D., 'The Population Statistics of China AD 2-1953', *Population Studies,* 13 (1959-60), pp.209-256

Ehrlich, Cyril, 'The Uganda Economy, 1903-45', in V. Harlow and E.M. Chilver (eds), *History of East Africa*, Vol.2 (Oxford: Clarendon Press, 1965), pp.395-475.

Explorations in Economic History, 11 (1974), pp.317-444

Fairlie, J.A., 'The Economic Effects of Ship Canals', *American Academy of Political and Social Science, Annals,* Jan. (1898), pp.54-78

Fletcher, Max E., 'The Suez Canal and World Shipping, 1869-1914', *Journal of Economic History,* 18 (1958), pp.556-573

Ford, A.G., 'Notes on the Role of Exports in British Economic Fluctuations, 1870-1914', *Economic History Review,* 16 (1963), pp.332-337

Ford, A.G., 'Overseas Lending and Internal Fluctuations, 1870-1914', in A.R. Hall (ed), *The Export of Capital from Britain 1870-1914* (London: Methuen, 1968), pp.84-102

Glass, D.V., and E. Grebenik, 'World Population in 1800-1950', in H.J. Habakkuk and M. Postan (eds), *The Cambridge Economic History of Europe*, Vol.6, (Cambridge: Cambridge University Press, 1965), pp.60-138

Graham, G.S., 'The Ascendency of the Sailing Ship, 1850-85', *Economic History Review,* 9 (1956), pp.74-88

Hammond, R.J., 'Uneconomic Imperialism: Portugal in Africa before 1910', in L.H. Gann and Peter Duignan (eds), *Colonialism in Africa, 1870-1960,* Vol.1 (Cambridge: Cambridge University Press, 1969), pp.352-382

Harley, C.K., 'The Shift from Sailing Ships to Steamships, 1850-1890: A Study in Technology Change and its Diffusion', in D.N. McCloskey (ed), *Essays on a Mature Economy: Britain after 1840* (London: Methuen, 1971), pp.215-237

Henderson, W.O., 'German East Africa, 1884-1918', in V. Harlow and E.M. Chilver (eds), *History of East Africa,* Vol.2 (Oxford: Clarendon Press, 1965), pp.123-162

Hopkins, A.G., 'The Creation of a Colonial Monetary System: The Origins of the West African Currency Board', *African Historical Studies,* 3 (1970), pp.101-132

Hopkins, A.G., 'The Currency Revolution in South-West Nigeria in the Late Nineteenth Century', *Journal of the Historical Society of Nigeria,* 3 (1966), pp.471-483

Houghton, D.H., 'Economic Development', in Monica Wilson and Leonard Thompson (eds), *The Oxford History of South Africa,* Vol.2 (Oxford: Clarendon Press, 1971), pp.1-48

Ingram, J.C., 'Thailand's Rice Trade and the Allocation of Resources', in *The Economic Development of South-East Asia* (London: George Allen & Unwin, 1964), pp.102-126

Johnson, Marion, 'The Ounce in Eighteenth-Century West African Trade', *Journal of African History,* 7 (1966), pp.197-214

Johnson, Marion, 'The Cowrie Currencies of West Africa', *Journal of African History,* 11 (1970), pp.17-49, 331-53

Ken Wong, Lin, 'Western Enterprise and the Development of the Malayan Tin Industry to 1914', in C.D. Cowan (ed), *The Economic Development of South-East Asia,* (London: George Allen & Unwin, 1964), pp.127-153

Knoll, Arthur J., 'Taxation in the Gold Coast Colony and in Togo: A Study in Early Administration', in Prosser Gifford and W.M. Roger Louis (eds), *Britain and Germany in Africa: Imperial Rivalry and Colonial Rule* (New Haven: Yale University Press, 1967), pp.417-453

Kuznets, Simon, 'Long Swings in Population Growth and Related Economic Variables', in S. Kuznets, *Economic Growth and Structure: Selected Essays* (London: Heinemann, 1965), pp.328-79

Kondratieff, N.B., 'The Long Waves in Economic Life', *The Review of Economic Statistics,* 17 (1935), pp.105-115

Kuper, Leo, 'African Nationalism in South Africa, 1910-1964', in Monica Wilson and Leonard Thompson (eds), *The Oxford History of South Africa,* Vol.2 (Oxford: Clarendon Press, 1971), pp.424-476

Landes, D.S., 'Introduction', in D.S. Landes (ed), *The Rise of Capitalism*

(New York: Macmillan, 1966), pp.1-25

Latham, A.J.H., 'Currency, Credit and Capitalism on the Cross River in the Pre-Colonial Era', *Journal of African History,* 12 (1971), pp.599-605

Latham, A.J.H., 'Witchcraft Accusations and Economic Tension in Pre-Colonial Old Calabar', *Journal of African History,* 13 (1972), pp.249-60

Latham, A.J.H., 'A Trading Alliance: Sir John Tobin and Duke Ephraim', *History Today,* Dec. (1974), pp.862-867

Mangolte, Jacques, 'Le chemin de fer de Konakry au Niger, (1890-1914)', *Revue Francaise d'Histoire d'Outre-Mer,* 55 (1968), pp.37-105

McCloskey, Donald N., and J. Richard Zecher, 'How the Gold Standard Worked', in Jacob A. Frenkel and Harry G. Johnson (eds), *The Monetary Approach to the Balance of payments* (London: Allen & Unwin, 1976), pp.357-385

Morris, M.D., 'Towards a Re-interpretation of Nineteenth Century Indian History', *The Indian Economic and Social History Review,* 5 (1968), pp.1-15

Morris, M.D. and G.B. Dudley, 'Selected Railway Statistics for the Indian Subcontinent, 1853-1946/7', *Artha Vijnana,* 17 (1975), pp.187-304

Nugent, J.B., 'Exchange-Rate Movements and Economic Developments in the Late Nineteenth Century', *Journal of Political Economy,* 81 (1973), pp.1110-1135

Paish, George, 'Great Britain's Capital Investments in Individual Colonial and Foreign Countries', *Journal of the Royal Statistical Society,* 74 (1911), pp.167-199

Phimister, I.R., 'Peasant Production and Underdevelopment in Southern Rhodesia, 1890-1914', *African Affairs,* 73 (1974), pp.217-228

Rajaratnam, S., 'The Growth of Plantation Agriculture in Ceylon, 1886-1931', *Ceylon Journal of Historical and Social Studies,* Jan-June (1961), pp.1-19

Rajaratnam, S., 'The Ceylon Tea Industry, 1886-1931', *Ceylon Journal of Historical and Social Studies,* July-Dec. (1961), pp.169-202

Raum, O.F. II, 'German East Africa. Changes in African Life under German Administration, 1892-1914', in V. Harlow and E.M. Chilver (eds), *History of East Africa,* Vol.2 (Oxford: Clarendon Press, 1965), pp.163-208

Remer, C.F., 'International Trade between Gold and Silver Countries: China 1885-1913', *Quarterly Journal of Economics,* 40 (1926), pp.597-643

Saini, Krishnan G., 'The Growth of the Indian Economy: 1860-1960', *Review of Income and Wealth,* 15 (1969), pp.247-263

Sandhu, K.S., 'Some Preliminary Observations of the Origins and Characteristics of the Indian Migration to Malaya, 1786-1957', in K.G. Tregonning (ed), *Papers on Malayan History* (Singapore: *Journal of South-East Asian History,* 1962), pp.40-72

Simon, Mathew, 'The Pattern of New British Portfolio Foreign Investment, 1865-1914', in A.R. Hall (ed), *The Export of Capital from Britain 1870-1914,* (London: Methuen, 1968), pp.15-44

Singer, H.W., 'Economic Progress in Underdeveloped Countries', *Social Research,* 16 (1949), pp.1-11

Singh, H.L., 'The Indian Currency Problem, 1885-1900', *Bengal Past and Present,* 80 (1961), pp.16-37

Stillson, R.T., 'The Financing of Malayan Rubber 1905-1923', *Economic History Review,* 24 (1971), pp.589-598

Stover, Charles C., 'Tropical Exports', in W.A. Lewis (ed), *Tropical Development 1880-1913, Studies in Economic Progress* (London: George Allen & Unwin, 1970), pp.46-63

Thorner, D., 'Great Britain and the Development of India's Railways', *Journal of Economic History,* 11 (1951), pp.389-402

Williams, David, 'The Evolution of the Sterling System', in C.R. Whittlesey and J.S.G. Wilson (eds), *Essays in Money and Banking in Honour of R.S. Sayers* (Oxford: Clarendon Press, 1968), pp.266-297

Wright, C.P., 'India as a Producer and Exporter of Wheat', *Wheat Studies,* 3 (1926-7), pp.317-412

Wrigley, C.C., 'Kenya: The Patterns of Economic Life, 1902-1945', in V. Harlow and E.M. Chilver (eds), *History of East Africa,* Vol.2 (Oxford: Clarendon Press, 1965), pp.209-264

Zimmerman, L.J., 'The Distribution of World Income, 1860-1960', in Egbert De Vries (eds), *Essays on Unbalanced Growth* ('S-Gravenhage: Mouton & Co. 1962), pp.28-55

Periodical Publications

Fairplay

Railway Year Book

Statistical Abstracts for British India

Statistical Abstracts for the British Colonies

The Economist

ADDITIONAL READING

Articles

Adas, Michael, 'Immigrant Asians and the Economic Impact of European Imperialism: The Role of the South Indian Chettiars in British Burma', *Journal of Asian Studies,* 33 (1974), pp.385-401

Soff, Harvey, G., 'Indian influence on Kenya's Nyanza Province 1900-1925', *Journal of Indian History,* 46 (1968), pp.369-386

Books

Adas, Michael, *The Burma Delta: Economic Development and Social Change on an Asian Rice Frontier, 1852-1941* (Madison, Wisc.: University of Wisconsin Press, 1974)

Bagchi, A.K., *Private Investment in India 1900-1939* (Cambridge: Cambridge University Press, 1972)

Bhattacharyya, Dhires, *A Concise History of the Indian Economy* (Calcutta: Progressive Publishers, 1972)

Cheng, Siok-Hwa, *The Rice Industry of Burma, 1852-1940* (Singapore: University of Malaya Press, 1968)

Gadgil, D.R., *The Industrial Evolution of India in Recent Times, 1860-1939,* 5th ed (Bombay: Oxford University Press, 1971)

Mangat, J.S., *A History of the Asians in East Africa, c.1886-1945* (Oxford: Clarendon Press, 1969)

Macpherson, W.J., 'Economic Development in India under the British Crown, 1858-1947', in A.J. Youngson (ed), *Economic Development in the Long Run* (London: George Allen & Unwin, 1972), pp.126-191

Kumar, Dharma, *Land and Caste in South India: Agricultural Labour in the Madras Presidency during the Nineteenth Century* (Cambridge: Cambridge University Press, 1965)

Sandhu, K.S., *Indians in Malaya: Immiggation and Settlement, 1786-1957* (Cambridge: Cambridge University Press, 1969)

APPENDICES

Appendix 1: Freight Rates 1869-1913 (shillings)

	Homeward freights (lowest fix)		Outward freights (lowest fix)	
	Java-UK or Continent (sugar, etc.)	Burma-UK or Continent (rice, etc.)	Wales-Singapore (coals)	Wales-Bombay-(coals)
1869	57/6	60/-	24/-	—
1870	55/-	52/6	25/-	25/-
1871	60/-	60/-	20/-	22/-
1872	60/-	65/-	23/-	23/-
1873	95/-	72/6	26/-	24/-
1874	—	82/6	22/6	22/-
1875	—	72/6	—	—
1876	75/-	62/6	17/6	18/-
1877	70/-	65/-	19/-	17/6
1878	55/-	30/-	22/6	23/-
1879	60/-	40/-	24/-	25/-
1880	72/6	52/6	19/-	20/-
1881	75/-	56/3	17/-	14/6
1882	52/6	47/6	17/-	14/6
1883	47/6	41/3	20/-	14/6
1884	35/-	27/6	19/-	14/6
1885	32/6	30/-	16/6	14/3
1886	30/-	27/6	15/9	12/6
1887	32/6	30/-	16/6	14/-
1888	35/-	30/-	22/-	18/6
1889	42/6	30/-	19/3	14/9
1890	32/6	27/6	15/3	13/-
1891	31/3	32/6	10/3	6/9
1892	27/6	22/6	10/3	8/6
1893	27/6	22/6	10/6	7/6
1894	32/6	26/3	9/3	6/9
1895	25/-	21/3	9/-	7/3
1896	20/-	12/6	14/-	11/-
1897	22/6	15/-	12/6	10/6
1898	27/6	23/9	13/6	11/-
1899	27/6	22/6	12/6	11/-
1900	30/9	23/9	15/6	14/6
1901	20/6	20/-	12/-	9/-
1902	20/-	15/-	11/-	8/3
1903	20/6	20/-	8/3	9/-
1904	22/6	20/-	7/6	6/-
1905	21/9	16/3	8/-	6/6
1906	19/6	13/9	10/-	8/-
1907	25/-	20/-	10/-	8/-
1908	21/3	10/6	9/-	9/6
1909	24/-	17/6	8/-	7/-
1910	20/-	18/9	9/-	7/6
1911	25/-	21/3	12/3	8/9
1912	29/9	27/6	14/9	9/3
1913	—	22/6	11/6	10/6

Source: *Fairplay,* Jan.-June 1920

Appendix 2: The Fall of Silver and Silver Currencies, 1872-1913 (pence)

Year	Annual average price of bar silver per oz in London	Annual average exchange rate of Haikwan tael	Annual average exchange rate of rupee
1872	60.31	79.75	23.12
1873	59.25	77.00	22.75
1874	58.31	76.12	22.35
1875	56.88	74.20	22.22
1876	52.75	71.40	21.64
1877	54.81	72.00	20.49
1878	52.56	71.55	20.79
1879	51.25	67.33	19.76
1880	52.25	69.62	19.96
1881	51.69	66.50	19.95
1882	51.63	68.50	19.89
1883	50.56	67.25	19.52
1884	50.63	67.00	19.53
1885	48.63	63.50	19.30
1886	45.38	60.12	18.25
1887	44.13	58.25	17.44
1888	42.88	56.37	16.89
1889	42.69	56.75	16.39
1890	47.69	62.25	16.56
1891	45.06	59.00	18.08
1892	39.81	52.25	16.73
1893	35.63	47.25	14.98
1894	28.94	38.37	14.54
1895	29.88	39.25	13.10
1896	30.75	40.00	13.63
1897	27.56	35.75	14.45
1898	26.94	34.62	15.40
1899	27.44	36.12	15.97
1900	28.25	37.25	16.06
1901	27.19	35.56	15.97
1902	24.06	31.20	15.98
1903	24.75	31.66	16.00
1904	26.38	34.40	16.04
1905	27.81	36.06	16.04
1906	30.88	39.50	16.04
1907	30.19	39.00	16.08
1908	24.38	32.00	16.02
1909	23.69	31.18	15.96
1910	24.63	32.31	16.04
1911	24.56	32.25	16.06
1912	28.03	36.62	16.08
1913	27.56	36.25	16.05

Source: G. F. Shirras, *Indian Finance and Banking* (London: Macmillan, 1919), pp.449-50, Table 6, 458, Table 12; C. F. Remer, *The Foreign Trade of China* (Shanghai: Commercial Press, 1926), p.250, Table 6.

Appendix 3: New British Portfolio Foreign Investment, 1865-1914 (£ million)

Year	Africa	Asia	Africa & Asia	Total World	Africa & Asia as % total
1865	8.5	11.2	19.7	42.5	46.35
1866	4.1	4.5	8.6	25.3	33.99
1867	0.5	7.5	8.0	18.3	43.71
1868	1.5	8.1	9.6	29.1	32.98
1869	–	6.3	6.3	21.9	28.76
1870	2.2	7.1	9.3	44.8	20.75
1871	0.4	3.7	4.1	70.2	5.84
1872	1.9	2.2	4.1	94.0	4.36
1873	1.2	4.1	5.3	68.7	7.71
1874	0.5	5.9	6.4	74.5	8.59
1875	4.5	4.0	8.5	46.1	18.43
1876	2.1	5.1	7.2	30.4	23.68
1877	1.7	6.7	8.4	19.5	43.07
1878	3.2	5.0	8.2	31.7	25.86
1879	5.6	0.7	6.3	30.3	20.79
1880	2.7	3.2	5.9	41.7	14.14
1881	5.8	10.6	16.4	73.9	22.19
1882	4.5	9.4	13.9	67.5	20.59
1883	2.6	4.6	7.2	61.3	11.74
1884	6.7	5.8	12.5	63.1	19.80
1885	4.7	11.0	15.7	55.2	28.44
1886	2.5	9.6	12.1	69.9	17.31
1887	1.5	10.5	12.0	84.4	13.57
1888	4.2	10.7	14.9	119.1	12.51
1889	8.9	11.2	20.1	122.9	16.35
1890	4.6	10.8	15.4	116.6	13.20
1891	6.6	5.7	12.3	58.1	21.17
1892	3.3	4.1	7.4	39.8	18.59
1893	2.6	2.5	5.1	32.2	15.83
1894	5.2	13.1	18.3	48.3	37.88
1895	14.9	10.4	25.3	77.7	32.56
1896	9.6	15.4	25.0	68.5	36.49
1897	10.8	27.2	38.0	78.4	48.46
1898	11.6	21.1	32.7	76.5	42.74
1899	21.3	21.7	43.0	78.1	55.05
1900	7.2	11.9	19.1	49.8	38.35
1901	9.2	4.6	13.8	49.6	27.82
1902	24.7	10.8	35.5	89.4	39.70
1903	42.4	6.6	49.0	82.7	59.25
1904	32.0	15.2	47.2	88.1	53.57
1905	29.9	35.6	65.5	128.9	50.81
1906	10.5	15.8	26.3	85.0	30.94
1907	9.5	23.4	32.9	116.3	28.28
1908	13.9	29.6	43.5	147.4	29.51
1909	18.7	25.4	44.1	175.6	25.11
1910	16.3	32.9	49.2	198.1	24.83
1911	9.4	24.7	34.1	169.1	20.16
1912	9.8	21.5	31.3	200.7	15.59
1913	8.1	17.4	25.5	217.5	11.72
1914	12.9	16.4	29.3	203.4	14.40

Source: Mathew Simon, 'The Pattern of New British Portfolio Foreign Investment, 1865-1914', in *The Export of Capital from Britain, 1870-1914*, ed. A. R. Hall (London: Methuen & Co., 1968), pp.39-40, Appendix Table.

Appendix 4: Indian Trade (by Sea), 1864-1914 (rupees x 10 million)

Year*	Merchandise exports	Merchandise imports	Trade surplus	Net treasure inflow	Net gold inflow
1864	65.6	27.1	38.4	21.6	8.8
1865	68.0	28.1	39.8	19.9	9.8
1866	65.4	29.5	35.8	24.3	5.7
1867	41.8	29.0	12.8	10.8	3.8
1868	50.8	35.7	15.1	10.2	4.6
1869	53.0	35.9	17.0	13.7	5.1
1870	52.4	32.9	19.5	12.9	5.5
1871	55.3	34.4	20.8	3.2	2.2
1872	63.2	32.0	31.1	10.0	3.5
1873	55.2	31.8	23.3	3.2	2.5
1874	54.9	33.8	21.1	3.8	1.3
1875	56.3	36.2	20.1	6.5	1.8
1876	58.0	38.8	19.1	3.1	1.5
1877	61.0	37.4	23.5	7.4	0.2
1878	65.2	41.4	23.7	15.1	0.4
1879	60.9	37.8	23.1	3.0	0.8
1880	67.2	41.1	26.0	9.6	1.7
1881	74.5	53.1	21.4	7.5	3.6
1882	81.9	49.1	32.8	10.2	4.8
1883	83.4	52.0	31.3	12.4	4.9
1884	88.1	55.2	32.8	11.8	5.4
1885	83.2	55.7	27.5	11.9	4.6
1886	83.8	55.6	28.2	14.3	2.7
1887	88.4	61.7	26.6	9.3	2.1
1888	90.5	65.0	25.5	12.2	2.9
1889	97.0	69.4	27.6	12.0	2.8
1890	103.4	69.1	34.2	15.5	4.6
1891	100.2	71.9	28.2	19.8	5.6
1892	108.1	69.4	38.7	11.4	2.4
1893	106.5	66.2	40.3	10.0	−2.8
1894	106.5	77.0	29.4	14.3	0.6
1895	108.9	73.5	35.3	1.3	−4.9
1896	114.3	72.9	41.3	9.1	2.5
1897	103.9	76.1	27.8	8.1	2.2
1898	97.6	73.6	23.9	13.3	4.9
1899	112.7	72.1	40.6	10.4	6.5
1900	109.0	75.3	33.7	13.0	9.4
1901	107.7	80.8	26.8	10.3	0.8
1902	124.8	88.7	36.1	9.1	1.9
1903	129.3	85.8	43.5	15.7	8.7
1904	153.5	92.5	60.9	23.5	9.7
1905	157.7	104.4	53.3	22.9	9.7
1906	161.8	112.1	49.7	16.1	0.4
1907	177.0	118.1	58.9	38.8	14.8
1908	177.4	136.6	40.8	36.8	17.3
1909	153.1	128.7	24.3	16.4	4.3
1910	187.9	122.6	65.3	31.1	21.6
1911	209.9	133.7	76.2	32.6	23.9
1912	227.9	144.0	83.9	43.0	37.7
1913	246.2	166.6	79.5	51.1	34.0
1914	249.0	191.3	57.6	36.3	23.3

* Year ended 30th April up to and including 1866-1867 onwards year ended 31st March.

Source: *Statistical Abstracts for British India.*

Appendix 5: Indian Balance of Private Merchandise Trade with Major Regions, 1868-1914 (rupees x 10 million)

Year ending 31st March	UK	Europe	Africa	America	Asia	Australasia	Total*
1868	−3.2	2.2	0.1	1.1	15.1	−0.2	15.2
1869	−1.4	4.0	0.3	1.4	12.9	−0.1	17.1
1870	1.1	4.6	0.0	1.5	12.6	−0.3	19.5
1871	2.2	3.4	0.5	2.5	13.3	−0.1	21.9
1872	7.3	7.0	0.2	2.3	15.6	−0.1	32.3
1873	3.0	4.6	0.8	2.1	14.0	0.0	24.7
1874	1.8	5.1	0.3	2.0	13.8	0.0	23.3
1875	−1.6	6.7	0.8	1.9	13.7	0.0	21.6
1876	−2.4	7.1	0.3	1.8	13.9	0.0	20.9
1877	−1.7	8.3	1.2	1.9	15.7	0.0	25.5
1878	−2.5	9.4	1.2	1.9	15.5	0.1	25.8
1879	−3.0	6.7	0.6	2.1	17.4	0.3	24.3
1880	−4.6	8.7	1.4	3.1	18.3	0.2	27.4
1881	−10.2	12.0	1.6	2.4	17.9	0.4	24.2
1882	−3.6	16.1	1.9	2.5	17.3	0.5	34.9
1883	−4.9	16.3	2.4	2.8	16.1	0.6	33.3
1884	−5.8	18.0	4.3	3.1	15.7	0.0	35.4
1885	−8.5	17.1	2.4	2.7	15.9	0.3	30.0
1886	−7.3	16.1	3.5	2.7	16.6	0.1	32.0
1887	−12.4	19.1	2.3	2.5	18.0	0.1	29.7
1888	−13.9	17.7	3.1	3.3	17.1	0.6	28.0
1889	−15.1	19.8	3.1	3.1	18.4	0.8	30.4
1890	−11.1	21.2	4.4	2.9	18.5	0.6	37.5
1891	−19.3	20.4	5.1	3.3	20.5	0.9	31.0
1892	−13.7	22.2	8.0	3.9	20.2	0.6	41.4
1893	−10.6	21.2	5.9	5.0	21.5	0.8	43.9
1894	−17.3	25.1	4.4	2.6	16.7	0.2	32.4
1895	−17.2	20.9	5.4	6.6	21.7	1.0	38.6
1896	−11.0	18.8	6.3	6.1	23.5	0.9	44.9
1897	−17.6	13.8	6.2	5.0	23.9	0.7	32.1
1898	−16.2	10.7	5.0	6.3	21.5	0.9	28.2
1899	−14.1	11.7	8.3	5.5	27.0	0.9	44.3
1900	−17.0	12.2	6.4	8.1	27.2	1.1	38.2
1901	−16.6	12.3	5.2	7.5	21.4	1.1	31.0
1902	−21.4	14.4	6.5	9.2	32.9	1.3	42.9
1903	−19.9	19.3	9.0	9.6	30.9	0.9	50.0
1904	−13.8	32.0	1.8	10.7	35.9	1.2	68.1
1905	−19.9	29.1	2.2	11.9	36.5	0.8	60.8
1906	−28.0	27.6	2.6	14.9	39.9	1.4	58.6
1907	−24.3	37.7	3.1	16.8	32.9	2.1	68.6
1908	−40.8	40.3	2.5	14.9	27.8	2.5	47.3
1909	−39.0	26.5	2.3	14.2	25.6	1.9	31.7
1910	−24.1	42.6	2.1	14.9	32.7	2.4	70.8
1911	−27.0	49.9	2.4	14.3	38.1	2.6	80.5
1912	−26.3	51.3	4.1	14.5	43.1	2.4	89.2
1913	−39.6	52.2	2.9	20.5	46.1	2.8	85.0
1914	−59.2	55.0	3.7	24.1	37.8	4.0	65.6

*The difference between the total in this table, and the trade surplus recorded in Appendix 6, Indian Trade, is accounted for by Government transactions not included here. The columns do not add up to the total because of rounding.

Source: *Statistical Abstracts for British India.*

Appendix 6: Indian Trade Balances with Asia (by Sea), 1868-1914 (rupees x 10 million)

Year ending 31st March	Ceylon	China	Japan	Java	Straits	Others	Total*
1868	0.7	12.8	–	–	0.6	0.9	15.1
1869	0.8	10.3	–	–	0.5	1.2	12.9
1870	0.9	10.8	–	–	0.4	0.4	12.6
1871	0.8	10.7	0.0	0.0	0.8	0.9	13.3
1872	0.8	12.4	0.0	0.0	1.3	1.0	15.6
1873	1.0	10.7	0.0	0.0	1.2	0.9	14.0
1874	1.4	10.0	0.0	0.0	1.2	1.0	13.8
1875	1.0	10.1	0.0	0.0	1.3	1.1	13.7
1876	1.1	9.9	0.0	0.0	1.6	1.1	13.9
1877	1.7	11.5	0.0	0.0	1.4	0.9	15.7
1878	2.0	11.3	0.0	0.0	1.5	0.7	15.5
1879	2.3	12.2	0.0	0.0	1.5	1.1	17.4
1880	1.5	13.9	−0.1	0.0	1.4	1.5	18.3
1881	1.2	12.9	0.0	0.0	1.6	1.9	17.9
1882	1.2	12.0	0.1	0.0	1.9	1.8	17.3
1883	0.8	11.0	0.2	0.0	2.0	1.8	16.1
1884	0.9	11.0	0.2	0.0	1.4	1.9	15.7
1885	1.4	10.6	0.0	0.0	1.7	2.0	15.9
1886	1.4	10.8	0.2	0.0	2.0	2.1	16.6
1887	1.3	11.2	0.3	0.0	2.5	2.5	18.0
1888	1.4	10.6	0.6	0.0	2.0	2.2	17.1
1889	1.5	12.2	1.0	0.0	2.0	1.5	18.4
1890	1.6	11.4	1.1	0.0	2.3	1.8	18.5
1891	1.9	12.0	1.0	0.0	3.4	2.0	20.5
1892	2.2	10.9	1.2	0.0	2.8	2.9	20.2
1893	2.6	11.7	1.5	0.0	2.3	3.3	21.5
1894	2.5	7.5	1.1	0.0	2.3	3.1	16.7
1895	2.9	10.0	1.3	−0.1	3.5	3.8	21.7
1896	3.1	11.1	2.4	0.0	4.1	2.6	23.5
1897	2.5	11.6	3.4	0.0	4.5	1.7	23.9
1898	3.0	10.5	3.6	0.0	2.1	2.2	21.5
1899	3.6	11.1	4.6	−0.1	3.9	3.7	27.0
1900	3.6	12.6	5.8	−0.2	3.8	1.4	27.2
1901	4.1	9.2	1.2	0.0	4.7	2.0	21.4
1902	3.6	15.8	6.2	0.0	4.2	2.8	32.9
1903	3.8	13.7	4.9	−0.1	5.4	3.0	30.9
1904	4.0	16.0	7.1	−0.7	4.9	4.5	35.9
1905	4.4	17.7	8.5	−1.5	3.4	3.9	36.5
1906	5.0	19.7	8.6	−0.7	3.8	3.5	39.9
1907	5.6	17.5	5.4	−2.3	3.8	2.7	32.9
1908	5.2	12.9	6.6	−4.6	4.0	3.5	27.8
1909	5.2	15.6	5.0	−5.5	2.1	3.0	25.6
1910	5.8	16.1	10.1	−6.4	3.2	3.8	32.7
1911	7.2	16.7	10.1	−5.4	4.6	4.7	38.1
1912	7.8	15.8	13.2	−5.2	5.8	5.5	43.1
1913	8.4	17.4	14.6	−6.2	6.1	5.7	46.1
1914	8.2	10.8	17.9	−8.8	3.3	6.3	37.8

* The columns do not add up to the total because of rounding.

Source: *Statistical Abstracts for British India.*

Appendix 7: Chinese Balance of Trade, 1868-1914 (Haikwan taels x 1 million)

Year	Exports	Imports	Balance
1868	61.8	63.2	–1.4
1869	60.1	67.1	–6.9
1870	55.2	63.6	–8.3
1871	66.8	70.1	–3.2
1872	75.2	67.3	+7.9
1873	69.4	66.6	+2.8
1874	66.7	64.3	+2.3
1875	68.9	67.8	+1.1
1876	80.8	70.2	+10.5
1877	67.4	73.2	–5.7
1878	67.1	70.8	–3.6
1879	72.2	82.2	–9.9
1880	77.8	79.2	–1.4
1881	71.4	91.9	–20.4
1882	67.3	77.7	–10.3
1883	70.1	73.5	–3.3
1884	67.1	72.7	–5.6
1885	65.0	88.2	–23.1
1886	77.2	87.4	–10.2
1887	85.8	102.2	–16.4
1888	92.4	124.7	–32.3
1889	96.9	110.8	–13.9
1890	87.1	127.0	–39.9
1891	100.9	134.0	–33.0
1892	102.5	135.1	–32.5
1893	116.6	151.3	–34.7
1894	128.1	162.1	–33.9
1895	143.2	171.6	–28.4
1896	131.0	202.5	–71.5
1897	163.5	202.8	–39.3
1898	159.0	209.5	–50.5
1899	195.7	264.7	–68.9
1900	158.9	211.0	–52.0
1901	169.6	268.3	–98.6
1902	214.1	315.3	–101.1
1903	214.3	326.7	–112.3
1904	239.4	344.0	–104.5
1905	227.8	447.1	–219.2
1906	236.4	410.2	–173.8
1907	264.3	416.4	–152.0
1908	276.6	394.5	–117.8
1909	338.9	418.1	–79.1
1910	380.8	462.9	–82.1
1911	377.3	471.5	–94.1
1912	370.5	473.0	–102.5
1913	403.3	570.1	–166.8
1914	356.2	569.2	–213.0

Source: Ping-Yin Ho, *The Foreign Trade of China* (Shanghai: Commercial Press, 1935), pp.15-16, 20-2.

Appendix 8: Chinese Treasure Balances, 1888-1913 (Haikwan taels x 1 million)

	Gold	Silver	Gold and silver
1888	−1.6	−1.9	−3.5
1889	−1.6	+6.0	+4.3
1890	−1.7	−3.5	−5.3
1891	−3.6	−3.1	−6.8
1892	−7.3	−4.8	−12.1
1893	−7.4	+10.8	+3.3
1894	−12.7	+26.3	+13.6
1895	−6.6	+36.6	+30.0
1896	−8.1	+1.7	−6.3
1897	−8.5	+1.6	−6.8
1898	−7.7	+4.7	−2.9
1899	−7.6	+1.2	−6.3
1900	+1.2	+15.4	+16.6
1901	−6.6	−6.0	−12.7
1902	−9.4	−13.8	−23.2
1903	–	−6.0	−6.0
1904	+8.4	−13.6	−5.1
1905	+7.0	−7.1	−0.1
1906	+3.8	−18.6	−14.8
1907	+2.4	−31.2	−28.7
1908	−11.5	−12.2	−23.7
1909	−6.8	+6.8	0.0
1910	+0.1	+21.7	+21.9
1911	+1.5	+38.3	+39.8
1912	+7.4	+19.2	+26.7
1913	−1.3	+35.9	+34.5

Source: C. F. Remer, 'International Trade between Gold and Silver Countries: China 1895-1913', *Quarterly Journal of Economics,* 40 (1926), p.630.

Appendix 9: Chinese Trade Balances with Major Countries, 1868-1914
(Haikwan taels x 1 million)

Year	UK	India	Hong Kong	Japan	US	Others
1868	16.3	–22.9	–5.9	–1.4	5.1	7.3
1869	7.0	–17.5	–8.1	–0.7	6.7	5.7
1870	4.8	–17.6	–9.0	1.1	7.2	5.0
1871	9.7	–18.5	–11.5	–0.7	–9.9	7.9
1872	12.4	–16.2	–8.8	–1.5	11.5	10.5
1873	16.2	–14.3	–17.1	–2.0	7.2	12.8
1874	13.5	–17.4	–12.3	–0.6	6.1	13.0
1875	8.0	–14.6	–14.7	–0.5	6.6	16.3
1876	14.3	–16.4	–12.8	–1.4	6.5	20.4
1877	7.7	–19.1	–12.3	–1.6	6.8	12.7
1878	12.6	–20.7	–12.4	–2.3	4.3	14.9
1879	5.7	–24.1	–12.2	–1.1	6.4	15.3
1880	5.9	–19.6	–13.6	–1.2	7.9	19.2
1881	–1.0	–26.3	–13.5	–1.9	6.9	15.3
1882	3.5	–17.7	–12.5	–2.6	5.1	13.9
1883	7.6	–16.5	–10.2	–2.3	4.6	13.5
1884	2.5	–15.7	–13.5	–1.8	5.8	17.0
1885	–1.9	–15.5	–19.3	–3.7	4.9	12.5
1886	–2.2	–16.4	–12.3	–4.4	5.0	20.2
1887	–9.1	–4.7	–26.3	–3.4	5.5	21.8
1888	–13.6	–5.5	–36.2	–2.2	5.8	19.5
1889	–5.5	–6.8	–28.1	–0.1	3.2	23.4
1890	–11.5	–9.2	–39.1	–2.5	4.4	18.0
1891	–15.8	–10.9	–30.4	0.0	1.3	22.7
1892	–18.3	–12.4	–29.1	1.3	4.7	21.3
1893	–16.4	–14.0	–32.6	1.4	6.2	20.5
1894	–18.4	–17.3	–31.6	0.1	7.1	26.1
1895	–23.3	–14.1	–33.4	–2.3	10.2	34.6
1896	–33.2	–20.8	–37.3	–6.0	–0.8	26.7
1897	–27.0	–19.0	–29.7	–5.9	5.3	37.0
1898	–24.2	–17.8	–35.1	–11.2	–5.1	43.1
1899	–26.1	–30.1	–46.2	–18.6	–0.6	52.9
1900	–36.1	–13.9	–29.8	–8.8	–1.9	38.6
1901	–32.6	–25.8	–48.8	–15.6	–6.9	31.3
1902	–47.2	–30.8	–50.8	–6.6	–5.1	39.5
1903	–40.5	–31.9	–47.3	–19.8	–6.3	33.6
1904	–41.9	–29.8	–54.2	–12.1	–2.0	35.7
1905	–68.4	–32.0	–66.6	–25.8	–49.8	23.6
1906	–65.4	–30.5	–62.1	–27.7	–18.7	30.9
1907	–65.4	–29.7	–58.4	–18.1	–10.3	30.0
1908	–60.0	–26.4	–58.1	–15.3	–17.4	59.5
1909	–48.6	–34.6	–53.5	–8.4	–0.1	66.2
1910	–52.2	–39.4	–62.7	–6.1	7.4	70.9
1911	–72.7	–31.2	–44.5	–17.4	–6.8	78.6
1912	–58.9	–39.0	–44.4	–35.7	–1.1	76.7
1913	–80.5	–42.1	–54.5	–53.8	2.2	61.8
1914	–82.6	–32.3	–73.5	–62.5	–1.0	39.0

Source: Ping-Yin Ho, *The Foreign Trade of China* (Shanghai: Commercial Press, 1935), pp.20-22, 70-1, 112, 162-3, 436-7, 632-3.

Appendix 10: Indian Exports of Rice and Wheat, 1868-1914

Year ending 31st March	Rice (million cwt)	Wheat (million cwt)
1868	12.6	0.2
1869	15.3	0.2
1870	10.6	0.0
1871	16.0	0.2
1872	17.3	0.6
1873	23.2	0.3
1874	20.2	1.7
1875	17.3	1.0
1876	20.4	2.5
1877	19.9	5.5
1878	18.4	6.3
1879	21.2	1.0
1880	22.1	2.2
1881	27.2	7.4
1882	28.8	19.9
1883	31.2	14.1
1884	27.0	21.0
1885	22.0	15.8
1886	28.2	21.0
1887	26.8	22.2
1888	28.5	13.5
1889	23.1	17.6
1890	27.0	13.8
1891	34.9	14.3
1892	33.1	30.3
1893	27.9	14.9
1894	24.6	12.1
1895	34.4	6.8
1896	35.1	10.0
1897	28.2	1.9
1898	26.8	2.3
1899	37.9	19.5
1900	32.2	9.7
1901	31.3	0.0
1902	34.0	7.3
1903	47.4	10.2
1904	45.0	25.9
1905	49.4	43.0
1906	43.0	18.7
1907	38.7	16.0
1908	38.2	17.6
1909	30.2	2.1
1910	39.2	21.0
1911	47.9	25.3
1912	52.4	27.2
1913	55.2	33.2
1914	49.0	24.0

Source: *Statistical Abstracts for British India*

Appendix 11: Terms of Trade of India and UK, 1861-1914

	India	UK
1861	92.6	83.7
1862	92.6	90.2
1863	82.4	91.4
1864	78.0	89.3
1865	80.0	91.2
1866	87.2	93.8
1867	82.2	91.9
1868	87.8	85.5
1869	111.3	87.9
1870	110.5	87.2
1871	108.0	93.3
1872	111.0	96.4
1873	100.0	100.0
1874	103.0	96.5
1875	105.5	95.2
1876	99.0	99.9
1877	125.0	84.0
1878	135.7	87.3
1879	135.0	86.7
1880	125.0	85.3
1881	115.0	82.5
1882	111.8	84.9
1883	112.0	84.0
1884	123.0	85.2
1885	121.3	87.4
1886	116.2	89.0
1887	113.2	90.7
1888	106.5	87.2
1889	114.5	87.8
1890	114.3	93.0
1891	122.5	91.6
1892	131.0	91.2
1893	126.0	93.2
1894	131.0	97.6
1895	127.6	94.5
1896	124.6	94.5
1897	144.2	93.8
1898	127.5	93.2
1899	115.0	95.7
1900	129.1	102.3
1901	120.8	100.7
1902	131.5	97.3
1903	117.0	95.9
1904	111.8	96.6
1905	120.8	96.0
1906	132.4	97.6
1907	125.0	98.0
1908	142.4	97.8
1909	134.3	93.3
1910	116.5	92.0
1911	120.0	96.0
1912	124.0	95.9
1913	131.0	99.1

Sources: B. R. Mitchell and Phyllis Deane, *Abstract of British Historical Statistics* (Cambridge: University Press, 1971), pp.331-2; B. M. Bhatia, 'Terms of Trade and Economic Development: A Case Study of India 1861-1939', *Indian Economic Journal,* 14 (1969), pp.417-8.

Appendix 12: British Home-Produced Exports to Major Markets, 1865-1914 (£ million)

Year	Industrial Europe	Africa	Asia	USA
1865	38.9	3.7	29.0	21.2
1866	40.4	3.7	34.7	28.5
1867	46.3	4.3	36.0	21.8
1868	48.7	4.0	35.0	21.4
1869	51.3	3.9	32.0	24.6
1870	50.0	4.5	35.4	28.3
1871	68.2	4.8	33.3	34.2
1872	73.9	6.7	34.5	40.7
1873	71.0	7.5	35.7	33.6
1874	63.7	7.3	39.4	28.2
1875	59.5	7.4	41.0	21.9
1876	55.3	6.9	37.6	16.8
1877	50.1	7.1	42.2	16.4
1878	50.8	7.9	37.6	14.6
1879	49.8	8.7	36.7	20.3
1880	49.3	9.4	48.9	30.9
1881	52.5	9.9	48.3	29.8
1882	55.2	10.5	45.3	31.0
1883	56.6	8.3	48.2	27.4
1884	56.2	8.0	46.9	24.4
1885	49.8	6.7	46.0	22.0
1886	46.5	6.1	46.1	26.8
1887	46.5	7.7	48.5	29.5
1888	48.2	8.8	52.1	28.9
1889	52.5	12.5	48.8	30.3
1890	56.2	13.1	53.5	32.1
1891	55.1	12.0	50.0	27.5
1892	50.7	11.7	44.7	26.5
1893	50.1	12.7	44.6	24.0
1894	50.7	12.5	45.6	18.8
1895	52.0	14.7	42.3	27.9
1896	55.7	18.9	50.6	20.4
1897	55.8	18.8	46.6	21.0
1898	56.9	17.8	48.6	14.7
1899	64.0	17.9	56.2	18.1
1900	72.9	19.7	55.7	19.8
1901	60.7	24.4	59.4	18.4
1902	58.7	31.4	54.8	23.8
1903	59.9	33.9	56.2	22.6
1904	61.1	25.8	67.5	20.2
1905	69.3	25.3	78.6	23.9
1906	81.8	25.3	84.9	27.8
1907	99.1	24.7	92.0	30.9
1908	86.1	22.5	83.2	21.3
1909	86.2	25.4	75.5	29.8
1910	93.3	34.5	82.2	31.4
1911	100.6	34.5	94.7	27.5
1912	105.7	37.3	101.8	30.1
1913	109.4	38.6	125.7	29.3
1914	79.0	32.5	105.2	34.0

Source: B. R. Mitchell and Phyllis Deane, *Abstract of British Historical Statistics* (Cambridge: Cambridge University Press, 1971), pp.315-327.

Appendix 13: New British Portfolio Foreign Investment to Major Areas, 1865-1914 (£ million)

Year	Europe	North America	Asia
1865	7.5	7.1	11.2
1866	4.5	4.4	4.5
1867	4.6	1.5	7.5
1868	11.7	3.5	8.1
1869	8.0	4.8	6.3
1870	18.6	10.0	7.1
1871	29.2	13.0	3.7
1872	34.9	30.8	2.2
1873	25.4	26.8	4.1
1874	24.7	33.1	5.9
1875	10.1	12.2	4.0
1876	5.0	9.3	5.1
1877	3.7	4.3	6.7
1878	6.1	6.2	5.0
1879	3.3	7.2	0.7
1880	2.7	18.3	3.2
1881	20.6	22.2	10.6
1882	12.1	28.6	9.4
1883	4.7	16.6	4.6
1884	7.3	15.1	5.8
1885	3.4	14.1	11.0
1886	5.0	14.0	9.6
1887	12.9	23.9	10.5
1888	10.1	37.2	10.7
1889	11.2	37.2	11.2
1890	12.3	52.8	10.8
1891	5.0	18.7	5.7
1892	2.7	14.9	4.1
1893	1.7	13.1	2.5
1894	1.8	17.0	13.1
1895	3.6	26.0	10.4
1896	2.7	13.2	15.4
1897	8.1	16.7	27.2
1898	10.1	19.8	21.1
1899	8.6	12.1	21.7
1900	6.9	10.7	11.9
1901	5.8	14.1	4.6
1902	5.2	37.3	10.8
1903	2.1	17.3	6.6
1904	0.8	31.3	15.2
1905	3.0	43.9	35.6
1906	14.7	19.1	15.8
1907	7.0	42.7	23.4
1908	10.4	62.7	29.6
1909	13.6	68.4	25.4
1910	18.8	82.5	32.9
1911	14.5	73.5	24.7
1912	22.8	89.9	21.5
1913	18.9	116.9	17.4
1914	43.5	82.5	16.4

Source: Matthew Simon, 'The Pattern of New British Portfolio Foreign Investment', in *The Export of Capital from Britain 1870-1914,* ed. A. R. Hall (London: Methuen, 1968), pp.39-40.

Appendix 14: Rice Prices and British Home-Produced Exports to Asia 1874-1914

Year	Rice (Hk tael) per picul	Rice (pence) per picul	British home-produced exports (£ million)
1874	1.33	101.2	39.4
1875	1.25	92.7	41.0
1876	1.14	81.3	37.6
1877	1.51	108.7	42.2
1878	1.76	125.9	37.6
1879	1.34	90.2	36.7
1880	1.46	101.6	48.9
1881	1.24	82.4	48.3
1882	1.23	84.2	45.3
1883	1.19	80.0	48.2
1884	1.32	88.4	46.9
1885	1.47	93.3	46.0
1886	1.70	102.2	46.1
1887	1.41	82.1	48.5
1888	1.35	76.0	52.1
1889	1.40	79.4	48.8
1890	1.51	93.9	53.5
1891	1.40	82.6	50.0
1892	1.47	76.8	44.7
1893	1.36	64.2	44.6
1894	1.51	57.9	45.6
1895	1.54	60.4	42.3
1896	1.59	63.6	50.6
1897	1.90	67.9	46.6
1898	2.24	77.5	48.6
1899	2.41	87.0	56.2
1900	1.83	68.1	55.7
1901	1.59	56.5	59.4
1902	2.42	75.5	54.8
1903	2.73	86.4	56.2
1904	2.49	85.6	67.5
1905	3.83	138.1	78.6
1906	2.50	98.7	84.9
1907	2.69	104.9	92.0
1908	3.94	126.0	83.2
1909	4.12	128.4	75.5
1910	3.34	107.9	82.2
1911	3.52	113.5	94.7
1912	4.32	158.1	101.8
1913	3.39	122.8	125.7
1914	3.24	106.1	105.2

Sources: Hsaio Liang-lin, *China's Foreign Trade Statistics 1864-1949* (Cambridge: Mass.: Harvard University Press, 1974), pp.32, 190-1; B.R. Mitchell and Phyllis Deane, *Abstract of British Historical Statistics* (Cambridge: Cambridge University Press, 1971), pp.315-327.

INDEX